China's "Belt and Road" Initiative (BRI) in the Pacific Island Countries (PICs)

The Belt and Road Initiative
Interdisciplinary Perspectives

Series Editor

Wenshan Jia

Vol. 5

Lei Yu and Sophia Sui

China's "Belt and Road" Initiative (BRI) in the Pacific Island Countries (PICs)

Geo-economic and political implications for China–PICs relations

PETER LANG

New York · Berlin · Bruxelles · Chennai · Lausanne · Oxford

Bibliographic information published by the Deutsche Nationalbibliothek.
The German National Library lists this publication in the German National Bibliography; detailed bibliographic data is available on the Internet at http://dnb.d-nb.de.

Library of Congress Control Number: 2025010843

The book is funded by China Social Sciences Fund: 24BGJ001

Cover design by Peter Lang Group AG

ISSN 2689-7970
ISBN 978-3-0343-5429-5 (print)
ISBN 978-3-0343-5430-1 (ebook)
ISBN 978-3-0343-5431-8 (epub)
DOI 10.3726/b22968

Published by Peter Lang Publishing Inc., New York (USA)
info@peterlang.com

This publication has been peer reviewed.

www.peterlang.com

Contents

List of Figures and Tables

Interviewees in the Book

Chen Dezheng is a professor and former director of the China-PICs Climate Change Action Cooperation Center, Liaocheng University.

Chen Hong is a professor and the director of the Center for Australian Studies, East China Normal University.

Guo Chunmei is deputy director and associate research professor in the Institute of Southeast Asian and Oceanian Studies, China Institutes of Contemporary International Relations.

Kang Jian is an associate professor and research fellow in the Center for the Pacific Island Countries, Liaocheng University.

Li Jianjun is director of the Center for Australian Studies at Beijing Foreign Studies University.

Lyu Guixia is a professorial research fellow at the Center for the Pacific and Pacific Countries History, China Academy of Social Sciences.

Ni Peng is an associate professor at the Research Center for the Pacific Island Countries, Liaocheng University.

Niu Li is director of Pacific Center, Beijing Foreign Studies University.

Xu Xiujun, a professorial research fellow on the Pacific islands affairs at the China Academy of Social Sciences.

Yang Honglian, a research fellow in the Center for the Pacific Island Countries, Liaocheng University.

Yu Changsen is an associate professor and former vice director of the Center for Oceanian Studies, Sun Yatsen University.

Zhao Shaofeng is a professor and director of the Research Center for Pacific Island Countries, Liaocheng University.

The interviews conducted are aimed to help explore the dynamics that contributes to the rapid intensification of China-PICs economic cooperation and their strategic partnership, and the constraints that hamper China-PICs cooperation particularly in the spheres of security and military cooperation. Some IR academics in China were interviewed. The criteria of choice are as follows: (1) interviewees are academically specialized in the China-PICs relations; (2) interviewees have been committed to the studies on China-PICs relations for more than a decade; (3) interviewees had field work or academic exchanges in the counterpart countries in the last decade. The authors concluded from the interviews that the growing economic cooperation and trade between China and the PICs have helped intensify their relations whereas aroused concerns and worries among the traditional players.

1 The Rise of China and Its Strategy of Peaceful Rise

Introduction

One of the most important events in international relations in the 21st century is the rapid rise of China at the systemic (global) level, which has altered, and will most likely continue to change the global geoeconomic and geo-political landscape. It is no denial that China's rise at the systemic (global) level has benefited much from the post-Cold War global system that is characterized by globalization and economic integration (Khan & Yu 2013, p. 81). The global system with the new features provides an international environment, in which the status quo powers and the rising powers might have cooperative interactions despite their differentiated interests. Some scholars of international relations, such as Robert Keohane and Josef Nye (2000, p. 104), note the fast-growing cooperation between countries, and propose the theory of complex interdependence.

It is truism to argue that China's rise in a relatively peaceful way shall give credit to globalization and economic integration, which makes it possible for China and its global partners to formulate a cooperative relationship of complex interdependence, and help China incorporate into the existing global system (Khan & Yu 2013, p. 87; Sui & Yu 2023a, p. 43). As well, the rise of China shall give credit to the strategy of "economic growth priority" adopted by Deng

Xiaoping and other Chinese policy makers who perceive economic growth as a basis underlying China's "hard" and "soft" power as well as its rise at the systemic (global) level (Sui & Yu 2020, p. 239). To sustain China's economic growth, Deng Xiaoping (1993, p. 380) advised China to create cooperative relations with countries across the world regardless of their political systems and ideological values. In so doing, China may gain entry to their partners' markets, capitals, technologies and resources that China needs to sustain its economic growth.

The main argument of the chapter is that as a rising big power, the primary objective of China, like that of other rising powers, is to ensure its rise at the systemic (global) level without being delayed or completely disrupted. This objective of China and other rising powers might contradict that of the status quo superpower and even some status quo middle powers. To ensure their undisrupted rise, the rising powers would more or less reform or adapt the existing system and order to accommodate their expanding interest. The moves of the rising powers will most likely undermine the vested interest of the status quo superpower and some status quo middle powers, arising from the existing system and order created and dominated by the status quo superpower. The chapter finds that the Chinese authorities have stuck to the strategy of "economic growth priority" that contributes to China's rise in the early 2010s as the largest economy at GDP PPP and the second one at nominal GDP (Department of Foreign Affairs and Trade of Australia 2011). Deng Xiaoping adopted the strategy in the late 1970s and launched a market reform, which will change China's economic landscape and the world's forty years later. Deng (1993, p. 370) theorizes that sustained economic growth and modernization constitutes a basis underpinning China's "hard" and "soft" power, particularly its military and high-technology capabilities, and the restoration of China's historical glory as a great power. China's economic rise has indeed augmented the country's "hard" power, including its military capabilities through heavy investment in military buildups and military-related technology. The chapter concludes that China has increasingly become a "revisionist", or more accurately, a "reformist" of the existing global system and order alongside its rapid increase on the "hard" and "soft" power and in response to the growing containment imposed on it by the United States, the established superpower.

It is noteworthy that China has been focusing domestically on its economic growth and internationally on the reform of global economic governance and the existing economic system and mechanism. To this end, China has been committed to the creation of its own global network of Free Trade Areas (FTA) (e.g., China-ASEAN FTA), and new financial institutions (e.g., Asia Infrastructural Investment Bank and the BRICS Bank) to boost its economic growth and increase its say in global economic and financial systems (Peng & Tok 2016, p. 736; Yu 2022, p. 1633). Unlike the United States that frequently launches wars across the world both over the Cold War era and the post-Cold War era, China has to date shown little interest in pursuing military hegemony as Deng Xiaoping (1993, p. 371) advised China to refrain from seeking military hegemony. China has now risen as one of the few economic superpowers as exemplified by its global network of bilateral and multilateral FTAs (e.g., China-Australia FTA & Regional Comprehensive Economic Partnership, RCEP) and new financial institutions (e.g., the BRICS Development Bank, jointly founded by Brazil, Russia, India, China and South Africa, and the Asian Infrastructure Investment Bank, AIIB).

Politically, China has pursued the strategy of creating strategic partnerships with states and states groupings with strategic significance, such as Russia, the BRICS, the African Union, and the Pacific Island Countries (PICs) (Papageorgiou 2021, p. 51; Yu 2023, p. 217). In so doing, China is aimed to win their political backing at the international arena, and work together to reform the existing system and order in their favor, or in the official Chinese terms, "a more rational and fairer" world order. Despite a dozen of strategic partnerships having been established, China has to date refused to formulate a formal military alliance with other states as the Chinese authorities insist that its strategic partnership shall not target at any third party. For instance, Beijing has long emphasized that its strategic partnership with Moscow is by no means a military alliance though Beijing and Moscow have much shared interest in counterattacking their perceived U.S. threat and containment, and in reshaping the world order more to their liking (Sui & Yu 2023b). Noticeably, Beijing has persistently refused the definition of China-Russia relationship by President Putin and others as "de facto allies" though Beijing and Moscow hold regular military drills in Asia, Europe and other parts of the world (Lukin 2019; Glosny 2016, p. 28).

Concurrent with the partnership strategy, China has pursued the strategy of "South-South" cooperation that was first proposed by Deng Xiaoping (1993, p. 380) in the early 1980s, who envisions the developing states and states groupings as the strategic assets of China's international power and influence. As noted, China has established and institutionalized fora on China-Africa Cooperation, China-Latin America Cooperation, China-Arabic Countries Cooperation, China-PICs Cooperation, etc. These fora have now grown as multilateral infrastructure with strategic significance, through which, China has markedly increased its economic, and, by extension, political cooperation with African, Latin American, Arabic and South Pacific countries (Yu 2018, p. 489). Waldron (2008, p. 12) notes that 'Beijing has the possibility of winning almost fifty friends in Africa... with a collection of such friends, China can create her own sphere of influence, secure her own resources, and develop military and political leverage'. The China-Pacific Island Countries (PICs) Economic Development and Cooperation Forum was formally set up in 2006 by President Jiang Zemin (1989-2003) who transplants to the PICs his experience gained in setting up the fora with Africa and Latin America. The forum has grown as a major platform for China and the PICs to conduct economic and political cooperation on issues of their common interest.

Militarily, China has since the beginning of the early 21st century accelerated the modernization of the People's Liberation Army (PLA) by markedly increasing its investment in military-related high technology and build-ups of hardware. China's pursuit of military modernization is primarily aimed to protect the country's "core interest", such as territory integrity and China's rise without being disrupted, rather than to seek a global hegemony by pursuing interventionism and hegemonism (Sui & Yu 2023c, p. 217). After the demise of the former Soviet Union, Deng Xiaoping (Leng & Wang 2004, p. 1078) advised China to keep a "low profile" in the radically changed international environment by adopting the strategy of "concealing China's ability and biding its time (*taoguang yanghui*)". In so doing, the Chinese authorities aspire to concentrate on economic growth and avoid any military confrontation with other countries, especially with the United States, the status quo superpower. China has not been involved in any war over the last four decades and its last war was with Vietnam in 1979, as a result of their territorial disputes. Deng Xiaoping observed that those countries having good relations with the United States in the post-War era (e.g., Japan, South Korea and Taiwan) have become rich whereas those having adversarial ties with the United States (e.g., China, Vietnam and North Korea), have become poor (Yu 2015, p. 1047). China's economic rise has, to a large extent, relied on its access to overseas markets, capitals and technology, including those of the United States (Khan & Yu 2013, p. 81). This partially explains why Deng Xiaoping advised China to keep a low profile in the international affairs especially before China's obvious rise in the early 2000s. Some Chinese academics of international relations are of the view that the strategy makes it possible for China to concentrate on economic development and modernization without being targeted by the established powers, and particularly by the superpower in the system (Leng & Wang 2004, p. 1078).

Alongside its economic rise and its marked increase on the "hard" power, China has redoubled its efforts to reinforce its "soft" power by showcasing its "economic model" particularly in the developing areas and its traditional culture throughout the world. It is noteworthy that China insists on its long-term foreign policy of "non-interference" that has helped China win diplomatic support of the developing states (Chaziza 2023, p. 41; Yu 2018, p. 489). China hence refuses to impose its economic model on other developing countries. Neither does it use its "economic model" to entice others to follow its model. Instead, China prudently advises other developing countries to choose their own path of development that best serves their country's interest.

The Dynamics of Rising Powers and China's Strategy

In the viewpoints of Hans J. Morgenthau (1966, p. 25), a theorist of realist international relations, international politics is essentially "a struggle for power" as he notes that "whatever the ultimate aims of international politics, power is always the immediate aim". The argument of Morgenthau displays his profound understanding of the essence of international politics from the realist perspectives as intimated by the post-War bipolar system that was created in the wake of the Second World War by the then superpowers, namely, the United States and the former Soviet Union. The bipolar system is undoubtedly an outcome of the "struggle for power" between the two superpowers for global hegemony (power), further complicated by their competing political systems, security interests and ideological beliefs. As the then superpowers, the United States and the former Soviet Union stayed high on the top of the power hierarchy in the post-War system primarily by virtue of their "hard" power, which was mainly based on their formidable military capabilities and economic might, and by their political, cultural and ideological influence over the rest of the world ("soft" power). Other states in the post-War world were roughly categorized as 'middle powers (regional) and the bottom-layer states' by virtue of their "hard" and, to a lesser degree, "soft" power (Khan 2012, p. 52). The disintegration of the former Soviet Union marked the end of the post-War II bipolar system that had lasted for more than half a century, and signaled the onset of the U.S.-dominated unipolar system. Russia that inherits the most assets of the former Soviet Union is no longer a superpower, but plummets into the grouping of middle powers as a consequence of its markedly weakened "hard" and "soft" power in comparison with that of the former Soviet Union.

The primary objectives of the superpower(s) that sat on the top of the global power hierarchy in either the former bipolar, or dominates the current unipolar system remain the same: to keep their dominated system and order and their supremacy by blocking the rise of any emerging powers to the level capable of challenging their system and status (Ratuva 2014, p. 409; Tow & Hay 2001, p. 37). In so doing, the superpowers will be able to keep their monopoly on "power" that is defined by Morgenthau as "the immediate and ultimate aims of international politics". As well, the superpowers will be able to keep their vested interest arising from the "power". The superpowers either in the former bipolar system or in the unipolar system are surely unpleasant to see the rise of any powers inside or outside their dominated systems to the level capable of challenging their monopoly on power. This provides insight into the fact that neither the United States nor the former Soviet Union was pleasant to see the rise of any power though they competed fiercely for power and hegemony in the Cold War era. As Morgenthau summarized, the rising powers might someday challenge the monopoly of the superpowers on power as China did to the former Soviet Union in the late 1950s and 1960s, Japan did to the United States in the 1980s, and China is now doing to the United States (Sui & Yu 2023b). Not out of expectation, Beijing was excluded by Moscow from its dominated system (the so-called "Socialist family") in the early 1960s, as a result of Beijing's challenge to the former Soviet Union (Radchenko 2010, p. 349). Likewise, Japan has suffered from the "lost decades" of economic stagnancy caused by the Plaza Accord imposed on it by the United States since the early 1990s, due to its challenge to the U.S. supremacy in the 1980s (Tyers 2012, p. 517; Zhang 2016, p. 57). Alongside China's rise in the 21st century, a growing number of Chinese foreign policy elites (e.g., Gao & Zhang 2017, p. 32; Liu 2019, p. 61) claim that China is suffering increasing U.S. containment, such as the "pivot to Asia", the "Indo-Pacific" strategy and the "quadrilateral alliance" composed by the United States, Australia, Japan and India despite Washington's denial (Panetta 2012).

The grouping of "middle powers" may roughly be categorized as the "established middle powers" and the "rising powers" in view of the growing momentum of particularly their "hard" power. This categorization is of analytical significance and contributes to specifically analyzing the primary objectives of the established and rising powers as states with differentiated "hard" and "soft" power are bound to pursue varied objectives to best serve their countries' interest. Under the normal circumstances, the established middle powers are most likely to pursue the objectives of ensuring their survival, interest and status in the existing global system, and take them as their primary objectives. To this end, the established middle powers would like to formulate an alliance with the superpower of the system in exchange for the latter's military protection, political endorsement and economic assistance in achieving their primary objectives (Yu 2023). As the dominator of the existing global system, the superpower, in turn, needs a global network of political and military alliances composed mainly of middle powers to help it keep its status and its dominance in the system and order. In this context, the objectives of the established middle powers dovetail those of the established superpower, which prompts the established superpower and established middle powers to work in synergy with each other to maintain the status quo of the existing system and order.

It is no denial that the established middle powers would like to help the established superpower in an explicit, or implicit way to maintain the status quo of the existing system and order and to hamper the rise of any emerging power from challenging the status of the established superpower and the existing system. By allying with the superpower, the established middle powers are more likely to keep their interest and reputation arising both from the alliance with the superpower and the global system and order dominated by the superpower. This is the way that the Chinese foreign policy elites (Jiang 2013, p. 69; Wang 2014, p. 36) conceive the military alliance dominated by the United States in the Asia-Pacific region (e.g., the U.S.-Japan alliance and the AUKUS), and the motivations of some established middle powers (e.g., Japan and Australia) behind their involvement in U.S. containment of China. From the perspectives of Japan and Australia, the rapid rise of China has generated profound impacts on the geopolitical landscape in the Asia-Pacific region and incurred radical changes to the regional order and power hierarchy. Japan has long viewed itself as the leading state in East Asia before China's rise in the early 21st century, and Australia has to date viewed itself as the "deputy sheriff" in the Asia-Pacific. In this context, the rise of China has undoubtedly undermined the status and vested interest of some established middle powers arising from the U.S.-dominated regional order and system (Tow & Hay 2001, p. 37).

Radically different from the established middle powers, the rising middle powers are eager to grow into a full-fledged superpower in an early date lest their process of rise be delayed or disrupted either by the established superpowers, or by a coalition of the established superpowers and some established middle powers. In this sense, to ensure their rise at the systemic (global) level is obviously the objectives of the rising powers. Vis-à-vis the "containment" by superpowers, or a coalition, some rising middle powers (e.g., Hitler's Germany and militarized Japan) decide to complete their process of rise by launching a "duel" against the superpower and its coalition, and re-creating a new world system and order dominated by themselves. Others, such as the United States, luckily completed their process of rise without major wars with the superpower, or its coalition due to a confluence of factors, such as their geographical remoteness, or their "smart" foreign strategy to avoid conflict with the established superpowers, or the lack of enough willingness or strength of the established superpowers to intervene in their rise. This partially explains why the Chinese authorities had stuck to the strategy of "keeping a low profile in international affairs" ("hiding China's ability and biding its time") throughout the 1990s and 2000s before China's rise as the second largest economy at current price (Leng & Wang 2004, p. 1078). The strategy, to a large extent helps China improve its relations with the rest of the world by avoiding offending the established superpower and its allies, and by avoiding inviting an early containment by the established superpower, namely, the United States.

The conceptualization of China by President Bush Jr. as U.S. strategic competitor in 2001 prior to the "9/11" event surprised the Chinese foreign policy makers and academics (Tull 2006, p. 459). However, the "9/11" event and the subsequent wars on terror launched by President Bush Jr. in Iraq and Afghanistan in the early 2000s ensnared the United States, the status quo superpower in the post-Cold War era. In a sense, it is fortunate for China, a rapidly rising power in the post-Cold War era as the decade-long wars on terror distracted the United States, and provided an invaluable opportunity for China's peaceful rise in the first decade of the 21st century without incurring much containment from the United States and its allies (Sui & Yu 2020, p. 239). The "peaceful" rising states, i.e., the United States, could hardly claim that there is no such thing as the so-called "Thucydides" trap between them and the established superpowers despite the possibility that they might rise without major wars with the established superpower. Thucydides was said to conclude that "the inevitability of the Peloponnesian war was the rise of Athens and the fear that it inspired in Sparta" (Foot 2014, p. 121). Likewise, the "fear" of the rising powers for a "duel" launched by the superpower and its allies to block them from rising as superpowers spurs the rising powers to increase their military capabilities and to be poised for a "duel" befalling them. This provides insight into the decision made by Theodore Roosevelt, President of the United States, to dispatch the well-known "White Fleet" to Australia in 1908 with a secret mission of surveying Australian harbors and military forts, in an attempt to occupy them once a British-America "duel" took place (Parkin & Lee 2008, p. 54).

In the viewpoints of the Chinese historians, the process of China's rise had twice been disrupted by militarized Japan that concerned with China's rapid economic growth and strong momentum of national rejuvenation. The Chinese historians hence argue that militarized Japan hence launched wars on Qing China and the Republic of China respectively in the late 1890s and 1930s, in an attempt to disrupt China's rise (Feng 2016, p. 176; Yu 2023, p. 217). In this context, it is not hard to understand why there has long existed a widely-claimed "Thucydides" trap between the established superpowers and the rising middle powers as a result of their mutual "fears" (Kirk 2016). It is frequently argued by some scholars of international relations that the increase of the might of the rising middle powers indicates the relative decline of that of the established superpower. Moreover, the expanding interest, influence and footprints of the rising middle powers across the world might undermine those of the established superpowers as well as some established middle powers. As a result, the rising middle powers may find it imperative to reshape, revise, or reform the existing global system dominated by the established superpower to better serve their interest although the rising middle powers rise in and benefit much from the existing system and order (Khan 2012, p. 52). Under normal circumstances, the moves of the rising middle powers to reshape, reform or adept the existing global system and order to their expanding interest would inevitably undermine the interests of the established superpower and probably the established middle powers (Nayar 1979, p. 117). Without enough power to immediately challenge the established superpower and its allies, the rising powers may more likely create their own system at the sub-systemic (regional) levels to satisfy their interest partially. The rising middle powers may wait for an appropriate time and opportunity to further expand their interest and influence at the systemic (global) level lest an early clash of interest with the established superpower occur.

China's rise and its strategies

China had been a great power for most part of the last 2000 years particularly in East Asia (Pant 2011, p. 9). China had long been a prominent economy in the world and its GDP remained around one third of global totals prior to the first Opium War (the first Sino-British Trade War) that took place in 1839-1841(Bregolat 2015, p. 64). The Chinese historians refer to the one hundred years starting from the first Opium War to the founding of the People's Republic of China (PRC) in 1949 as the "Chinese century of humiliation". They explain that the "Old Chinas", namely Qing China and the Republic of China (ROC) was frequently bullied and invaded by the then imperialist powers (Hsu 2000, p. 129). Mao Zedong, the founder of the PRC, and Deng Xiaoping, the launcher of China's market reform, had both witnessed their country's miserable experiences and cherished strong aspirations for their country's rejuvenation. However, Mao and Deng adopted different strategies to restore their country's status at the systemic (global) level (Scott 2008, p. 371). Mao Zedong was in favor of an alignment with the former Soviet Union, a superpower in the post-War bipolar system, as a result of a confluence of factors, such as shared ideological value and geopolitical interest.

Moreover, Mao's alignment with Moscow made it possible for the newly-established government to gain from Russia's economic assistance, diplomatic recognition, political endorsement and, most importantly, military protection to secure China's survival and safety[1]. The Beijing government was granted by the Soviet Union large quantities of economic and military assistance, as a result of its strategy of alignment with Moscow (Lüthi 2008, p. 35). The strategy also helped the PRC survive the Korean War by rolling back the U.S.-headed UN forces on the Korean Peninsula that, in the eyes of Mao Zedong, might serve as a springboard for U.S. invasion of China[2]. Some Chinese scholars defend Mao's

1 Between the spring and summer of 1949, Mao Zedong advanced the principle of "leaning to one side". The official Chinese IR literature believes that this is a major decision made in the light of China's historical and realistic situation and in accordance with the existing international environment at that time. The strategy of "leaning one side" is to declare that China would lean to the side of socialism as during the Chinese civil war the United States stood on the opposite side of the Chinese Communist Party and supported the Kuomintang. After the birth of New China, the U.S. might carry out armed intervention against China. Thus the above-mentioned situation necessitated China's allying with the socialist countries. For more details, see Ministry of Foreign Affairs of the PRC 2015, *Formulation of foreign policy of new China on the eve of its birth*, FMPRC, Beijing, <http://www.fmprc.gov.cn/mfa_eng/ziliao_665539/3602_665543/3604_665547/t18057.shtml>.

2 The mainstream perceptions of Chinese academics on China's involvement in the Korean War are radically different from those of the West. Many Chinese scholars characterize China's involvement in the war as inevitable. They argue that China's involvement was not merely a logical outcome of the Communist ideology that Mao Zedong upheld, but was more related to China's geopolitical interests, territorial security and economic rehabilitation from its long-term wars. In their eyes, after the U.S.-headed UN forces crossed the 38th parallel into North Korea and quickly pushed forward towards the Chinese border, Mao Zedong was left with only one option: to roll back the UN forces to the 38th parallel by sending troops to North Korea. For more details, see Qin, Xiaofan 2010, 'Mao Zedong and China's decision on the war to resist American aggression and aid Korea, *Foreign Affairs Review*, No. 1, pp. 4-10; Sha, Jiansun 2010, 'The war of resisting American aggression and aiding Korea and its historic meaning', *Journal of Ideological & Theoretical Education*, Vol. 139, No. 7, p. 33-37.

strategy of aligning with the Soviet Union, arguing that it would bring enormous security and economic interest for the newly-born PRC. They contend that otherwise, the "new China" might not be able to survive the political isolation, economic embargo, and military intervention imposed on it by the imperialist powers (Yu 2007, p. 81). Neither could the new-founded republic restore China's status as a middle power in the post-War bipolar system (Xia 2014, p. 61; Academy of Military Science of the PLA 2000, p. 207).

It is noteworthy that some other scholars do not share this point of view and beg to differ. They contend that China had over the decade of the 1950s subjected its national interest to that of the Soviet Union, as the consequence of the strategy of alignment with Moscow. This strategy therefore hurt China's sovereignty as an independent state and precluded China's rise as an independent center of power (Zhang 2000, p. 48; Yu 2015, p. 1047). Much worse, these scholars contend that the strategy of alignment with Moscow resulted in a long-term antagonism and animosity with the U.S.-headed West, which contributed to China's isolation from the Western world, the most advanced and dynamic part of the then global economy. In the viewpoints of these scholars, the long-term animosity and isolation caused China to lag far behind the developed countries particularly in terms of economic development, and science and modern technology (Sui 2004, p. 49).

Mao Zedong had to shift his strategy of alignment with Moscow to an alignment with Washington after the border clashes between China and the former Soviet Union occurred in the late 1960s. Mao and the Chinese political leaders conceived the Soviet military threat as 'most dangerous and imminent' following the border clashes that claimed hundreds of lives on both sides (Sutter 2000, p. 62). Some Chinese academics of international relations acclaim this policy shift as the rapprochement between China and the United States helped contain the Soviet attempt to launch a military invasion into China (Niu 1999, p. 69). The rapprochement also helped China fit into the U.S.-dominated Western system and provided China an invaluable opportunity to gain access to Western market, technology and capitals, which laid groundwork for China's economic take-off that started in the early 1980s and throughout into the 21st century. Other scholars nonetheless beg to differ, counter-arguing that this policy shift in alignment with Washington had likewise undermined China's efforts to grow as an independent center of power in global power hierarchy (Liu 1997, p. 7).

Different from Mao Zedong, Deng Xiaoping was apparently eager to elevate China as an independent center of power in the global power hierarchy.

To this end, he committed himself to advancing Chinese economic growth and modernization that he identified, among others, as the base underlying China's "hard and soft power" (Voge 2013, p. 36; Ye 2004, p. 13). Deng Xiaoping masterminded China's foreign policy shift in international relations by pursuing an "Independent Foreign Policy" without formulating any alliance with other powers to achieve the goal of growing as an independent "pole" at the systemic level[3]. Deng announced to cultivate relations of economic cooperation with states throughout the world "regardless of what their ideologies and political systems are" (Fujita 1993, p. 464; Liu 1997, p. 7).

History repeats itself and this seems particularly true of Beijing's foreign strategy, which had tilted to Moscow in the 1950s, and to Washington in the 1980s. Beijing has once again tilted to Moscow (the Soviet Union and then Russia) since the Tiananmen Incident and the onset of the *Pax-Americana* unipolarity in the early 1990s. These two events changed the geopolitical and strategic environment in which China and the U.S.-headed West had collaborated since the early 1970s to contain the Soviet expansion in Asia and beyond. In its place, a strong sense of crisis prevailed among the Chinese political leaders and communist ideologues following the Soviet disintegration that China was doomed to be the next target of U.S. "peaceful evolution"[4]. Deng Xiaoping obviously foresaw the strategic pressure on China from the upcoming U.S. unipolarity after the demise of the former Soviet Union, and felt it a policy necessity, rather than a policy

3 The fundamental goals of the Independent Foreign Policy of Peace are, according to the Chinese Government, to preserve China's independence, sovereignty and territorial integrity, to create a favorable international environment for China's reform and modernization and to maintain world peace. For more details, see Huang, Wenyong 1998, 'Lun dulizizhu heping waijiao zhengce (On China's Independent Foreign Policy of Peace)', *Journal of China Foreign Affairs University*, No. 3, pp. 29-36.

4 'Peaceful evolution' is a term generally used by Chinese academics to describe an alleged strategy of the United States and its western allies to either overthrow or westernize socialist states, including China, through peaceful means if or when they fail to achieve the same goal through economic embargoes, military interference or outright invasion. For an elaboration of this term, see Fuke Zhao, 'Mao Zedong Deng Xiaoping fangzhi he fandui heping yanbian de lilun yu shijian shuxi' [On the theories and practices of Mao Zedong and Deng Xiaoping for preventing and combating peaceful evolution], *Journal of Jiangxi Normal University* 42:1, 2009, pp. 110-114.

option to accelerate China's rise at the systemic (global) level as an independent "pole" on an early date (Ye 2004, p. 14). To buy the time that China needs to rise as a global power, Deng Xiaoping proposed the strategy of 'hiding China's capability and biding its time (*tao guang yang hui* 韬光养晦)' to avoid an early U.S. containment and keep an international environment favorable for China's economic growth and modernization in the changed global geopolitics (Leng & Wang 2004, p. 1078).

Deng Xiaoping held a view of the Soviet fall that is radically different from the U.S.-headed West. He theorized the tragedy of the Soviet fall as the corollary of the Soviet economic incapability of buttressing its "imperial over-expansion" and its hegemonic rivalry with the United States (Meisels 2013; Liu & Xue 2002, p. 78). Deng's perception apparently contradicts the prevalent one in the United States and other western countries that the Soviet disintegration signaled the triumph of America-style democracy over the Soviet authoritarian communism and the universalization of liberal democracy as the final form of human government (Fukuyama 1992, p. 2). Many Chinese policy elites and political scientists share Deng Xiaoping's view, arguing that the former Soviet Union and other communist countries in Eastern Europe have long lagged far behind the United States and other western countries in terms of economic development. The Chinese political elites insisted that the economic inferiority of those countries in the Soviet bloc be the major cause resulting in the fall of the communist regimes. This provides insight into Deng Xiaoping's adherence to the belief that China should prioritize economic growth and catch up with the United States in terms of particularly "hard power" (i.e., economic and military capabilities) sooner than later. In so doing, China may win the hearts and minds of the Chinese people by improving their livelihoods and avoid a doom similar to that of the Soviet Union befalling China (Deng 1993, p. 370). To expedite its economic growth and rise, China has since the beginning of the 21st century adopted several strategies to boost its rise as a great power at the systemic (global) level, usher in a multi-polar world, and re-shape the current global order more to its liking.

China's strategies

China has been committed to economic growth since the late 1970s and has expedited its economic rise in the first decade of the 21st century by adopting a series of strategies. Since the onset of the 21st century, China has adopted the strategy of Free Trade Area (FTA) in pursuit of a global network of FTAs to sustain its economic growth that Deng Xiaoping and other Chinese policy makers define as the basis underpinning China's "hard" power (Deng 1993, p. 371; Khan & Yu 2013, p. 86). In pursuing this strategy, China aspires of augmenting its say in global economic reform and governance and helping reforming the current global economic order (Xi 2013). China's pursuit of a global network of FTAs comes against the backdrop of the long-term deadlock of global free trade talks, the growing protectionism in the advanced markets and the ABC strategy adopted by the Western countries (meaning that the U.S.-headed West would like to conclude free trade agreements with any country but China)[5]. The Chinese foreign policy elites and economists have long complained that the United States and the EU have to date refused to grant China a market economy status and conclude with Beijing any free trade agreements (Ewert & Poter 2016; Hornby & Donnan 2016). In this way, the U.S.-headed West attempts to exclude China from their free trade network, decouple their economic links with China and undermine China's economic take-off.

By 2024, China has concluded or implemented 20 bilateral and multilateral FTAs with 18 more under negotiation and consideration (Ministry of Commerce of the PRC 2024). Of the concluded FTAs, the most noteworthy one is the RCEP (Regional Comprehensive Economic Partnership, or ASEAN +5), which is composed of China, Japan, the ROK, Australia and New Zealand and the 10 member nations of ASEAN. The enormous FTA covers almost half of the world's population with an aggregate GDP of $26.3 trillion and an export of $5 trillion, both of which account for about one third of the world's totals (Department of Foreign Affairs and Trade, Australia 2021). There is a wide-spread estimate

5 Chinese scholars and economists argue that the advanced nations, particularly the United States and EU, have tacitly adopted a strategy to exclude China from their FTA networks, or in the Chinese phrase, an "ABC" strategy (they may conclude FTAs with all but China). In their view, the ABC strategy is designed to perpetuate the predominance of the EU and the United States in the world trade and economics. They tend to validate their argument by pointing to the US-dominated TPP that excludes China whereas incorporating Vietnam whose economy is widely perceived as far less open than China's. For more details, see Song, Guoyou 2013, 'quanqiu ziyou maoyi xieding jingzheng yu zhongguo de zhanlue xuanze (global FTA competition and China's strategic choice), *Contemporary International Relations*, No. 5, pp. 30-35; Liu, Qing 2012, 'meiyue guanxi xin fazhan ji qianjing (the new development of the US-Vietnam relationship and its prospect)', *International Studies*, No. 2, pp. 90-99.

among regional economists that the RCEP is likely to re-shape global economic and, by extension, political landscape by speeding up the shift of global economic gravity from the Atlantic to the Pacific, and sustain China's economic growth (Zhang 2015, p. 11; Petri & Plummer 2020). A close examination of China's global network of FTAs will easily find that the FTA strategy is specifically designed as such by the Chinese foreign policy makers and economists as an important and practical path to the restoration of the country's wealth and power. The Chinese policy makers have reached an agreement that China's economic rise requires the country to secure access to overseas markets, resources and investment destinations to sustain its economic growth and modernization (Khan & Yu 2013, p. 87).

This FTA strategy is also aimed to help upgrade China's labor-intensive manufacturing system to a capital- and technology-based structure that is widely assumed by the Chinese policy makers and economists as a "key" step to rank China among the advanced nations by the mid-21st century (Liu & Zhang 2015, p. 135; Khan & Yu 2013, p. 83). China has remained the world's largest trader and manufacturer in terms of commodities since the onset of the 21st century, and aspired for a greater say in global economic governance and reform. The Chinese policy makers and economists have long complained about its limited say and voting rights in the world's economic, trading and financial institutions. They claim that their country's rights in these international institutions are much less commensurate with China's contribution to global economics, trade and finance (Lyu 2014, p. 48). China's FTA strategy reveals China's growing awareness of the importance to reform the existing global economic governance by competing with the United States for the leading role in setting new rules and regimes governing global trade, finance and investment (*Japan Times* 2015). The Chinese policy makers and economists anticipate the reform of the existing global economic governance as "vital" in sustaining China's economic growth and increasing its "hard" and "soft" power globally (Xi 2014; Huo 2015, p. 45). Sustained economic growth is highly relevant to China's dream of *fuqiang* (wealth and power) and its rise at the systemic (global) level, and equally importantly, to the legitimacy of the communist rule of China (Holbig & Gilley 2010, p. 396). This explains why the Chinese government at various levels has prioritized economic growth and modernization to win the hearts and minds of the Chinese people by improving their livelihoods.

In the financial area, the Chinese government has resonated with other emerging powers and worked together with them to propel the reform of the international financial system and mechanism. China and other emerging powers (e.g., the member countries of the BRICS, Brazil, Russia, India and South Africa) have articulated their demand for a substantial increase on its share, voting rights and representation in international financial institutions. It is noted that China has suffered from U.S. blockage in such international financial institutions as the World Bank (WB) and International Monetary Fund (IMF) from increasing its representation and influence. As a way out, China is adopting a "starting anew" strategy to create new international financial institutions unilaterally and multilaterally with various ends in view. For instance, China has recently created the Development Fund for its African partners and the "Silk Road" Fund for member states of Shanghai Cooperation Organization (SCO). China has also created and dominated the newly-founded SCO Bank, BRICS Bank and AIIB (Asian Infrastructure Investment Bank). These recently-established funds and banks not only provide financial support for regional infrastructure development and other economic projects but also help expand China's economic and by extension, political influence across the world (Haga, Allison 2021, p. 31; Reuters 2016). In a sense, these funds and banks have served as an important fulcrum for China's rise as a major financial player in the international arena.

In the monetary area, the Chinese currency Renminbi (RMB), commonly known as the yuan, has acquired the conditions to rise as an international currency in view of China's rapid increase on its nominal GDP and international trade that respectively took up 16 percent and 11.4 percent of the world's totals in 2018 (Woetzel et al 2019, p. 27). It is in this context that the Chinese policy makers and economists have reached consensus that it is time for China to push for the yuan's internationalization. The Chinese economists argue that China should fasten yuan's internationalization as they note that the United States has been abusing its position as the controller of the main reserve currency (Blackwill & Harris 2016, p. 78). As a result, China has tried to mitigate its reliance on the U.S. dollar and encouraged its global partners to use Yuan as the means of settlement for their bilateral trade and investment. In trade settlement, cross-border yuan settlement reached a record high in 2023, with the yuan accounting for 4.43 percent of global trade at the year's end, a 34.18 percent year-over-year increase (*Global Times* 2024). In international financial transactions, the yuan used in direct investment grew steadily, as well as in credit loans and bond financing, leading to a 28.80 percent year-over-year rise. Parallel to trade and investment, the People's Bank of China, China's Central Bank, has concluded dozens of bilateral agreements with its counterparts across the world, and encouraged them to take yuan as part of their foreign exchange reserves. The yuan has now risen as the fifth most-used currency in global goods and services payments, and the seventh largest foreign reserve currency (Wright 2016, p. 186). The internationalization of yuan has been described by some international economists as 'the most important monetary event' as they believe that 'it will change the international monetary landscape' (Jiang 2014, p. 18). Obviously, the Chinese policy makers and economists are employing the international funds, banks and FTAs created by Beijing and its global partners as an instrument to boost yuan's internationalization and China's rise as a global financial player (Zen & Li 2015, p. 81; Khan & Yu 2013, p. 86).

Politically, China has selectively created partnerships with strategically significant states and states groupings that might assist China in overcoming U.S. containment of China's rise and boosting its economic growth. China has to date created strategic partnerships with Russia, Africa, Latin America, Central Asia and most recently, the Pacific Island countries that geographically sprawl across the central part of the Pacific. The growing significance of China's strategic partnerships with these states and states groupings comes against the backdrop of China's rapid rise in the 21st century. It is well-noted that China's rise has apparently given birth to sensitive periods of "power shift" between the rising and established powers as exemplified by the growing rivalry between China and the United States for global supremacy. China has now risen as the largest economy in terms of Purchasing Power Parity (PPP) (Department of Foreign Affairs and Trade, Australia 2023) after decades of commitment to economic growth since Deng Xiaoping launched a market reform in the late 1970s. By the late 2010s, China has reached a vital juncture of national rejuvenation and resurgence at the systemic (global) level as a great power (Zhang 2015, p. 11). The Chinese authorities expect the states and groupings of states that have formulated strategic partnerships with China to work together for a new international order that they deem favorable for their economic development, and more rational and fairer for their interest.

It is noteworthy that many Chinese foreign policy elites are issuing warning calls that China is most likely to encounter unprecedented containment from the established superpower, namely, the United States. This is partially due to the structural conflicts between the rising and the established superpowers, and to the U.S. strategy of blocking the rise of any power capable of challenging its hegemony (Tow & Loke 2009, p. 442; Ratuva 2014, p. 409). Not surprisingly, the Chinese foreign policy elites are of the view that the fall of the former Soviet Union in 1991 and the economic stagnancy of Japan over the last decades since the early 1990s to U.S. strategy of "containment". They argue that the U.S. containment put an end to the rise of both the Soviet Union and Japan, as a result of their challenge to U.S. hegemony[6]. The Chinese foreign policy elites articulate concerns that as a rising power, China is bound to confront U.S. containment similar to those befalling the former Soviet Union and Japan. In their views, the U.S. strategy of "pivot" to Asia, "freedom of navigation" operation in the South China Sea, and the "quadruple alliance" headed by the United States are containment of its kind (Xin 2014, p. 68; Sui & Yu 2020, p. 239).

Policy watchers and IR scholars within and without China note with concern that relations between these two superpowers have approached a "tipping point" where the United States could no longer tolerate China's rise that has undermined U.S. hegemony particularly in the Asia-Pacific region (Medeiros 2019, p. 119; Clad & Manning 2014; Lampton 2015). In the viewpoints of some IR academics, the United States, the established superpower, wishes a rising China to follow Japan's mode: 'economically powerful and politically cooperative but strategically dormant and militarily inhibited' (Lee 2010, p. 10). Judged by the past three decades, 'there's no worse fate than getting touted as the next global superpower' (Lowry 2011). To overcome the perceived U.S. containment, some Chinese policy elites and IR scholars (e.g., Zhang 2015, p. 11; Wang 2014, p. 42) advise China to continue to focus on economic growth and modernization as Deng Xiaoping suggested. They share Deng's view that China's "hard" and "soft" power, including its military capabilities, depends on the country's sustained economic growth.

Concurrent with its economic rise, these Chinese political elites suggest to further enhance China's strategic partnerships with states and states groupings that have much significance in terms of geopolitics and geo-economics. They also suggest China to narrow its distance from the United States by investing more in high-technology and military-related technology. Apart from economic motivations, such as trade, resources and investment, China perceives its strategic partnerships with states and states groupings with geopolitical and economic significance as a way to coordinating their stances on international affairs and enhancing their political and strategic cooperation in the world arena. The

6 In the view of some Chinese IR scholars, the Soviet Union, the once second powerful country was 'sent into the garbage heaps of history' by the United States through half a century's Cold War. The United States did not tolerate the rise of Japan, its docile and obedient ally in political and military terms, and imposed on it the Plaza Accord, which plunged Japan into the 'lost decades'. For more details, see Jiang, Yong 2010, 'dang xin shi jie lao er de mo zhou (Beware of the curse upon the world's No. 2 Power)', *World Affairs*, No. 22, pp. 52-54 and Ye, X.W. 2011, 'Comments on China's GDP surpassing Japan's', *People's Daily* (Overseas Edition), 22 February, p. 1.

Chinese foreign policy elites forecast that the more powerful China grows in terms of economic and military power, the more containment it will confront from the United States (Zuo 2014, p. 28). Based upon what we have learnt from the world's history, particularly since the British Industrial Revolution, transitional periods of global hegemony are frequently characterized with intense competition, and even wars between powers for dominance and interest (Ross 2009, p. 43; Guo 2005, p. 66).

International watchers and IR academics across the world have voiced their concerns that the strategic competition between China and the United States may escalate and eventually result in a vehement clash. Some realist scholars, such as John Mearsheimer (2006, p. 162) predict that a "security competition" is most likely to take place between the United States and China given the mounting tensions triggered by the US-China competition for hegemony and dominance. Several Chinese foreign policy analysts and IR scholars have voiced suspicions of the viewpoints of Henry Kissinger, former State Secretary of the United States, that US-China relations are in the "foothills of a Cold War" and "could be headed toward a conflict worse than World War I" (Evans 2019). The Chinese foreign policy elites, however, do take the view that the US-China relationship will hardly remain good, and may become very bad in view of their hegemonic competition, the ongoing trade war and a possible economic disconnection (Wu 2019, p. 20; Xie 2018, p. 20). The Chinese foreign policy elites (e.g., Zhu 2019, p. 14; Zhang 2020, p. 89) are increasingly voicing their concerns over the likelihood of a rapid worsening of China-US relations and, much worse, a military confrontation.

It is in this context that the Chinese foreign policy makers realize more deeply now than ever the importance of China's strategic partnerships with states and states groupings with strategic significance across the world in counterattacking US containment of China's rise. Of these partnerships, the China-Russia partnership is of much strategic significance, which explains why President Xi Jinping has personally advanced China-Russia strategic partnership by undertaking intense summit diplomacy (Sui & Yu 2023). Xi and Putin have to date had more than 40 face-to-face meetings since early 2013, about five meetings per year, which is rarely seen in state-to-state relations, particularly between powers (Kottasova 2017; Wang 2019). As a result, the China-Russia partnership has been extremely intensified under Xi's "personal influence" especially after the Ukraine crisis broke out in 2014. Noticeably, the partnership between these two historical foes is now hailed by foreign policy makers and IR scholars in both states as being at "an unprecedented high level" (Gvosdev & Marsh 2014, p. 132; Fu 2016). A number of political leaders and scholars in the Western countries hold fast to the belief that the nature of the Sino-Soviet partnership is no more than a "convenience of marriage", or more accurately, an "axis of convenience" (Lo 2008, p. 3; Clarke & Ricketts 2016). This argument sounds plausible if a glance is cast upon China-Russia geopolitical competition particularly in Central Asia and eastern Siberia.

However, this argument reveals a fact that these scholars and politicians fail to understand the Chinese political culture and the long-cherished dream of the Chinese people to restore their nation's past glory of *fuqiang* (wealth and power). The Chinese people long for their country's re-rise as a great power as some Chinese scholars (e.g., Li Xiaokang) highlight that 'after more than a century's sufferings and humiliations, the Chinese people have strong aspirations for their country's rejuvenation and they thereby elevate it [*rejuvenation*] to their nation's first priority'. In this sense, China's cooperation with the United States is primarily out of economic motivations, which is defined by IR textbooks as "low politics" whereas that with Russia is obviously for China's strategic interest of rise at the systemic (global) level, which is defined as "high politics" in international politics and international relations. This sheds light on the perception of the Chinese foreign policy elites of the China-Russia partnership that is defined by the foreign policy makers of both China and Russia as 'the ballast stone of world peace and strategic stability' and a pillar for China's "peaceful" rise (Xi 2013b, p. 2; Foreign Ministry of the People's Republic of China 2016). By enhancing their strategic partnership, China attempts to economically gain entry to Russia's resources and energy as well as its investment opportunities to advance China's economic growth and modernization. Politically, China attempts to counterattack US containment and reform the US-dominated world order in a fashion more to its liking and favorable for its rise as a global power (or in the official Chinese terms, a fairer and more rational order) (Sui & Yu 2023). As far as the Asia-Pacific region is concerned, China plans to increase its political and military wherewithal by playing the "Russia card" to wrestle with the US-led military allies that have more than 300 military bases in the region to encircle China. The Chinese foreign policy elites have long viewed the US military alliance and those military bases as testament to US containment and encirclement of China.

Africa is another area with strategic significance that the Chinese authorities have persistently deepened its strategic partnerships with. A large number of African states have provided political backing of China at the international arena, which has long been considered as an indispensable component of China's global power and influence (Luo 2013, p. 117). This explains why China attaches strategic significance to the developing states and identifies its relations with the developing states and particularly African states as the "basis of its international relations". This also explains why China has been committed to creating an "all weather" partnership with Africa since the PRC was founded in 1949[7]. China initiated the Forum on Chinese-Africa Cooperation (FOCAC) in 1999 to institutionalize its summit diplomacy with Africa, and coordinate their stances on major international issues and advance their economic cooperation and trade. The FOCAC has now grown into a 'platform and mechanism for the China-Africa high-end dialogue and effective cooperation' (Xia 2007, p. 9). President Xi Jinping expanded China's presence and influence in Africa and endeavored to create a "Community of Shared Future (命运共同体)", which is, in Xi's view, aimed to seek common development, shared prosperity and collective security by intensifying economic integration, political trust and security cooperation[8]. The new world order that China is now committed to creating with other rising powers would be less legitimate and representative without the political backing of African states. This partially explains why China has always preferred to acquire loyal friends in Africa who would now and in the future back it in international fora everywhere and always (Rotberg 2008, p. 11).

It is truism to argue that China is now enjoying enormous competitive advantages over other peer competitors in the developing world that have no structural conflict or territorial disputes with China. This is particularly true in Africa, which is partially reflected by the remarks of Jacob Zuma, former President of South Africa: "we are particularly pleased that in our relationship with

7 China formulated a diplomatic strategy in 2009 that identified "relations with major powers as the key, neighbors as top priority and developing countries the basis (大国是关键、周边是首要、发展中国家是基础)". More details see Zhang, Qingmin 2009, 'Liu shi nian lai xin zhong guo wai jiao bu ju de fa zhan—dui dang dai hui zheng zhi bao gao de wen ben fen xi' (Diplomatic composition of China in the last sixty years—a text analysis of the political reports to Chinese Communist Party National Congress), Foreign Affairs Review, Vol. 26, No. 4, pp. 32-42.

8 Some Chinese IR scholars believe that "the community of common destiny" is a new strategy proposed by Xi Jinping, reflecting China's concept of its relations with African countries: to seek common development and shared prosperity through economic regional cooperation and interdependence. For more details see Xi, Jinping 2013, *Trustworthy friends and sincere partners forever–speech at the Julius Nyerere International Convention Center*, Foreign Ministry of the PRC, 25 October 2013, <www.fmprc.gov.cn/mfa_eng/wjdt_665385/…/t1027951.shtml>; Liu, Hongwu and Lu, Lingyu 2013, 'Chinese dream and African dream:building of China-Africa common destiny', *West Asia and Africa*, No. 6, pp. 19-33.

China…China's intention is different to that of Europe, which to date continues to intend to influence African countries for their sole benefits' (Hanauer & Morris 2014). As a rational player in the world politics, China will most likely make use of its advantages to consolidate and enhance its predominance in Africa. Waldron observes that 'Beijing has the possibility of winning almost fifty friends in Africa… with a collection of such friends, China can create her own sphere of influence, secure her own resources, and develop military and political leverage' (Waldron 2008, p. 246). Equally importantly, China has impressively expanded its economic involvement in Africa and their bilateral trade volume has rapidly risen to the level of amounting to the total amount of trade between Africa and the United States and the EU combined. Looking ahead, it is safe to predict that the African states are most likely to play an even more important role in the process of China's rise in view of their abundance in resources, and their economic potential and political influence.

On the Eurasian continent, China worked with Russia to create the Shanghai Cooperation Organization (SCO) in 2001, which helps China in the 21st century to expand its footprints and influence in Central Asia in terms of geopolitics, security and economics. President Xi Jinping proposed the "Belt and Road" initiative (BRI) after his presidency began in 2013 to reinforce China's involvement and interest in Central Asia. The BRI is designed to revitalize the cross-continental and marine "silk roads" connecting ancient China to West Asia and Europe respectively through Central and South Asia[9]. The BRI has been widely conceived by international watchers and policy analysts as China's Marshall Plan as once completed, China is expected to transform the geopolitical landscape and play a dominant role in Eurasia (De Conti 2019; Andresen 2019, p. 135). The SCO is composed of two permanent members (Russia and China) of the United Nations Security Council (UNSC) and three members of the BRICS (Russia, China and India). President Nursultan Nazarbayev announced that 'the leaders of the member states [of the SCO] sitting at this negotiation table are representatives

9 In concrete terms, the Belt and Road initiative is an ambitious development proposal through which China wishes to sustain its economic growth by prompting trade and economic cooperation with the rest of the world. To this end, China is committing itself to infrastructure development in the hopes of connecting it to countries in Asia and beyond. It is estimated that China plans to invest $150 billion dollars into infrastructure each year. For more details see Cai, Peter 2017, *Understanding China's Belt and Road Initiative*, Lowy Institute for International Policy, Australia, March, Melbourne.

of half of humanity' given the SCO's large population (Moran 2013, p. 164). The Chinese foreign policy makers have tasked the SCO with a significant mission to rise as a new regional "center of power" with profound influence in political, security and economic spheres (Ministry of Foreign Affairs of the PRC 2014).

The Chinese foreign policy makers have adopted a two-pronged approach to boosting the SCO's rise as a new center of power in global system. Politically, China enlarges the SCO in a step-by-step way by first accepting the participation of India and Pakistan, the two most influential states in South Asia, in the SCO (Michel 2017). China's motivations behind this move are first to employ the SCO as a means to expand its presence and influence in South Asia and second to create a regular platform for China, India and Pakistan to communicate and manage their territorial disputes. Most recently, the SCO accepts Iran as its member, and Saudi Arabia as an observer, which helps China extend its presence in and influence on the Middle East. Economically, China proposed to create the SCO Bank to bolster regional infrastructure development and intra-regional economic cooperation and trade with the use of Chinese currency RMB as the means of settlement in regional trade and investment (Hakans & Phill 2017).

Different from the perceptions held by some scholars in the West to view the SCO as a vehicle of "human rights violation", the mainstream viewpoints reflected in the Chinese IR literature on the one hand acknowledge the numerous challenges that the SCO is facing, such as internal competition and solidarity (Deng 2021, p. 47); On the other hand, the Chinese academics (Pan & Li 2009, p. 67) acclaim the creation of SCO in the early 21st century as a far-sighted move with strategic significance for China as it contributes to keeping peace and stability in the Chinese border areas, and serves as fulcrum for China's rise at the systemic (global) level in the 21st century. The Chinese foreign policy elites argue that China is likely to face critical territorial disputes with its neighbors in Central Asia as what it is now experiencing in the East and South China Seas should the SCO not been created a couple of decades ago.

There is an agreement among the Chinese foreign policy elites (e.g., Zeng & Li 2018, p. 66, Gao 2012, p. 74) that the peace and stability in Northwest China are of strategic significance for China's rise. In their viewpoints, SCO provides China with vast and stable interior territories, ensuring China's commitment to economic growth that underlies China's "hard" power and its rise as a global power. In the line of the Chinese logic, it is truism to argue that a stabilized Chinese Northwest helps China avoid a strategic dilemma of military confrontations simultaneously in East and West China. As well, the Chinese foreign policy elites see the peace in Northwest China make it possible for China to shift its strategic and military resources to East China to deal with the territorial disputes over the East and South China Seas, and equally importantly, to meet the military challenges arising from the US "pivot to Asia" and its military operations in the South China Sea.

China's relations with most states in the Latin American and Caribbean region have long faltered at the commercial level in comparison with the intimate relationships between China and the majority states in Africa (Taylor 2011, p. 53). This is not because China is unwilling to intensify its cooperation with the states in Latin American and Caribbean region, but mainly due to China's reluctance in giving offence to the United States by intruding into Latin America and the Caribbean region, the 'backyard' of the United States, which might undermine the China-America economic ties and trade. However, the strategic thinking of the Chinese foreign policy makers has markedly changed since Xi Jinping's Presidency began in 2013, and the United States started to pursue the strategy of "pivot to Asia" in early 2013. Xi created the China–CELAC (China-Latin America Cooperation) Forum and a regular China–CELAC summit meeting as the institutional underpinnings of a strategic partnership. The Beijing Declaration issued at the first ministerial conference of the China–CELAC Forum held in 2015 announced their 'comprehensive partnership' and their jointed commitment to 'a multipolar world and greater democracy in international relations' (China–CELAC Forum 2015). The declaration reveals that neither China nor Latin America is satisfied with the U.S.-dominated unipolar system and that they will work together to create a new world order deemed by both sides 'more reasonable and fairer'.

Apparently, Beijing is taking measures to counterattack the U.S. containment as particularly exemplified by U.S. strategy of 'pivot to Asia' and its military operations in the South China Sea. Beijing is issuing a warning call to Washington by intruding Latin America and the Caribbean region, the U.S. 'backyard', and by extending their cooperation from the economic and commercial spheres to the political, military and strategic spheres (Vadell 2018, p. 107). In so doing, the Chinese foreign policy elites signal the United States that they have their own ways to counterattack U.S. containment and encirclement of their country by 'ganging up' its Cold War era allies in the Asia–Pacific region, notably Japan and Australia (Lim 2003, p. 142). The Chinese foreign policy elites have long described Japan and Australia, the two military "anchors" of the United States in the Asia-Pacific region, as the two 'crabs' claws' of the United States (Tang 2015, p. 32, Sui & Yu 2023a, p. 32).

It is noteworthy that China's expanding presence and influence in Latin America and the Caribbean region has aroused concerns in the United States though China has to date hardly had the capability of subverting or marginalizing the United States in the region (Piccone 2016, Ellis 2011, p. 87). An article published in the *Wall Street Journal* claimed that 'China is becoming a political rival of the United States in its own backyard' and that 'some of these [Latin American] nations may try to use the Chinese alternative to challenge U.S. hegemony' (O'Grady 2004, p. 7). General Bantz Cradock, former head of the U.S. Southern Command, warned that China's presence in Latin America and the Caribbean region was 'an emerging dynamic that could not be ignored' (Hsiang 2008, p. 121, Pablo 2005). The United States is apparently unlikely to sit on its hands and do nothing about its declining influence in its own 'backyard', and China's growing involvement there despite the statement of John Kerry, former U.S. Secretary of State, that the 'Era of the Monroe Doctrine' is over (Kerry 2013).

Since the onset of the 21st century, China has committed itself to formulating a strategic partnership with the Pacific Island Countries (PICs) by persistently providing them with economic assistance and, more importantly, extending its economic and political involvement there (Smith & Wesley-Smith 2019, p. 56). China's rapidly increasing involvement and influence in the South Pacific displays its desire for intensifying its economic cooperation and political relations with the PICs, and its goal of creating a meaningful strategic partnership with the PICs in the forms of "a community of shared future". China satisfies the PICs' demands for self-determination and assistance by pursuing the strategy of "non-interference" (in official Chinese terms "the five principles of peaceful co-existence") and "aids without strings" (Sui & Yu 2024, p. 3). China's strategy and its respect for the PICs' sovereignty and self-determination help distance the PICs from the United States and its military allies by providing the PICs with an alternative and therefore cement its strategic partnership with the PICs. In this sense, China may reap not only economic but also geopolitical interest from its intensified economic, and by extension, political and strategic relations with the PICs, which will assist China's rise at the systemic (global) and sub-systemic (regional) levels.

China has since the late 1990s changed its previous strategy of focusing on economic growth by allocating much more resources to speed up the modernization of the People's Liberation Army (PLA) and military build-ups, as a result of its perceived U.S. military containment of its rise. 1996 saw a U.S. aircraft carrier sail through the Taiwan Strait to deter China's attempt to preclude Taiwan's separation; 1998 witnessed the United States bomb the Chinese embassy in Belgrade; 2001 saw a fatal mid-air collision of a U.S. spy plane with a Chinese jet fighter. Humiliated and conversely given incentives, the Chinese authorities took advantage of these incidents leading the Chinese public opinions to supporting their devotion to economic and military modernization to boost China's rise at the systemic (global) level (Sun & Guo 2013, p. 125). The Chinese authorities have since invested heavily in education, high-tech and military build-ups in response to the 'menacing' U.S. unilateralism and containment, and, in an attempt to modernize the People's Liberation Army (PLA) to narrow the distance from the United States sooner rather than later (Shambaugh 2003, p. 3). It is well noted that after a couple decades of heavy investment, China has now moved from one of the major global arms importers to a position where it can aboriginally develop and produce world class weaponry system and keep abreast of the latest military innovations in the United States and elsewhere. The PLA's progress in hardware build-ups is impressively exemplified by the most recent development of stealthy jet fighters F-20, anti-satellite missiles and hypersonic glider vehicle (HGV) (Mizokami 2014).

Alongside its military modernization, the PLA is undergoing a revolutionary transformation from ill-equipped armed forces to one of the world class forces capable of winning over any rival even in the sphere of high technology. Noticeably, China set up its first overseas naval base in Djibouti, marking a significant shift in China's military strategy that no longer merely focuses on defending her territories, but also on protecting her overseas interest. Equally importantly, the PLA regularizes joint military drills with Russia to hone the PLA's skill, and their joint naval drills in the last couple of years were held as far away as in the Mediterranean and the Baltic Seas (Korolev 2018, p. 233). These joint drills are evidently meant to display the joint capacity of the two forces to back up the policies of the China-Russia partnership effectively, and signal to Washington of Beijing and Moscow's shared stance against its unilateralism and hegemony in the global affairs (Gady 2015). Some military analysts (e.g., Haas 2013, p. 43) note that these joint military exercises though held in Europe serve as a showcase of force, showing others, particularly the United States, that who is in control of the Asia–Pacific region.

China has tried to enhance its "soft power" in the 21st century in tandem with its rapidly growing "hard" power, by particularly showcasing the rest of the world its "economic growth mode", diplomatic conceptions and traditional culture (Khan 2012, p. 57). The Chinese foreign policy makers and academics boast of the Chinese mode of "economic priority" and diplomatic principles, such as "non-interference", as the indispensable components of China's "soft power". It is no denial that these Chinese conceptions have helped Beijing reap political and diplomatic benefits particularly in the developing world as evidenced by the Pew global polling that finds China is mostly welcomed in emerging markets and the developing countries (Pew Research Global Attitudes Project 2019). The Chinese foreign policy makers and IR scholars are of the view that these new modes and principles provide an alternative to the developing states of their development modes and their roles in the international affairs (Sui & Yu 2024, p. 19). The alternative provides an explanation of why the developing states in Africa, Latin America and Asia (with exception to those with territorial disputes with China, e.g., Vietnam and India) view China's rise as a counterbalance to U.S. hegemony and power politics.

The Chinese government has over the post-Cold War era impressed the world that Beijing is committed to advancing economic cooperation and trade with the rest of the world. Beijing's move contrasts that of the United States that is busy in reinforcing its hegemony in the post-Cold War era by frequently launching wars and military interventions in the name of anti-terrorists and democracy promotion. These wars and interventions were viewed by the Chinese foreign policy elites as evidence of U.S. pursuit of global hegemony and power politics in the guise of democracy promotion and antiterrorism, thereby posing severe challenges to world peace and stability (Zhao 2011, p. 6). As Francis Fukuyama (2011) highlights, the wars launched by the United States and the close association they created between military invasion and democracy promotion tarnished the latter. Contrary to the U.S. interventionism and hegemonism, China sticks to the pursuit of its traditional strategy of "the five principles of peaceful co-existence (commonly known as "non-interference" overseas)[10] in dealing with its relations

---

10 The Five Principles of Peaceful Co-Existence are: mutual respect for sovereignty and territorial integrity, mutual non-aggression, non- interference in each other's internal affairs, equality and mutual benefit, and peaceful coexistence. These ideas were first put forward by then Chinese Premier Zhou Enlai in December 1953 when he met an Indian Government Delegation. In June 1954, Zhou visited India and Burma (now Myanmar). The joint Statement of the Prime Ministers of China and India issued in June and the Joint Statement of the Prime Ministers of China and Burma issued both affirmed that the Five Principles of Peaceful Co-Existence as guiding principles in their bilateral relations and then the Five Principles were formally proposed as the norms for handling international relations. In 1955 the Asian-Africa Conference convened in Bandung, Indonesia adopted Ten Principles for conducting international relations, in which the Five Principles of Peaceful Co-Existence were included. In 1970, the General Assembly of the United Nations adopted the "Declaration on Principles of International Law concerning Friendly Relations and Co-operation among States in accordance with the Charter of the United Nations". This declaration included the content of the Five Principles of Peaceful Co-Existence. For more details, see Li, Shihua 1995, "The Five Principles of Peaceful Co-Existence" constitutes the basis for a new international order", *Scientific Socialism*, No. 3, pp. 41-51.

with the developing countries, including the Pacific Island countries. This strategy has helped China seek solidarity with other developing countries by distancing itself from the colonial and imperialist powers that pursue "hegemonic" policies by interfering in the internal affairs of the developing countries (Sui & Yu 2024, p. 7). In this sense, China's strategy of "non-interference" allows Beijing to present itself to the other developing countries as a benevolent alternative to the western powers.

China has gone to great lengths to promote overseas a positive image of itself for the sake of political profit by making full use of its abundant cultural wealth. China has spent an enormous amount of money in the 21st century, trying to expand cultural exchanges with the rest of the world by establishing a global network of mass media and educational institutions (Khan 2012, p. 67). Of them, the program of Confucius Institutes is most notable as a form of cultural and linguistic diplomacy that has been widely employed by other culture-rich nations, such as the Alliance Française for French, the Goethe-Institut for German and the British Council for English. The Confucius program started in 2004 and has around 500 institutes in the Universities worldwide and more than 1000 Confucius Classrooms located in overseas primary and secondary schools, which outnumber the Goethe-Institut (around 160 schools) and the Alliance Française (850 schools) (Luk & Zhou 2016, p. 629). The Confucius Institutes bring the world resources for Chinese culture and serve as a vehicle for cultural diplomacy and a way for China to expand its soft power overseas. China has to date set up dozens of Confucius classrooms in the middle schools and universities in the PICs, such as those in the National University of Samoa and the University of South Pacific. China perceives its increasing influence and popularity particularly in the developing world (e.g., Africa and Latin America) as China's strategic assets that should be valued and smartly employed in the international politics (Yu 2018, p. 489). It is no denial that China has to date made impressive progress in enhancing its national prowess particularly in terms of "soft power".

It is noteworthy that China has over the last decade increasingly responded to the concerns with climate change particularly articulated by the 14 Pacific Island Countries (PICs) that have long been neglected by the U.S.-headed West in the post-Cold War era but valued by the Chinese authorities. The responses made by the Chinese academia and the Chinese authorities to climate change help China win the hearts and minds of the PICs' political elites and general public alike and intensify China-PICs strategic partnership. To address the challenges arising from climate change, the PICs collectively propose the *2050 Strategy for the Blue Pacific Continent* that announces to harness technology and scientifically-based research to 'secure our ocean and derive economic benefits from its resources' in a manner that will maintain environmental integrity and drive sustainable economic prosperity and development' (Pacific Islands Forum 2022). As part of the strategy, the PICs announce to advance their blue economy in a way of keeping green and sustainable development, which will contribute to promoting social and economic progress as well as environment and ecosystem conservation in the region (Pacific Islands Forum 2022). The World Bank defines the "blue economy" as the "sustainable use of ocean resources for economic growth, improved livelihoods, and jobs while preserving the health of the ocean ecosystem" (World Bank 2017).

The concept of the blue economy has also been accepted by the United Nations Sustainable Development Goals that set a target that by 2030 the economic benefits will be increased to small island developing states (SIDS) and least developed countries (LDCs) from the sustainable use of marine resources, including sustainable management of fisheries, aquaculture, and tourism (Spalding 2016). The Blue Economy has become a focal point of the PICs for fostering economic growth, societal advancement, and environmental conservation. The pursuit of blue economy is based on its potential to create employment, reduce poverty and enhance nutrition and food security, and drive economic growth, as recognized by various international organizations and researchers. The PICs describe the Pacific as a vast blue continent, to which their economic landscape is closely linked. The PICs depend more heavily on the marine resources for feeding their people and providing their income than other countries in the world. In this vein, it is hard to overstate the importance of a healthy Pacific continent. This partially explains why the PICs commit themselves to the "blue economy" to advance their economic and social progress, and environmental protection. It is noted that the PICs have prioritized the blue economy sector as a key component for achieving their economic and social development goals outlined in the *2050 Strategy* for the Blue Pacific Continent.

The PICs are widely considered the frontline of climate change and more vulnerable to it than most countries in the other parts of the world, as a result of their land size, geographic location in the vast Pacific prone to tropical cyclones, and equally importantly, incapacity to adapt to climate change. The PICs as a whole have significant vulnerability and are facing seminal challenges arising from climate change that leads to rising sea temperatures, ocean acidification and other disasters, which are worsened by El Niño cycles. Climate change and resultant disasters, such as sea-level rise, floods and tsunamis, give rise to seminal challenges to the PICs in general and to the sustainability and resilience of the blue economy in particular. Rising sea level has been a significant threat to the low-lying coastal areas of the South Pacific, and has resulted in increased coastal erosion, flooding, and saltwater intrusion. The degradation of vital coastal ecosystems like seagrass beds and mangroves further threatens marine biodiversity and the livelihoods of coastal communities. The risks are particularly high in some low-lying area, with potential inundation of a significant portion of some atolls and islands, and substantial economic losses projected. The climate change might destroy the PICs' ocean-based economy, local livelihoods, and the ecosystem and biodiversity as evidenced by the reduced fish populations within the waters of the PICs, which is detrimental to local economy and regional ecosystem (Charlton 2016, p. 12).

The Chinese government and academia have made prompt responses to the PICs' concerns with climate change as exemplified by the training program offered by the Liaocheng University located in China's Shandong Province in cooperation with the Chinese Ministry of Ecology and Environment and the Chinese Ministry of Natural Resources. The China-PICs Climate Change Cooperation Center (The Research Center for PICs Studies) based at the Liaocheng University works with other Chinese universities and research institutions to provide the PICs training opportunities to the scholars and officials from the PICs on climate change. The Chinese government provides fundings annually to the Chinese universities and research institutions, which are earmarked for China-PICs cooperation on climate change and climate change assistance to the PICs. The Chinese government and relevant universities have to date provided hundreds of training opportunities on the climate change with the aim to help the PICs remain resilient to the impacts of climate change and disasters, and be able to lead safe, secure and prosperous lives. At invitation by the Center, the authors have annually lectured the trainees on the China-PICs green energy cooperation since 2018. China's prompt responses to climate change have contributed to China-PICs strategic partnership and constituted a significant component of China's "soft" power particularly in the developing world.

Conclusion

The main argument of the chapter is that under normal circumstances, the primary objectives of the rising middle powers likely contradict those of the established superpower and some established middle powers as intimated by the rising powers of the past centuries. Acutely aware of this by engaging in historical learning, the Chinese foreign policy makers have deliberately adopted the strategy of "concealing China's ability and biding its time" in pursuit of China's resurgence at the systemic (global) level without drawing much attention and containment from the established superpower, namely, the United States. China pursued this strategy particularly before the end of the first decade of the 21st century in pursuit of its century-long goal of restoration of its past glory of *fuqiang* (wealth and power) and its revival at the systemic (global) level. At the same time, China has prioritized economic growth as a result of its belief in the significance of economic modernization for its rise at the systemic (global) level.

To speed up its rise, China has economically increased its commercial presence throughout the world, and its say in global economic reform and governance alongside its economic rise. Politically, China is intensifying its partnerships with strategically significant states and states groupings to counterattack its perceived U.S. containment and reshape the world order more to its liking. China also places much importance on its relations of cooperation with the developing states and states groupings as it views the relationships with the developing countries as the "basis" of China's international relations. Militarily, China expedites the modernization of the PLA to meet the challenges arising from U.S. military threat and containment and, more importantly, to protect China's rise from being disrupted by any established power. China also tries to enhance its "soft power" by showcasing its "growth model" and its culture alongside its rise. An important point emerges from the discussions in the chapter is that the continuity of China's strategies of rising at the systemic (global) level is reflected in China's decades of commitment to enhancing its "hard power" by advancing its economic and military modernization and its "soft power" by increasing its popularity and influence particularly in the developing world.

References

Academy of Military Science of the PLA 2000, *the History of the War to Resist U.S. Aggression and Aid Korea*, Military Science Publishing House: Beijing, p. 207.

Andresen, Joshua 2019, 'China's Military and the Belt and Road Initiative: a View from the Outside', *The Chinese Journal of Global Governance*, Vol. 5, No. 2, pp. 122-135.

Blackwill, Robert D. and Harris, Jennifer M. 2016, *War by Other Means: Geoeconomics and Statecraft*, The Belknap Press of Havard University Press: Cambridge, p. 78.

Bregolat, Eugenio 2015, *the Second Chinese Revolution*, Palgrave Macmillan: New York, p. 64.

Charlton, Karen E.; Russell, Joanna; Gorman, Emma et al 2016, Fish, food security and health in Pacific Island countries and territories: a systematic literature review, *BMC Public Health*, Vol. 16, No. 285, pp. 2-26.

Chaziza, M. 2023, 'The Non-interference Principle and the BRI Grand Strategy in the GCC', *China Report*, Vol. 59, No. 1, pp. 40-57.

China–CELAC Forum 2015, *The Beijing Declaration*, 21 January, http://www.chinacelacforum.org/chn/zywj/t1230231.htm.

Clad, J. and Manning, R.A. 2014, 'China and America: At a Dangerous Tipping Point', *National Interest*, 10, June, http://nationalinterest.org/feature/china-america-dangerous-tipping-point-10632.

Clarke, Michael and Ricketts, 2016, 'Should America Fear the China-Russia Relationship?', *National Interest*, 1 February, http://nationalinterest.org/feature/should-america-fear-the-china-russia-relationship-15075.

Cui, Shoujun and Liu, Zuoli 2018, 'the current situation, characteristics and impacts of the China-Latin America military exchanges', *Journal of Latin American Studies*, Vol. 40, No. 6, pp. 96-108.

De Conti, B., Sequetto Pereira, M. an Prates, D. M. 2019, 'Belt and Road Initiative: a Chinese Marshall plan?', *Papel Político, Vol. 24, No.* 2, https://doi.org/10.11144/Javeriana.papo24-2.bric.

Deng, Hao 2021, 'The political cooperation within the SCO: the achievement, challenge and prospects', *International Studies*, No. 3, pp. 47-66.

Deng, Xiaoping 1993, *Selected works of Deng Xiaoping*, vol. 3, People's Press: Beijing.

Department of Foreign Affairs and Trade of Australia 2011, *China fact sheet*, Commonwealth of Australia, Canberra, December, http://www.dfat.gov.au/geo/fs/chin.pdf.

Department of Foreign Affairs and Trade, Australia 2021, *Regional Comprehensive Economic Partnership*, https://www.dfat.gov.au/trade/agreements/not-yet-in-force/rcep.

Department of Foreign Affairs and Trade, Australia 2023, *China Factsheet*, https://www.dfat.gov.au/geo/China.

Ellis, R. 2011, 'Chinese soft power in Latin America', *Joint Force Quarterly*, No. 60, 1st quarter, pp. 85-91.

Evans, Z. 2019, Kissinger warns U.S. and China in "foothills of a Cold War", *National Review*, 21 November, https://www.nationalreview.com/news/kissinger-warns-u-s-and-china-in-foothills-of-a-cold-war/.

Ewert, Insa & Poter, Jan Philipp. 2016, 'Market Economy Status for China: The Views From Brussels and Beijing: A closer look at the market economy debate between China and the EU', *Diplomat*, 25 July, <http://thediplomat.com/2016/07/market-economy-status-for-china-the-views-from-brussels-and-beijing/>.

Feng, Bing 2016, *The "Belt and Road": to connect and upgrade global economics*, China Publishing Group: Beijing, p. 176.

Foot, Rosemary 2014, 'Constraints on conflict in the Asia-Pacific: balancing the War Ledger', *Political Science*, Vol. 66, No. 2, pp. 119-142.

Foreign Ministry of the People's Republic of China 2016, 'Wang Yi: China-Russia Strategic Coordination Has Become the Ballast Stone of Safeguarding World Peace and Stability', FMPRC News, 3 December, <http://www.fmprc.gov.cn/mfa_eng/zxxx_662805/t1421647.shtml>.

Fu, Y. 2016, 'How China sees Russia', *Foreign Affairs*, January/February, https://www.foreignaffairs.com/articles/china/2015-12-14/how-china-sees-russia.

Fukuyama, F. 2011, 'U.S. democracy has little to teach China', *Financial Times*, 17 January, http://www.ft.com/cms/s/0/cb6af6e8-2272-11e0-b6a2-00144feab49a.html#axzz1DXPgVQ22.

Fujita, Kimio 1993, 'China and its Asian neighbors: a Japanese perspective', Kau, Michael Ying-Mao and Marsh, Susan (eds), *China in the era of Deng Xiaoping: a decade of reform*, M.E. Sharp: New York, p. 464.

Fukuyama, F. 1992, *The end of history and the last man*, Hamilton, London, p. 2.

Gady, Franz-Stefan 2015, 'China and Russia Conclude Naval Drill in Mediterranean', *Diplomat*, 22 May, http://thediplomat.com/2015/05/china-and-russia-conclude-naval-drill-in-mediterranean/.

Gao, Fei and Zhang, Jian 2017, 'the triangular relationships of China-the United States and Russia in the post-Cold War era', Gao, Fei and Li, Mingjiang (eds), *China's neighborhood diplomacy: peaceful development vs strategic hedging*, Beijing: Global Publishing.

Gao, Zugui 2012, 'shanghe zuzhi fazhan jianzheng zhongguo duiwai zhanlue chuangxin (the development of SCO witnesses the innovation of Chinese foreign strategy)', *Ziguangge*, No. 7, pp. 72-74.

Global Times 2024, 'Chinese yuan's internationalization continues to display strong momentum: university report', 29 July, Beijing, https://www.globaltimes.cn/page/202407/1316953.shtml.

Glosny, Michael A. 2016, 'Chinese Assessments of China's influence in developing Asia', Goh, Evelyn (eds), Rising China's influence in developing Asia, Oxford University Press: Oxford, p. 28.

Guo, Wanchao 2005, China's road to peaceful development, *Studies on the Socialism with Chinese Characteristics*, Vol. 68, No. 6, pp. 62-66.

Gvosdev, N. K. & Marsh, C. 2014, *Russian foreign policy: Interests, vectors and sectors*, New Delhi: SAGE Publications India, p. 132.

Haga, Allison 2021, 'The Asian Infrastructure Investment Bank: A Qualified Success for Beijing's Economic Statecraft', *Journal of Current Chinese Affairs*, Special Issue, pp. 1-31.

Hakans, Erik and Hynes Phill 2017, 'China's Challenge to the World Economic Order', *Asia-Pacific Research*, 17 January, <http://www.asia-pacificresearch.com/chinas-challenge-to-the-world-economic-order/5569175>.

Haas, Marcel de 2013, *Russian–Chinese Security Relations: Moscow's Threat from the East?* Netherlands Institute of International Relations Clingendael Institute: Hague, p. 43.

Holbig, H. and Gilley, B. 2010, 'Reclaiming Legitimacy in China', *Politics & Policy*, Volume 38, No. 3, pp. 395-422.

Hornby, Lucy & Donnan, shawn 2016, 'China fights for market economy status', 9 May, *Financial Times*, 9 May, <https://www.ft.com/content/572f435e-0784-11e6-9b51-0fb5e65703ce>.

Hsiang, Antonio C. 2008, 'China challenges the United States in Latin America', *Tamkang Journal of International Affairs* 11: 4, pp. 121-52.

Hsu, Immanuel, C.Y. (Xu, Zhongyue) 2000, *the rise of modern China*, Oxford University Press: New York, p. 477. Liu, Ye 2004, *Chinese Intellectuals and Chinese revolutions*, Tianjin People's Press: Tianjin, p. 129.

Huo, Jianguo 2015, 'zimaoqu kuoda shidian de zhanlue shenyi (the strategic implications for enlarging experiments on free trade areas)', *People's Tribune*, Vol. 473, No. 6, pp. 43-45.

Japan Times 2015, 'Obama warns TPP failure would let China write trade rules', 18 April, <http://www.japantimes.co.jp/news/2015/04/18/business/economy-business/obama-warns-tpp-failure-would-let-china-write-trade-rules/#article_history>.

Jiang, Xinfeng 2013, 'the development of Japan's military forces and its impact on China's security', *Japanese Studies*, No. 3, pp. 69-86.

Jiang, Xueqing 2014, 'Nation looks to boost international use of yuan for trade', *China Daily*, 15 August, p. 18.

Keohane, R.O. and Nye, J. S. 2000, 'Globalization: What's new? What's not? (And so what?)', *Foreign Policy*, spring, Issue 118, pp. 104-119.

Kerry, John 2013, *Remarks on U.S. policy in the western hemisphere*, U.S. Department of State, 18 November, http://www.state.gov/secretary/remarks/2013/11/217680.htm.

Khan, Shamsul 2012, "Middle Powers and the Dynamics of Power Shift", *Harvard Asian Quarterly*, Vol. XIV, No. 3, p. 52.

Khan, Shamsul and Yu, Le 2013, 'Evolving China-ASEAN Relations and CAFTA', *European Journal of East Asian Studies*, Vol. 12, No. 1, pp. 81-107.

Kirk, Hugo 2016, 'No Bigger Question: How Should the U.S. Handle the Rise of China?', *National Interest*, 30 September, http://nationalinterest.org/blog/the-skeptics/no-bigger-question-how-should-the-us-handle-the-rise-china-17885.

Korolev, Alexander 2018, 'on the verge of an alliance: contemporary China-Russia military cooperation', *Asian Security*, Vol. 15, Issue 3, pp. 233-252.

Kottasova, I. 2017, Putin meets Xi: Two economies, only one to envy, CNN, 2 July, http://money.cnn.com/2017/07/02/news/economy/china-russia-putin-xi-meeting/index.html.

Lampton, D.M. 2015, 'A Tipping Point in U.S.-China Relations is Upon Us', *US-China Perception Monitor*, China Program, Carter Center, 6 May, http://www.uscnpm.org/blog/2015/05/11/a-tipping-point-in-u-s-china-relations-is-upon-us-part-i/>

Lee, John 2010, 'Don't rush to back Beijing over Delhi', *Australian*, 13 September, p. 10.

Leng, Rong & Wang, Zuoling 2004, *Deng Xiaoping Nian Pu (A chronicle of Deng Xiaoping's life) (1975-1997)*, Central Literature Press, Beijing, p. 1078.

Li, Xiaokang 2010, 'On China's choice of the path of constitutional government and the retrospection', *New West*, No. 16, pp. 87-88.

Lim, Robyn 2003, *The Geopolitics of East Asia: search for equilibrium*, Routledge: London, p. 142.

Liu, Guo hua and Xue, Xiaorong 2002, 'An analysis on the disintegration of the Soviet Union', *East European & Central Asian Studies*, No. 6, pp. 75-81.

Liu, Huaqiu 1997, 'Zhong guo shi zhong bu yu de feng xing du li zi zhu de he ping wai jiao zheng ce (China adheres to the independent foreign policy of peace)', *Journal of Qiushi*, No. 23, pp. 2-9.

Liu, Xiaofeng 2019, "An analysis on U.S. containment of China from a geopolitical perspective", *Foreign Theoretical Trends*, Vol. 524, No. 10, pp. 60-71.

Liu, Xiaofeng and Zhang, Zongwu 2015, 'houwuji shidai zhongguo daguimo duimei zhijie touzi dongyin yanjiu (analysis on China's large-scale investment in the United States in the post-crisis era)', *People's Tribune*, Vol. 479, No. 9, pp. 132-135.

Lo, Bob 2008, *Axis of Convenience: Moscow, Beijing, and the New Geopolitics*, Brookings Institutuin Press: Washington, p. 3.

Lowry, R. 2011, 'China without illusions', 18 January, *National Review Online*, 18 January, <http://www.nationalreview.com/articles/257334/china-without-illusions-rich-lowry>.

Lu, Yan 2014, 'meiou mouqiu zimao xieding dui shijie jingmao de yingxiang yu zhongguo yingdui celue (the impact of an FTA between the United States and EU on global economics and trade and China's countermeasures)', *Intertrade*, No. 2, pp. 44-48.

Luk, Sabrina and Zhou, Ying 2016, 'Establishing Confucius Institutes: a tool for promoting China's soft power?', *Journal of Contemporary China*, Vol. 25, Issue 100, pp. 628-642.

Lukin, Artyom 2019, 'The Implications of a True Russia-China Alliance', Australian Institute of International Affairs, 14 July, http://www.internationalaffairs.org.au/australianoutlook/implications-true-russia-china-alliance/.

Luo, Jianbo 2013, 'China's relations with African Union: the historical transition and its significance to the world', *West Asia and Africa*, No. 1, pp. 116 -131.

Lüthi, Loren. M. 2008, The Sino-Soviet Split: Cold War in the Communist World, New York: Princeton University Press, p. 35.

Mearsheimer, John 2006, 'China's unpeaceful rise', *Current History*, Vol. 105, No. 690, pp. 160-162.

Medeiros, Evan S. 2019, 'The Changing Fundamentals of US-China Relations', *The Washington Quarterly*, Vol. 42, No. 3, pp. 93-119.

Meisels, Greer 2013, 'Lessons learned in China from the collapse of the Soviet Union', China Studies Center, University of Sydney, *Policy Paper Series*, Paper 3, <https://sydney.edu.au/china_studies_centre/images/content/ccpublications/policy_paper_series/2013/Lessons-learned-in-China-from-the-collapse-of-the-Soviet-Union.shtml.pdf>.

Michel, Casey 2017, 'SCO Set to Expand, Adding India and Pakistan', *Diplomat*, 6 June, <http://thediplomat.com/2017/06/sco-set-to-expand-adding-india-and-pakistan/>.

Ministry of Foreign Affairs of the PRC 2014, Xi Jinping attends SCO summit in Dushanbe and Delivers Important Speech Stressing Gathering People's Will and Power and Coordinating Sincerely to Push SCO to a New Level, 12 September 2014, http://www.fmprc.gov.cn/mfa_eng/topics_665678/zjpcxshzzcygyslshdsschybdtjkstmedfsllkydjxgsfw/t1191482.shtml.

Ministry of Commerce of the PRC 2024, China's FTA, Beijing, July, http://fta.mofcom.gov.cn/.

Mizokami, Kyle 2014, 'Five Chinese Weapons of War America Should Fear', *National Interest*, 7 May, http://nationalinterest.org/feature/five-chinese-weapons-war-america-should-fear-10388.

Moran, Michael 2013, The Reckoning: Debt, Democracy, and the Future of American Power, Macmillan: New York, p. 164.

Morgenthau, H.J. 1966, *Politics among nations*, Knopf, New York, p. 25.

Nayar, Baldev R. 1979, "A World Role: the Dialectics of Purpose and Power" in *India: A Rising Middle Power*, ed. Boulder Mellor: Lynne Rienner, pp. 117-145.

Niu, Jun 1999, '1969 nian zhong su bian jie chong tu yu zhong guo wai jiao zhan lue de tiao zheng (the 1969 China-Soviet border dispute and China's shift in diplomatic strategy)', *Contemporary China History Studies*, No. 1, pp. 66-77.

O'Grady, Mary Anastasia 2004, 'The Middle Kingdom in Latin America,' *Wall Street Journal*, 6 September, p. A7.

Pablo, Bachelet 2005, 'China's Latin influence is growing, general says', *Miami Herald*, 10 March.

Pan, Zhengxiang and Li, Yong 2009, 'shanghe zuzhi buduan shenhua hezuo de dongyin fenxi (Analysis on the motivations for deepened cooperation among SCO member states)', *Contemporary World*, No. 12, pp. 63-65.

Panetta, Leon 2012, 'Secretary of Defense Speech: Shangri-La Security Dialogue', U.S. Department of Defense, 2 June, <http://www.defense.gov/speeches/speech.aspx?speechid=1681>.

Pant, Harsh V. 2011, *China's Rising Global Profile: The Great Power Tradition*, Sussex Academic Press: Eastbourne, p. 9.

Papageorgiou, M., dos Santos Cardoso, F. 2021, 'Chinese Diplomacy, Strategic Partnerships and Global Economic Supremacy', Spigarelli, F., McIntyre, J.R. (eds), *The New Chinese Dream. Palgrave Studies of Internationalization in Emerging Markets*, Palgrave Macmillan: Cham.

Parkin, Russel and Lee, David 2008, Great White Fleet to Coral Sea: naval strategy and the development of Australia–United States relations, 1900-1945, National Library of Australia: Canberra, p. 54.

Peng, Z. and Tok, S.K. 2016, 'The AIIB and China's Normative Power in International Financial Governance Structure', *Chinese Political Science Review*, Vol. 1, No. 1, pp. 736-753.

Petri, Peter A. and Plummer, Michael 2020, *RCEP: A new trade agreement that will shape global economics and politics*, November 16, https://www.brookings.edu/blog/order-from-chaos/2020/11/16/rcep-a-new-trade-agreement-that-will-shape-global-economics-and-politics/.

Pew Research Global Attitudes Project 2019, 'China's Economic Growth Mostly Welcomed in Emerging Markets, but Neighbors Wary of Its Influence', December, https://www.pewresearch.org/global/2019/12/05/attitudes-toward-china-2019/.

Piccone, T. 2016, *The Geopolitics of China's rise in Latin America*, The Brookings Institution, November, https://www.brookings.edu/wp-content/uploads/2016/11/the-geopolitics-of-chinas-rise-in-latin-america_ted-piccone.pdf.

Pacific Islands Forum 2022, *2050 Strategy for the Blue Pacific Continent*, Pacific Islands Forum Secretariat, Suva, Fiji.

Radchenko, S. 2010, 'The Sino-Soviet split', in M. Leffler & O. Westad (eds.), *The Cambridge History of the Cold War*, Cambridge: Cambridge University Press, pp. 349-372.

Ratuva, Steven 2014, 'A New Regional Cold War? American and Chinese Posturing in the Pacific', *Asia & the Pacific Policy Studies*, Vol. 1, No. 2, pp. 409-422.

Reuters 2016, Shanghai Cooperation Organisation to set up bank, Newsonline, 3 November, <https://search.yahoo.com/search;_ylt=A0LEV1nT01ZZIukA4wZXNyoA;_ylu=X3oDMTEzajVvczlrBGNvbG8DYmYxBHBvcwMxBHZ0aWQDBHNlYwNwYWdpbmF0aW9u?p=bank+of+shanghai+cooperation+organization&pz=10&fr=yfp-t&fr2=sb-top&bct=0&fp=1&b=1&pz=10&bct=0&xargs=0>

Ross, Robert, S. 2009, 'China's three rises, regional power transitions and East Asia security: 1949 to the 21st century', *World Economics and Politics*, Vol. 346, No. 11, 36-43.

Rotberg, R. 2008, 'China's quest for resources, opportunities and influence in Africa', Rotberg, R. eds, China Into Africa: Trade, Aid, and Influence, Brookings Institution Press: Baltimore, p. 11.

Scott, David 2008, *China and the International System, 1840-1949: Power, Presence, and Perception in a Century of Humiliation*, New York: State University of New York Press, pp. 371.

Shambaugh, D. 2003, *Modernizing China's military: Progress, problems and prospects*, University of California Press, Ewing, NJ, USA, p. 3.

Smith, G. and Wesley-Smith, T 2019, *The China Alternatives: changing regional order in the Pacific islands*, Canberra: Australian National University Press.

Sui, Shuying 2004, 'On the historical limitation of the policy of "standing on one side"', *Qilu Journal*, No. 6, pp. 48-56.

Sui, Sophia and Yu, Le 2020, 'Contending Chinese Perspectives on China-Russia Military Partnership', *Communist and Post-Communist Studies*, Vol. 53, No. 4, pp. 239-258.

Sui, Sophia and Yu, Lei 2023a, *Complex Interdependence and China-Australia relations*, New York: Routledge.

Sui, Sophia and Yu, Lei 2023b, 'China-Russia Strategic Partnership and the Oil and Gas Collaboration', *Innovation: The European Journal of Social Science Research*, https://doi.org/10.1080/13511610.2023.2289827.

Sui, Sophia and Yu, Lei 2024, 'Ontological Security in China–Pacific Islands Countries (PICs) Geopolitics', *Journal of Island and Marine*, Vol. 1, No. 1, pp. 1-23.

Sun, Xiaohui & Guo, Wenliang 2013, 'Xin zhong guo cheng li yi lai zhong zuo gong chan dang chu li zhong da she wai shi jian de jing yan yu qi di (The experience and revelation of the CCP in dealing with major international events since the founding of the PRC)', *Theoretical Investigation*, Vol. 171, No. 2, pp. 125-128.

Spalding, M. J. 2016, 'The new blue economy: The future of sustainability', *Journal of Ocean and Coastal Economics*, Vol. 2, No. 2, pp. 8-21.

Sutter, Robert 2000, *Chinese policy priorities and their implications for the United States*, Rowman & Littlefield: Lanham, p. 62.

Tang, Jun 2015, 'Ying jiang 21shiji haishangsichouzilu yanshen zhi lamei' [Expanding the 21st-century marine silk road to Latin America', *Contemporary World*, 399:2, pp. 32-34.

Taylor, Ian 2011, *The Forum on China–Africa Cooperation (FOCAC)*, Abingdon: Routledge, p. 12. Hakim, Peter, 'Is Washington losing Latin America?', *Foreign Affairs*, Vol. 85, No. 1, pp. 39-53.

Tow, William and Hay, Leisa 2001, 'Australia, the United States and a 'China growing strong': managing conflict avoidance', *Australian Journal of International Affairs*, Vol. 55, No. 1, pp. 37-54.

Tow, W. and Loke, B. 2009, 'Rules of engagement: America's Asia-Pacific security policy under an Obama administration', *Australian Journal of International Affairs*, Vol. 63, No. 4, pp. 442-457.

Tull, D.M. 2006, 'China's engagement in Africa: Scope, significance and consequences', *Journal of Modern African Studies*, Vol. 44, No. 3, pp. 459-479.

Tyers, Rod 2012, 'Japanese Economic Stagnation: Causes and Global Implications', *Economic Record*, Vol. 88, Issue 283, pp. 517-536.

Vadell, A. 2018, 'China in Latin America: South-South cooperation with Chinese characteristics', *Latin American Perspectives*, Vol. 46, No. 2, pp. 107-125.

Voge, Ezra F. 2013, *Deng Xiaoping and the Transformation of China*, Belknap Press: New York, p. 36.

Waldron, A 2008, 'China in Africa', Arthur Waldron (eds), *China in Africa*, The Jamestown Foundation, Washington, D.C., p. 12.

Wang, H. 2019, The 29 meetings between Xi and Putin over the last 6 years shows the intimacy of China-Russia relationship, *Observer* (Guanchazhe), 5 June, https://www.guancha.cn/internation/2019_06_05_504441.shtml.

Wang, Lianhe 2014, 'the new development of the US-Australian military alliance', *Contemporary International Relations*, No. 1, pp. 36-42.

Woetzel, Jonathan; Seong, Jeongmin; Ngai, Joe; Manyika, James; Madgavkar, Anu; Lund, Mumbai Susan; Mironenko, Andrey 2019, *China and the world: Inside the dynamics of a changing relationship*, McKinsey Global Institute: Brussels, p. 27.

World Bank 2017, *What is blue economy?* 6 June, https://www.worldbank.org/en/news/infographic/2017/06/06/blue-economy.

Wright, Sue 2016, Language Policy and Language Planning: From Nationalism to Globalisation, Palgrave Macmillan: New York, p. 186.

Wu, X. 2019, Competition-oriented U.S. China policy and the transformation of China-America relationship, International Studies, Vol. 191, No. 3, pp. 7-20.

Xi, Jinping 2013a, *shenhua gange kaifang gongchuang yatai meihao weilai (Deepening China's reform and opening up and creating a better future in the Asia-Pacific region)*, Xinhua News Agency, Beijing, 7 October, <http://news.xinhuanet.com/world/2013-10/08/c_125490697.htm>.

Xi, Jinping 2013b, '(shunying shidai chaoliu, chujin shijie heping fazhan (to keep pace with times and promote world's peace)', *People's Daily*, 23 March, p. 2.

Xi, Jinping 2014, 'jiakuai shishi ziyoumaoyiqu zhanlue, jiakuai goujian kaifangxing jingji xintizhi (speeding up the FTA strategy and creating an open economic system)', *People's Daily*, 7 December, p. 1.

Xia, J.S. 2007, 'A New Milestone in Sino-African Relationship', *West Asia and Africa*, No. 2, pp. 5-9.

Xia, Yafeng 2014, 'the People's Republic of China', Martray, James and Boose Jr, Donald (eds), *Ashgate Research Companion to the Korean War*, Ashgate: Burlington, p. 61.

Xie, T. 2019, 'China and the United States in the era of Trump', *Asia-Pacific Security and Maritime Affairs*, Vol. 26, No. 5, pp. 14-28.

Xin, Qiang 2014, '"Five No's" policy: the U.S. adjustment of the South China Sea Policy', *American Studies Quarterly*, No. 6, pp. 51-68.

Ye, Zicheng 2004, 'The legacy, development and reflections on Deng Xiaoping's diplomatic thought under the new conditions', *World Economics and Politics*, No. 11, pp. 8-14.

Yu, Huamin 2007, 'Three major policy and independent new China diplomacy', *Historical Research in Anhui*, No. 5, pp. 81-90.

Yu, Lei 2015, 'China-Latin America Strategic Partnership: a fulcrum in China's rise', *International Affairs*, Vol. 91, No. 5, pp. 1047-1068.

Yu, Lei 2018, 'China's expanding security involvement in Africa: a pillar for 'China-Africa community of common destiny', *Global Policy*, Vol. 9, Issue 4, pp. 489-500.

Yu, Lei 2022, 'China's FTA Strategy and Economic Regionalism', *The Journal of International Development*, Vol. 34, Issue 8, pp. 1633-1648.

Yu, Lei 2023, 'China-Russia Strategic Partnership: the strategic fulcrum of China's rise?', *International Journal*, 2023, Vol. 79, No. 1, pp. 217-239.

Zen, Bingyi and Li, Xiaoyu 2015, 'weilai 5nian waibu jingji huanjing yu zhongguo duiwai kaifang xinsilu (the international economic environment in the 5 years to come and China's new ideas about its opening-up), *International Studies*, No. 4, pp. 68-81.

Zeng, Xianghong and Li, Xiaotian 2018, 'the security cooperation in SCO and its prospects', *Foreign Affairs Review*, No. 1, pp. 66-97.

Zhang, H. 2020, 'Reviewing China-America relations in the new situation', *Literature of Chinese Communist Party*, Vol. 199, No. 1, pp. 85-90.

Zhang, Xiuhua 2000, 'dui jianguo chuqi yibiandao zhanlue de xinrenshi (re-considering the strategy of "leaning to one side" adopted at the beginning of the founding of the PRC)', *Collected Papers of History Studies*, No. 2, pp. 47-51.

Zhang, Yunhua 2016, *Macro-control and Economic Growth*, Beijing: China Social Sciences Press, p. 57.

Zhang, Yunling 2015, 'yatai jingji yitihua yu hezuo jincheng jiexi (analysis on economic integration and the process of economic cooperation in Asia-Pacific)', *Foreign Affairs Review*, No. 2, pp. 1-11.

Zhao, Gancheng 2011, 'Meiguo de nanya zhanlue yu zhongyin guanxi (America's strategy on South Asia and China-India Relations)', *Asia & Africa Review*, No. 5, pp. 1-6.

Zhu, F. 2019, 'Trade war and hi-tech war and the changing paradigm of China-America relationship', *Asia-Pacific Security and Maritime Affairs*, Vol. 26, No. 4, pp. 1-14.

Zuo, Xiying 2014, 'meiguo zhanlue shousuo yu yatai zhixu de weilai (the U.S. strategic withdrawal and the future order in the Asia-Pacific region)', *Contemporary Asia-Pacific Studies*, No. 4, pp. 4-28.

2

The "Belt and Road" Initiatives in the Pacific Islands

Introduction

Xi Jinping, Chinese President (2013-), proposed the "Belt and Road" Initiative (BRI) to advance "connectivity and communication" with countries across the world, and particularly on the Eurasian and African continents shortly after his presidency began in early 2013[11]. After the PICs expressed their willingness to actively participate in the BRI' four years later, Xi Jinping referred to the South Pacific islands as a 'natural' extension of the BRI, implying the increasing

11 The Chinese "One Belt and One Road initiative" (BRI) is aimed to create a global transport and investment infrastructure, which combines two projects – the Silk Road Economic Belt and the 21st-century Maritime Silk Road. BRI is an ambitious development proposal through which China wishes to sustain its economic growth by prompting trade and economic cooperation with the rest of the world. To this end, China is committing itself to infrastructure development in the hopes of connecting it to countries in Asia and beyond. It is estimated that China plans to invest $150 billion dollars into infrastructure each year. For more details see Cai, Peter 2017, *Understanding China's Belt and Road Initiative*, Lowy Institute for International Policy, Australia, March, Melbourne.

significance of the Pacific islands in the context of the great picture of the America-China competition for global supremacy and China's rise at the systemic (global) level (Szadziewski 2021, p. 295, Yu & Zhao 2019, p. 27). It is safe to say that the South Pacific islands were not meant to be incorporated into the BRI when it was first proposed in early 2013 before the U.S. "pivot to Aisa" had not yet played out. This is partially because China has been pursuing "peaceful rise" over the post-Cold War era and is reluctant to give offence to the United States by "intruding" the South Pacific--the backyard of the United States (Sui & Yu 2024, p. 3, Yu & Zhao 2019, p. 27).

A development strategy notwithstanding, the BRI is broadly assumed by policy analysts and scholars of international relations (IR) (e.g., Paal 2015, Zheng 2016, p. 107, Ma 2016, p. 9) as a strategy to counter the U.S. containment of China's rise. In their viewpoints, the BRI is most likely to expand China's presence and influence in the world by intensifying its economic and infrastructural cooperation, and, by extension, its political ties with the rest of the world. A number of Chinese foreign policy elites (e.g., Gao & Zhang 2017; Sui & Yu 2020) conceive the U.S. strategies, such as the "pivot to Asia", "the freedom of navigation operations" in the South China Sea and the ongoing trade war, as designed by the U.S. authorities to contain China's rise despite Washington's denial (Löfflmann 2016, p. 93). Against this backdrop, China's expanding footprints and involvement in the South Pacific islands, including the BRI, is widely conceived by IR scholars (e.g., Das 2016; Yu 2015, p. 1047) as a strategy to counterattack the U.S. containment by opening a "new battlefield" in the traditional U.S.' "sphere of influence".

The BRI primarily consists of the land-based Silk Road Economic Belt (the "Belt") that extends across Central and West Asia to Europe and the sea-based 21st Century Maritime Silk Road (the "Road") that starts from China to Europe via the Southeast Asia, and to those in Oceania and South America by crossing the Pacific. The BRI is an ambitious plan designed by China to link Asia, Europe and Africa with a network of ports, highways and railways and China is giving tens of billions of dollars in loans to countries, in a bid to build major infrastructure development projects in various participating nations (ZiroMwatela & Zhao 2016, p. 11). Since its implementation, the BRI has involved a massive amount of infrastructural and investment projects that the Chinese government expects will bring new opportunities for investors and enterprises home and abroad and further integrate the Chinese economy into the global economic system (Liu 2017, p. 21). More than 140 countries have to date signed on to the BRI, in which China has typically lent large sums of money to countries across the world for infrastructural development, such as the construction of roads, dams, railways, ports and sports facilities (ZiroMwatela & Zhao 2016, p. 15).

A report released by the World Bank shows that the building of the BRI demonstrates strong resilience and vitality, injecting strong impetus into global openness and cooperation and world economic development (Baniya et al 2019). The report predicts that the China-funded program could ultimately plug infrastructure gaps and boost global economic cooperation and trade. For example, the report notes that the shipment time from China to Central Europe is usually about 30 days, as most goods travel by sea. The shipment time by train is about half as long, but given the current infrastructure, it would be much costlier. The report concludes that the improvement of the capacity and network of rail infrastructure across the Eurasian continent could dramatically shorten the average travel time and reduce the cost. In this context, the report published by the World Bank shows its appreciation of the BRI and provides some advice for addressing the challenges arising from the BRI.

The data released by the Chinese government show that in 2023 alone, China's non-financial outbound direct investment in the countries participating in the BRI came in at US$31.8 billion, a year on year increase of 22.6 percent (The Central government of the PRC 2023); In terms of foreign contracted projects by the Chinese business, the value of newly signed contracts added up to US$227.16 billion in 2023, a year on year increase of 5.7 percent; The turnover reached US$132.05 billion, a year on year increase of 4.8 percent. Another World Bank analysis on the BRI finds that the BRI will contribute to the world's poverty reduction as if implemented fully, the BRI could lift 32 million people who live on less than $3.20 a day out of moderate poverty (Ruta et al 2019, p. 7). The report predicts that the BRI could boost global trade by up to 6.2 percent, and up to 9.7 percent for corridor economies, and global income by as much 2.9 percent. For low-income corridor economies, foreign direct investment could rise by as much as 7.6 percent.

Different from economists, a number of international watchers would like to see the BRI through the lens of geopolitics, predicting that the BRI projects are likely to alter, among others, the built environment and geopolitical landscape along the breadth of the "Belt" and "Road". The BRI, hence, encompasses a number of geopolitical elements as observed by some IR academics and analysts (e.g., Cau 2018, p. 39; Ehizuelen & Abdi 2017, p. 285). Not surprisingly, the BRI and China's expanding presence and influence in the South Pacific have given rise to heated discussion in the region and beyond, particularly among the United States, Australia and other traditional players. The topics are centered on the implications of the BRI and China's increasing involvement in the region for China, the Pacific islands and the traditional players, as well as the possible revision of the regional power structure and order (Sihaloho 2024, p. 57, Yu 2021, p. 81).

The main argument of this chapter is that China's BRI in the Pacific Islands is not merely an economic initiative, but one with a combination of economic, political and strategic objectives and consequences. The chapter finds that the BRI in the Pacific islands is, first and foremost, aimed to sustain China's economic growth by gaining access to overseas resources (particularly the marine resources in the region) and intensifying development cooperation, including economic and infrastructural collaboration with its partners in the South Pacific. Sustainable economic growth and modernization was identified by Deng Xiaoping (1993, p. 370), the late supreme Chinese political leader, as the basis underpinning China's "hard" and "soft" power and the country's rise at the systemic (global) level (Laursen 2009, p. 224). The BRI is secondly aimed to intensify China's political and strategic partnership with the Pacific Island Countries (PICs) by altering regionally geopolitical landscape and environment through the implementation of the BRI. A prevailing conception in the community of the Chinese foreign policy elites runs that vis-*à*-vis China's rapid ascent in the 21st century, the United States, the status quo superpower, has increasingly imposed containment on China (e.g., the "pivot to Asia" and the ongoing trade war), and "demonized" China's international image by spreading the "China threat thesis" (Swaine 2018, Liu 2019, p. 232). China wishes to display to its partners across the world, including the PICs, that its peaceful rise shall not be misconstrued as a threat, but an opportunity for economic prosperity both for China and for its economic partners across the world (Guo 2017, p. 3). The chapter concludes that China is increasingly able to reap economic and geopolitical interest in the South Pacific by intensifying "connectivity" and "exchanges of people" between China and the Pacific islands through the BRI.

The BRI was proposed by the Chinese policy makers at a time when the country is rapidly rising at the systemic (global) level, which produces a critical juncture of "power shift" from the established superpower to the rising one. A conception pervades the Chinese foreign policy and IR circles (e.g., Li 2018, p. 284; Gao & Zhang 2017, p. 13) that the United States is pursuing a strategy of containment of China as it is in U.S. interest to block any power's rise to the level capable of challenging its hegemony, particularly in the Asia-Pacific region (Tow & Loke 2009, p. 447, Ratuva 2014, p. 409). The Chinese foreign policy elites surmise the U.S. containment as the major motivations behind a series of U.S. strategies of containment, such as the "pivot to Asia", the "freedom of navigation operation in the South China Sea" the AUKUS alliance and the ongoing trade war (Xia & Zhong 2018, p. 22, Nie & Xia 2016, p. 28). The Chinese foreign policy elites caution against the U.S. strategies of containment as they harbor a deep-seated belief that the demise of the former Soviet Union and the fall of Japanese economy in the early 1990s are both the aftermaths of U.S. "containment" to stop their rise. In the view of the Chinese IR academics, the rise of the former Soviet Union and Japan challenged the U.S. hegemony and the vested interest arising from the hegemony. In this context, the United States had to keep its hegemony and interest by containing the rise of the former Soviet Union and Japan regardless of their ideological values and political systems.

Some international scholars (Lee 2010, p. 10) argue that the United States wishes a rising China to follow Japan's mode: 'economically powerful, and politically cooperative but strategically dormant and militarily inhibited'. Otherwise, Lowry (2011) argues that 'judging by the past three decades, there's no worse fate than getting touted as the next global superpower'. Keeping in mind the lessons learned from the fall of the Soviet Union and Japan, the Chinese foreign policy and IR elites are guarding against the U.S. strategy of containment similar to those by the United States towards the Soviet Union and Japan befalling China. In the face of the growing clashes of interest and hegemonic competition, some IR analysts (e.g., Paal et al 2019, Shambaugh 2023) note with concern that the two superpowers have reached a "tipping point" where the United States can hardly tolerate the rise of China as it has substantially undermined the former's hegemony in the Asia-Pacific region and elsewhere.

Against this backdrop, the Chinese academics advise the Chinese government to strategically stick to Deng Xiaoping (1993, p. 380)'s dictum of prioritizing economic growth and modernization. The Chinese policy elites have long reached consensus that China's sustained economic growth constitutes the basis underlying China's "hard" power, and particularly its military prowess. As this line of argument goes, China should further intensify its economic cooperation and interdependence with its partners around the globe, both of which are considered by the Chinese policy makers and economists as being contributable to sustaining China's economic growth and modernization (Wang 2018, p. 57). As far as the South Pacific is concerned, the Chinese academics specifically suggest that China intensify its strategic partnership with the PICs to extend its economic and political presence in the region, the traditional "sphere of influence", or the "backyard" of the United States. In so doing, China may enhance its relations of cooperation with the PICs and expand its presence and influence in the region to counterbalance the U.S. containment (Jiang 2018, p. 31, Fan & Tang 2016, p. 42).

The BRI in the South Pacific

President Xi Jinping's visit to Papua New Guinea (PNG) in 2018 led to the creation of a strategic partnership with PNG and other PICs that have diplomatic ties with China, agreeing to enhance their pragmatic cooperation particularly in the fields of infrastructural and economic development, and medical service in the framework of the BRI (Zhang 2019, p. 93; Yu 2021, p. 81). Due to their geographical isolation and relatively small-size economies, the PICs are facing a range of development challenges, including inadequate infrastructure, economic diversification, and climate change. The Asian Development Bank (2019) also estimates that the Pacific has enormous investment needs in the range of US$2.8 billion a year until 2030, on top of an additional US$300 million a year over the same period for climate mitigation and adaptation (see Fig 1). Emma Veve, director of social sectors and public sector management in the ADB's Pacific Department, highlighted that "investment on critical infrastructure like ports, bridges, roads, and connectivity is something that the Pacific cannot meet on its own". In her view, the economies of the PICs are too small and too isolated. So continued grant and concessional assistance from development partners will remain critical to supporting sustainable, inclusive, and resilient development in the region.

The Pacific islands are expected to remain one of the world's most aid-dependent regions as a result of the growing gap in their capacity to address these issues. Xi Jinping (2014) announced in his first visit to the PICs in 2014 that China would increase its economic and technological assistance and investment particularly in the local infrastructural development under the framework of the BRI. The paucity of infrastructure in the region explains why some PICs (e.g., PNG and the Solomon Islands) hold radically different views from the traditional players in the region by arguing the BRI an opportunity for their country's development and prosperity (Sihaloho et al 2024, p. 53, Zhao & Yu 2023, p. 27). The paucity of infrastructure also explains why a number of Chinese companies are able to expand their infrastructural and economic involvement in the region at such a rapid rate. Years after the BRI was implemented in the PICs, Australia, the "deputy sheriff" of the United States in the South Pacific, that has long viewed this region as its "backyard", finally pays attention to the lack of infrastructure in the region. The Australian government estimated in 2017 that the PICs required infrastructure investments of US$3.1 billion per year to 2030 to meet their needs (Clare 2022).

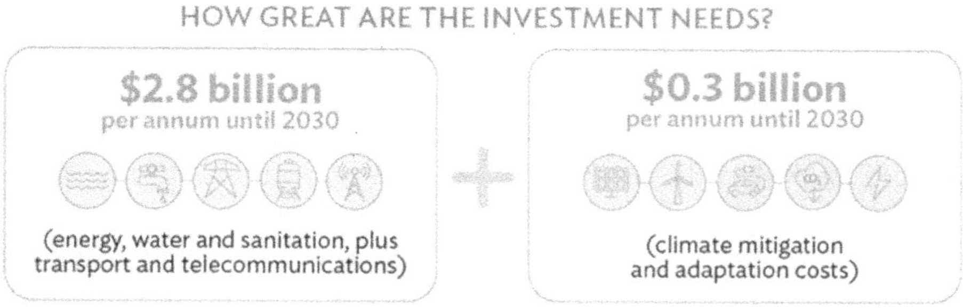

Fig. 1: How great are the investment needs?
Sources: Asia Development Bank 2019, The Pacific: Urgent Development Needs Remain Despite Stable Debt and Higher Revenues, 18 September, https://www.adb.org/news/features/pacific-urgent-development-needs-remain-despite-stable-debt-and-higher-revenues.

As far as the infrastructural development in the region is concerned, the authors had detailed talks with Professor Zhao Shaofeng and Professor Chen Dezheng in the Research Center for Pacific Island Countries, Liaocheng University[12], both of whom had much fieldwork in the PICs over the last decade since early 2010s. In their viewpoints, Xi Jinping's offer of infrastructural assistance and the BRI dovetail the needs of the PICs, which partially explains why China's expanding presence and influence in the South Pacific has been welcomed by the local governments and people. They both aired their voices that the former colonial powers have long neglected the regional demand for infrastructural development. They named Australia specifically, complaining that it has neither capacity nor willingness to meet the requirement of the PICs for infrastructural development though it has displayed a strong will to block the PICs' cooperation with China.

In their viewpoints, the traditional and new players in the South Pacific need cooperation, rather than confrontation, to help address regional challenges, including inadequate infrastructure and climate change. The authors and some

12 Zhao Shaofeng is a professor and director of the Research Center for Pacific Island Countries, Liaocheng University. Chen Dezheng is a professor and vice director of the Center for China-PICs Climate Change Action Cooperation Center, Liaocheng University.

scholars at the Research Center for Pacific Island Countries (China-Pacific Island Countries Climate Action Cooperation Center)[13], Liaocheng University, have done a lot of fieldwork in the Pacific islands over the decade since early 2010s. As well, the authors interviewed the local people during the fieldwork. The interlocutors from the local governments, universities, NGOs, and communities wish the developed countries and the international community to provide them assistance particularly in education, medical care, infrastructure and climate change. The BRI in the South Pacific islands is an umbrella initiative that is aimed at advancing hard infrastructural projects in the region to boost regional flow of goods, investment and people. Both China and the PICs that join the BRI reach consensus to synergize the BRI with the recently launched *2050 Strategy for the Blue Pacific Continent*, a roadmap for sustainable development in the Pacific region.

The ten PICs that have established diplomatic relations with China, have unexceptionally joined the BRI, and partnered China on sustainable development projects though the traditional players headed by the United States tried to block them from cooperating with China (Zhao & Yu 2023, p. 11). As mentioned before, the PICs are in great demand for infrastructure, which is imperative for regional connectivity and interaction with the rest of the world. The needs of the Pacific islands, to some extent, match the key target of the BRI: to boost connectivity and communication (Asia Development Bank 2019). China has to date invested billions of dollars in the region in funding infrastructural projects to advance the BRI, which is likely to unlock further finance to meet local infrastructure needs (Zhang 2019, p. 93). The fund that China provides for regional infrastructural development is broken down into several parts, such as infrastructural, economic and medical projects, and channeled to projects aligned to the BRI, primarily covering the construction of highways, seaports, electricity generation, telecommunications and industrial parks. China's BRI projects

13 The Research Center for Pacific Island Countries (RCPIC) at Liaocheng University is the first institute on the Pacific island countries in China. It is the pilot institute of the international and regional studies of the Ministry of Education of China. It holds the "High-level Forum for Pacific Island Countries Studies" every two years. The China-Pacific Island Countries Climate Action Cooperation Center (CACC) was set up by the Ministry of Foreign Affairs of China in April 2022, and located in the RCPIC. The RCPIC and CACC have held several training programs on climate change for a couple of hundreds of governmental officials and scholars from the PICs.

are mainly based in PNG, Fiji, the Solomon Islands and Vanuatu although 10 countries in the Pacific islands join the BRI (see fig. 2).

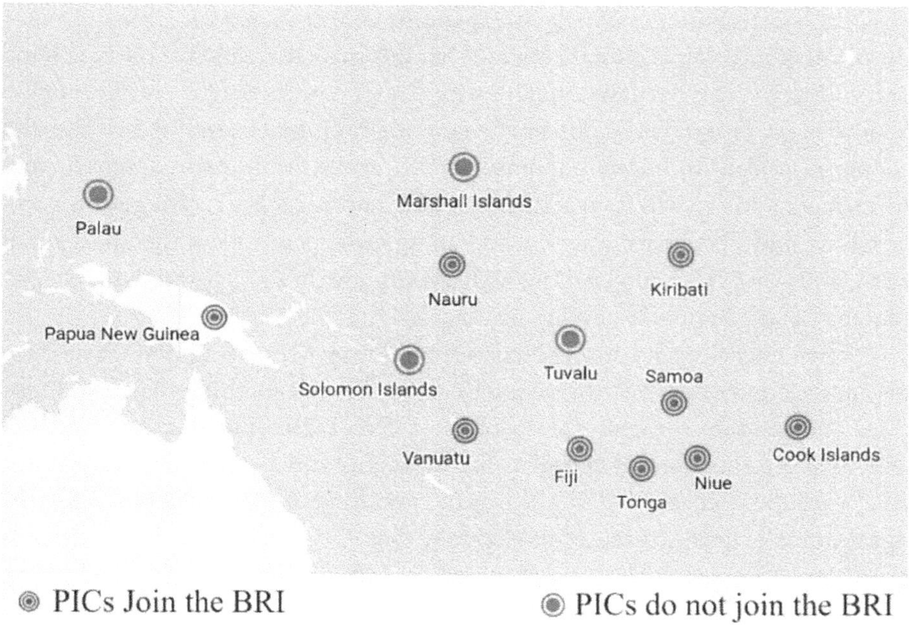

Fig. 2: The PICs that join the BRI. The Federated States of Micronesia, FSM as a country joining the BRI.

The construction of roads and bridges is one of the focuses of the BRI in the South Pacific where the Chinese authorities have proposed and provided hundreds of millions of dollars for the construction of roads and bridges to improve the local infrastructure (Zhao & Yu 2023, p. 11). To gain access to finance is crucial for infrastructural development in the region to boost connectivity and communication, which contributes to driving some PICs, such as PNG, Fiji, Samoa, Tonga, the Cook Islands and Vanuatu, to join the Asian Infrastructure and Investment Bank (AIIB) amid efforts to boost infrastructure, trade and investment. The South Pacific islands are literally a group of islands, scattering on the vast Pacific, which have many reasons why the infrastructure is crucial for the Pacific Island countries.

PNG is one of the most important partners of China in the South Pacific due first to its large surface area, second to its rich resources and economic potentials, and third to its close relationship with China economically and politically. Of the PICs, PNG is the largest in terms of surface area and population, and the second-largest country in Oceania only after Australia, which is rich in energy, minerals, fisheries, forestry, and tourism resources with great potential for economic development. Since the beginning of the 21st century, the government of PNG has displayed eagerness to expand its cooperation with China to boost the country's economic growth, upgrade her infrastructure, and lift the livelihood of her citizens. This partially explains why PNG becomes the first country in the South Pacific to sign with China a memorandum of understanding (MOU) and cooperation plan for jointly building the BRI and join the Asian Infrastructure Investment Bank (AIIB) (Lyu 2022, p. 71, Sihaloho 2024, p. 57). The governments of China and PNG have also reached an agreement to follow the concepts of open, green and clean cooperation, with a commitment to high-standard, people-centered, and sustainable development goals.

When interviewed, Peter O'Neill, former Prime Minister of PNG, expressed his appreciation of the BRI by saying that the BRI is something that is good for PNG and good for the region and globally. O'Neill (2023) predicts that the BRI will promote trade and investment for PNG and other countries. Jerry Agus, chief executive officer of PNG Tourism Promotion Authority, emphasizes the significance of infrastructure development for PNG and other Pacific islands countries: "Our (geological) environment is very unforgiving. We need roads, airports and bridges. you can do nothing without infrastructure". Actually, PNG has since the onset of the 21st century been undertaking infrastructural projects to meet the demand of its growing economy. Joseph Cajetan, acting administrator for the Southern Highlands Provincial Government in PNG, said "In our province, we are building a university, expanding an airport, and planning to build a new port. We also wanted to upgrade our hydro-power generation station, for the power generation capacity could not meet demand of the province." (State Council of the PRC 2018).

It is in this context that PNG has over the years worked with China to enhance synergy between the BRI and PNG's development strategies, such as *PNG Vision 2050*, *Development Strategic Plan 2010-2030*, and *Connect PNG*. Under the guidance by the governments of both PNG and China, a large number of Chinese enterprises have been involved in PNG in the infrastructural projects that are mainly in the areas of connectivity (Lyu 2022, p. 71, Zhao & Yu 2023, p. 35). Over the last decade since the launch of the BRI, the Chinese companies have constructed a number of roads, bridges, airports, ports, hospitals and schools, and the national power grid and undersea cables in PNG (Ministry of Commerce of the PRC 2023), which, in the viewpoints of the Zhao Shaofeng and Chen Dezheng, contribute to PNG's economic growth and social development.

For instance, the PNG National Power Grid Phase One Project is a crucial part of PNG's national power grid, with transmission lines starting from Mount Hagen in the Western Highlands Province, crossing rugged mountains and remote jungles to deliver electricity to Tari of Hela Province (Chinese Embassy in PNG 2018). The Chinese contractors completed this project and improved local grid connectivity, which contributes to powering local economic growth and making a better living standard for the local residents.

Ma Shuai is a managing director of the China State Construction Engineering Corporation (CSCEC) that entered the PNG market in 2014 after the BRI was launched and has been involved in the local construction of apartments, roads, bridges and schools. When interviewed by Zhao Shaofeng and Lei Yu (personal communication, August 17, 2019) in the Research Center for Pacific Island Countries, Liaocheng University, Ma said that PNG is rich in natural resources, such as minerals, agricultural products, fisheries and forestry, and the country is a popular tourist destination. He predicts that there is a great potential for PNG to boost its economic growth once the country has markedly improved its infrastructure in sectors. In his viewpoint, PNG's underdeveloped infrastructure in sectors like power, telecommunications, education, transportation and medical care, has substantially hampered the country's economic growth and social development. Zhou Wenjiang, general manager of the branch of the China Railway Construction Corporation (CRCC) in PNG, notes that the local governments and officials expect the BRI to bring jobs to their people, and development opportunities to their country.

The project of building The Edevu Hydropower Plant that was launched in February 2017 is an impressive project constructed on the mainstream of the Brown River in the Central Province by PNG Hydro Development Ltd, a subsidiary of the China Gezhouba Group (Zhang 2019). It is reported that more than 80 percent of PNG's population is inaccessible to the country's power grid, and Port Moresby, the capital city of PNG, has been subjected to constant blackouts, although the country is rich in hydropower resources that have to date remained largely untapped (Oeka 2023). Zhao Shaofeng and Ni Peng at Liaocheng University note that the inaccessibility of the large population in PNG and other PICs to electricity has long been one of the causes to local poverty and economic hardship. The Edevu powerhouse that is constructed and managed by China Gezhouba Group Company installs four turbines with a total capacity of 50 MW, which brings a reliable supply of electricity to about 40 percent of homes in the region and helps Port Moresby meet its growing energy demands (Zhang 2019, p. 27). James Marape, Prime Minister of PNG, expressed his gratitude to the Chinese investor––PNG Hydro Development Ltd–– for making the massive K750 million Project possible: "We are a nation in pursuit of development. In the power sector, we want 70 percent of our country – by 2030 – to have accessibility to cheap, reliable, and green energy to our country" (Kamus 2023). The hydropower plant is one of the country's biggest assets, whose construction has created hundreds of jobs and is expected to provide an abundance of business opportunities in the coming years.

The Kumul Submarine Cable Network Project (KSCNP) is another project with great potential for boosting the country's connectivity and economic growth. The project established a 5,457-kilometers submarine optic cable linking fourteen coastal provinces and Port Moresby, ending the country's reliance on high-cost, low-bandwidth networks like satellites and microwave (China National Development and Reform Commission 2020, Ministry of Commerce of the PRC 2019). The KSCNP is implemented in June 2020 by PNG DataCo Ltd, a wholesale subsidiary of Kumul Telikom Holdings and a state-owned commercial entity with concessional 85 percent loan financing from China through the Exports and Imports Bank, totaling an estimated amount of US$270 million. The project has improved PNG's communications infrastructure, enhanced communication quality, reduced costs, and made connectivity with the world more streamlined. John Kongoi, managing director of a small to medium technology company in PNG, complains that the cost for internet and for smaller enterprises to do business through internet is very high. He is pleased with the project and wishes his country to have more cooperation with China on digital infrastructure (Xinhua 2018).

Xu Xiujun, a professorial research fellow on the Pacific islands affairs at the China Academy of Social Sciences, views the large-scale project of infrastructural development as a signal of the upgrade of China-PICs cooperation under the framework of BRI. When interviewed by the authors (personal communication, June 19, 2022), he said that the cooperation between China and the PICs are going much beyond traditional sectors, such as agriculture, fishery, infrastructure and natural resources, into emerging sectors like the digital economy. In his viewpoints, the BRI will bring more opportunities for the PICs to enhance business ties and connectivity with China, among themselves and with the rest of the world, and for the PICs to take a greater part in economic globalization. As well, Xu predicts that more pragmatic cooperation between China and PNG will be conducted through the BRI as the political leaders of the two countries have decided to upgrade their relations of cooperation to the level of a strategic partnership. In the last fieldwork in the PICs in late 2022, the authors visited some

Chinese companies that have been involved in local infrastructural development, finding that the managers there were generally optimistic about the prospects of the BRI in the PICs.

Apart from infrastructural projects, the Chinese entrepreneurs and investors are encouraged by the Chinese government to set up economic and industrial parks in the Pacific islands countries to boost their economic cooperation and trade. Most recently, Fujian Zhonghong Fishery that has long been involved in fishing and seafood processing in PNG signed a memorandum of understanding in late 2020 with Lino Tom, PNG's fisheries minister, and Taboi Yoto, governor of Western province, to build a fishery industrial park on Daru Island (Ministry of Commerce of the PRC 2020). The project that is worth around US$150 million, is part of the BRI and signals a major boost to PNG's ambition to establish itself as a significant exporter of seafood to China and other countries, which is expected to boost the country's economic growth and brings hundreds of jobs to the local residents. PNG's fishing industry is much underdeveloped though the country has a huge potential to become a major exporter of seafood in view of the country's bountiful fish, prawn, and lobster stocks.

Leon Perera, CEO of international research and consulting firm Spire, argues that "The challenge for PNG is to create an effective made-in-PNG brand for the seafood industry" (Wilson 2021). As is the case with many poor countries, PNG could not work toward realizing its goal without financial help from outside, including international financial institutions and developed countries. China has recognized PNG's potential as a seafood exporter and an agreement concluded by China and PNG allows PNG seafood a fast and convenient access to the Chinese market, whose demand for overseas seafood is growing rapidly (Ministry of Commerce of the PRC 2022a). With China's assistance, Perera predicts that the fishery industrial park could create the foundation for PNG's seafood export industry, enhance PNG's ability to develop and utilize its own fishery resources, and help PNG realize its underdeveloped fishing industry potential.

In addition to the fishery industrial park, the PNG government is actively promoting the development of domestic downstream processing industries, aiming to transform its resource-rich advantages in energy, minerals, agriculture, forestry, and fisheries into sustainable development momentum. Prime Minister Marape and other senior officials have expressed a desire to attract more Chinese companies to invest and operate in the above-mentioned fields as they present new opportunities for cooperation between the two sides. The government of PNG has shown interest in learning from China's experience in developing special economic zones and attempted to establish several special economic zones to boost its own economic growth and development (Ministry of Foreign Affairs of the PRC 2022). To gain access to finance for infrastructural and economic development, PNG, among others, has joined the Asian Infrastructure and Investment Bank that is initiated and dominated by China. Moreover, the PNG government has recently introduced its first sovereignty bond and it was 600 percent over-subscribed.

Apart from the commercially-oriented projects, China has provided PNG with some infrastructural aids, such as the Independence Boulevard that is a "gift" given by the Chinese government to show "the goodwill of the Chinese people" to the PNG government and people. The Boulevard has now become a landmark road in Port Moresby, which is described by Zhao Shaofeng as a signal of the China-PNG friendship. The Enga Provincial Hospital is also a "gift" sent by China to the PNG people, which boasts itself of the most modern hospital in the South Pacific (Ministry of Commerce of the PRC 2022b). After having visited the hospital, Zhao Shaofeng is satisfied with the medical service and facilities in the hospital and calls for China and other countries to provide more medical aids to PNG as well as other PICs. China has dispatched a dozen of medical teams to PNG over the last 20 years consecutively, offering medical services to over 100,000 people, and conducting thousands of medical training sessions there.

In addition to medical aids, China has provided educational assistance and aids to PNG as exemplified by the Butuka Academy that is built by the China State Construction Engineering Corporation (CSCEC). The Academy is also a "gift" given by the Chinese government under the memorandum of the BRI, which is the largest and most well-equipped school in PNG with facilities for kindergarten and grades 1 to 12, accommodating more than 3,000 students (China State Construction Engineering Corporation 2022). This school not only helps solve the problem of limited access to education, but also elevates the standard of basic education in the area. Currently, admission to the school is highly competitive, with many parents from other provinces wanting to send their children to the school, and many local governments request China to build Butuka-like schools in their hometowns (Zeng 2023). When visiting the school, Zhao Shaofeng notes that the Chinese scholarships have become one of the most popular programs for local students to study in China.

As a newly industrialized country, China has long placed much importance on poverty reduction cooperation with the developing countries under the framework of the "South-South Cooperation". In this context, the poverty-reduction cooperation between China and the PICs, including PNG, has been a significant topic in their bilateral relations. China is rich in experience for poverty reduction as it has lifted more than 70 million of the Chinese people out of absolute poverty over the past decades since it launched a market reform in the late 1970s (Trankmann 2019). Poverty reduction is one of the projects of the most important cooperation between China and the PICs under the framework of "South-South Cooperation", and China has long provided economic and technological assistance within its capacity to PNG and other PICs (Yu 2021, p. 81). Chen Dezheng who has been in charge of some training programs on poverty reduction provided to the PICs' officials and scholars concludes that the economic and technological assistance provided by China to PNG and other developing countries help the recipients with their economic growth and social progress through a large number of economic and infrastructural projects. In Chen's opinion, China has provided aid and assistance to the developing countries based on its long-term principle of "non-interference" of the recipient's internal affairs.

China's adoption of the principle is primarily due to China's indelible memory of having been invaded and bullied by the colonial and imperialist powers in the Chinese century of "humiliation" that started from the First Opium War in 1839 to the founding of the PRC in 1949[14]. It is not quite surprising that the principle is appreciated by the authorities of the developing countries, including the PICs, as they have the same memory as the Chinese of their countries being colonialized and bullied by the European powers (Sui & Yu 2024, p. 4). This partially explains why China is increasingly expanding its involvement in the Pacific islands and other developing countries in Africa and Latin America without encountering much local resistance and opposition. The Pew Research Center based in the United States acknowledges that 'In global popularity contest, U.S. and China – not Russia – vie for first' with the United States standing at 50 percent while China, 48 percent (Vice 2017). The "popularity contest", to a certain degree, demonstrates that China has indeed gained "soft" power particularly in the developing world, including the PICs.

---

14 The Chinese historians dub the one hundred years following the first Opium War to the founding of the People's Republic of China (PRC) in 1949 as the "Chinese century of humiliation" in that the "Old Chinas", namely Qing China and the Republic of China (ROC), were frequently bullied and invaded by the imperialist powers. For more details, see Hsu, Immanuel, C.Y. (Xu, Zhongyue) 2000, *the rise of modern China*, Oxford University Press: New York, p. 477.

A decade after the implementation of the BRI, PNG has now risen as China's largest trading partner, investment destination, and project contracting market in the South Pacific region. Xu Xiujun at the China Social Sciences Academy predicts that the economic cooperation and trade between the two countries are expected to grow further given the two economies are highly complementary. According to *the International Business Daily*, a newspaper run by the Ministry of Commerce of the PRC, bilateral trade between the two countries was up 24.4 percent year-on-year to US$2.84 billion in 2017, and China's investment in the country reached US$3.04 billion as of October 2017 (Huang 2018) (see Table 1). In 2022, the bilateral trade doubled, around US$5.26 billion, a year-on-year increase of 29.9 percent. In the first half of 2023, PNG's exports to China rose to US$1.9 billion, a 6 percent increase year-on-year. It is well noted that PNG is rapidly expanding its market share in China by increasing its exports of liquefied natural gas, timber, minerals, coffee, palm oil, and other high-quality commodities to meet the Chinese market demands. China is providing an increasing number of affordable and good quality products to PNG, which, in the eyes of Xu Xiujun, contributes to the improvement of the local quality of life. China is expected to continue to increase its imports of PNG products and encourage the Chinese enterprises to invest more in PNG given the latter's economic potentials.

Table 1: China's trade with PNG (US$ billion)

years	aggregate volumes	growth rate%	China's exports	China's imports
2017	2.84	24.4	0.77	2.06
2018	3.62	27.1	0.79	2.83
2019	3.83	6.2	0.80	3.03
2020	3.21	-16.2	0.92	2.28
2021	4.02	25.2	1.05	2.97

Sources: Ministry of Commerce of China 2023, China's Outbound Investment and Cooperation (PNG), Beijing.

When interviewed by Zhao Shaofeng and the authors, Tang Qiaoliang, general manager of China Harbor Engineering in PNG, holds fast to the belief that as the BRI expands, more tie-ups between the two countries will help spur PNG's social and economic growth. The rapidly increasing economic cooperation and trade leads the two countries to actively advancing the negotiations on a bilateral free trade agreement that is assumed by the economists of two countries to boost their economic growth and bilateral trade (Ministry of Foreign Affairs of the

PRC 2023). Based on his long-term studies on PNG, Zhao Shaofeng shows confidence in China-PNG economic cooperation and trade, predicting that the bilateral trade and the Chinese investment in the PNG will markedly grow once the free trade agreement is concluded. Xu Xiujun anticipates that as the largest developing country and the largest Pacific Island country, China and PNG shall intensify their relations and make them go beyond commercial level, and hold increasing regional and strategic implications. In his view, the intensified relationship between the two countries may serve as a "locomotive" for China's economic cooperation and trade with the PICs, and further push forward China's relations with the PICs as a whole.

As a regional hub for transportation, Fiji is one of the most important partners of China in the South Pacific islands in terms of the BRI, as a result of its economic potentials and regional influence. Sitiveni Rabuka, Prime minister of Fiji, who has been cautious about China's expanding security footprint in the South Pacific, has recently changed his attitude towards China and praised China's record of aid to Fiji in fighting Covid-19, developing agriculture and revamping infrastructure (Cottrell 2023). Rabuka's comments came after his first meeting with Xi Jinping, Chinese President, on the sidelines of the APEC Forum that was held in San Francisco in late 2023. Rabuka told Xi Jinping at the meeting that he shared China's vision for global security and that he would like to see the two countries create a synergy for better infrastructural development in Fiji and beyond as the BRI "aligns with our nation's development agenda". Shortly afterwards, Rabuka addressed the Fijian Parliament that the modernization of Fiji's port facilities and shipyards is a "key focus" for the country's sustainable economic development. Rabuka surprised the Western policy analysts and regional watchers by adding that "I anticipate potential collaboration with China in that endeavor" in view of China's "globally competitive shipbuilding capacity". The shift in Rabuka's attitude towards China is primarily due to his need for China and the BRI to help boost the infrastructural development and economic growth in his country.

The Chinese companies and businessmen have long been involved in Fiji's economic and infrastructural development. China Railway First Group (Fiji) Company (CRFG) has been involved in Fiji for more than a decade, whose business covers Fiji and nearby countries, such as Samoa, Kiribati, Niue and Vanuatu. When interviewed by Zhao Shaofeng and Yu Lei (personal communication, August 19, 2019), Wang Gang, the general manager of the South Pacific regional headquarters of CRFG, said that "most of the engineering projects that the company has undertaken in the South Pacific islands are vital to the economic growth of the PICs and the better livelihoods of the local people." Signature projects that the Chinese companies have constructed in the region include the Nangali Bridge that is the first project in the history of Fiji's Roads Authority to be completed within the contract period. The 70 km highway connecting Labasa and Nabouwalu with 14 new bridges, along with another 30 km highway at the Buca Bay, is the largest infrastructure project in Fiji and constructed by CRFG. The two signature projects are both located in Vanua Levu, the second largest island in the northern part of Fiji, and both were completed in 2015, with the concessional loans provided by the Chinese banks.

According to Mr. Wang, the two projects provided employment to over 2,000 local workers during its construction and trained more than 300 machinery operators and over 1,000 skilled workers. In Wang's view, the Nabouwalu highway is a major boost to shipping services between the two main islands of Fiji, and have brought and will continue to bring a lot of business opportunities to the local people. Bainimarama, former Prime Minister of Fiji, attended the opening ceremony of the Nabouwalu project as he viewed the highways as a source of "national pride" (Bainimarama 2016, Zhang 2018). As well, the 18-story FHL Commercial Tower in the heart of Suva's Business District is being built by CRFG, which is going to be a new landmark in Suva. Apart from building large-scale landmark projects, Wang Gang told the authors that his company is well-known to establish "small but beautiful" projects tailored to the geography and development characteristics of these island nations. For instance, the low-cost housing projects that his company and other Chinese companies helped build in Fiji have markedly improved the housing conditions for Fiji's low-income groups. Wang refers to the pipeline project that his company worked on, saying that the project has brought clean water to the deep mountains of Fiji, improving the living environment in urban communities.

Power China that has constructed a lot of large-size hydropower plants in China and across the world, is a mega company headquartered in Beijing. The company entered the Fiji market in 2008 and has completed the construction of the Nadrewatu Renewable Energy Power Station Project and the Vinisaulu Dam Heightening Project. Recently, it completed the Rewa River Water Supply Project in early 2023, which is a key initiative to improve the quality of life of locals. The project improves the reliability of the urban water supply for about 273,000 residents (Power China 2023). The company won a new contract in early 2023 from the Water Authority of Fiji for the design and construction of the Fiji DN900 water supply pipeline.

The Stinson Parade Bridge, situated next to the bustling Suva Municipal Market in the Fijian capital city, was funded by the Chinese government and contracted by China Railway 14th Group Company (CRCC14) in 2018. The bridge and the Vatuwaqa Bridge, also funded by China and built by the CRCC14, serve as a crucial daily transit point for vendors, residents and commuters. When interviewed, Zhang Zihui, project director of the CRCC14, said that his company had hired around 600 workers from Fiji and 40 workers from China to work together on the bridges for months. In his viewpoints, the two bridges and the drainage, footpaths and traffic safety facilities, are built to international standards and meet the standard of 50 tons gross weight capacity and 14 tons axle loading. The pile foundation of the bridges penetrated nearly 50 meters into the seabed rock. In January 2018, Voreqe Bainimarama, Fijian Prime Minister, cut the red ribbon to open the bridges that, in his view, had been completely re-imagined and re-engineered to serve "a modern, growing, ambitious nation" (Zhang 2018).

In addition to infrastructural projects, China places a strong emphasis on the sustainable development and has increased its economic and technological assistance to Fiji under the banner of the BRI. The development assistance of Juncao is a case in point. Fujian Agriculture and Forestry University has set up a center in Fiji to promote the technology of mushroom planting by providing free technical training to local farmers and supplying them with mushroom bags. It is a patented project, easy to operate, profitable, and highly suitable for poverty alleviation, and has been promoted in several Pacific Island countries for years (Ren 2020). According to Lin Xingsheng, a professor at the Fujian Agriculture and Forestry University, this technology, known as "Juncao" technology, consists of the cultivation of grass that can be used as a substrate for mushroom production, feed for animals, windbreaks, and to minimize soil erosion. The Juncao technology has played a significant role in the Chinese poverty alleviation efforts and has extended its reach globally with the BRI as a solution to poverty alleviation and sustained economic growth in the developing world, including the Pacific islands.

The Juncao has showcased its adaptability to different climates and conditions, helping the efforts made by Fiji and other countries in poverty reduction and sustainable development. For instance, the Juncao and Upland Rice Project has been implemented in PNG for over 20 years and has benefited more than 40,000 local people. PNG's Prime Minister James Marape referred to Juncao technology as a "gift from China to the world", with Juncao now known locally as the "grass of prosperity" (Zeng 2023). Fanny Fiteli, the founder of Fiji's Mama's mushroom, is one of the leading local women to plant mushrooms, viewing the Juncao technology as an effective way for the local women in Fiji to have wage income. When interviewed, Professor Lin summarizes that to promote Juncao technology in the South Pacific countries by aligning with local natural conditions allows them to have a sustainable development key by acquiring new technology. Tagiyaco Vakaloloma is a senior technical assistant for mushroom research and development from Fiji's Ministry of Agriculture. She has worked together with the Chinese experts over the past five years and looks forward to cooperating closely with them in the third phase of the project in the coming three years. She said:

> I know Juncao is a very interesting and warmly welcomed project in Fiji for the sake of food sources, food security, income and also for the livestock farms in Fiji. We are looking forward to working with them in the next three years to help all the farmers in Fiji, to make them commercial and produce mushroom as a source of food and also the source of income for them.

Fiji has now risen as China's second largest trading partner, investment destination, and project contracting market in the Pacific Islands after PNG (Ministry of Commerce of China 2023) and China rises as Fiji's 4th largest source of imports and 7th largest exporting market. Data released by the Ministry of Commerce of China show that the economies of Fiji and China are highly complementary, which leads to an increasing momentum of trade and economic cooperation between the two countries. The bilateral trade in 2021 reached $453 million, up 31 percent year on year and almost 200 times the figure when the two countries first established diplomatic ties in 1975 (Chan 2022) (see Table 2). Fiji has attended the China International Import Expo since 2018, which is aimed to increase the publicity of high-quality foreign commodities to the Chinese consumers and their exports to China.

Table 2: China's trade with Fiji (US$ million)

years	aggregate volumes	growth rate%	China's exports	China's imports
2016	417	18.5	400	17
2017	383	-8.2	365	18
2018	482	25.9	457	25
2019	365	-24.3	350	14
2020	346	-5.2	322	24

Sources: Ministry of Commerce of China 2022, China's Outbound Investment and Cooperation (Fiji), Beijing.

Zhao Shaofeng and Ni Peng at the Research Center for the Pacific Island Countries, Liaocheng University have been to the Expo a couple of times, noting that the Fijian authorities have introduced specialties to the Chinese importers and consumers at the Expo, including Lami Kava, Pure Fiji, Taki Mai, Noni Essentials, Island Chill and Yofi Water, which have increasingly gained popularity in the Chinese market. In their last fieldwork in Fiji and other PICs in late 2024, Zhao and Ni observed that as a manufacturing power, China has provided a large number of affordable products to Fiji, which contributes to the improvement of local quality of life. The Chinese authorities are encouraging the country's enterprises to invest in Fiji given its economic potentials and its status as the regional economic and traffic hub. Data released by the Ministry of Commerce of China show that China's accumulative FDI in Fiji in 2020 rose to US$183 million (Ministry of Commerce of China 2023b).

It is noteworthy that the past years since their exchanges of diplomatic recognition witnesses a rapid growth of economic cooperation and trade between China and the Solomon Islands in the framework of the BRI. The Solomon Islands formally joined the BRI in 2019, less than one month after the two states announced the establishment of diplomatic relations. As Cheng Hong[15] at East China Normal University and Zhao Shaofeng at Liaocheng University note, the Chinese companies have rushed into the Solomon Islands over the last years and carried out thousands of infrastructural projects there. In their last fieldwork in late 2024, Zhao Shaofeng and Ni Feng at the Liaocheng University noted that these projects under the framework of the BRI had changed the infrastructural landscape of the country, boosted local economic growth and improved the livelihood of local people.

Of the newly-built infrastructural facilities stands a brand-new sports center, the 2023 Pacific Games Stadium in Honiara, the Capital of the Solomon Islands. The sports center was funded and constructed by the Chinese companies, allowing the Solomon Islands to be a host of the Pacific Games. The Pacific Games sports stadium is the largest-scale infrastructure project that China has to date assisted in building in the Pacific Island countries. The 2023 Pacific Games Stadium Project consists of seven separate project components, with the main venue being a 10,000-seat National Stadium complex with a full-size football and rugby field and running tracks that comply with international standards (Nanau 2021). The project has a two-story building housing a food court and office space, a swimming pool, a six-court tennis center, a five-a-side hockey field and a 90-meter-by-50-meter multi-purpose hall.

15 Cheng Hong is a professor and director of the Center for Australian Studies, East China Normal University.

The China Civil Engineering Construction Corporation (CCECC) and the Central South Architectural Design Institute have worked on the seven facilities funded by the Chinese government for the 2023 Pacific Games, which were handed over to the Solomon Islands in August 2023 (China Civil Engineering Construction Corporation 2023). It took more than two years for the Chinese companies to complete the project, during which time, the Chinese companies had hired and trained nearly a thousand Solomon Islands employees, and imparted professional skills to them. Zhao and Ni note that the Chinese companies have locally procured building materials and other supplies worth millions of Solomon Islands dollars, which boost the economic growth of the Solomon Islands. In their fieldwork, Zhao and Ni had conversations with the managers of the Chinese enterprises and found that the Chinese companies are increasingly focused on local operations, hiring and training local employees. Paul is a local worker and has been working at the Pacific Games sports stadium for two years. When interviewed by Zhao and Ni, he said: "To have such a stadium, which benefits many people here, makes us feel proud".

As part of the BRI program and at the request of the Solomon government, the Export-Import Bank of China provided a $100 million loan to the Solomon Islands to build 161 mobile communication towers across the country for the development of the national broadband network. The project is in cooperation with China Harbor Engineering Company and Huawei, a Chinese communications company, which will help 700,000 people scattered across hundreds of islands in the country achieve connectivity (Fildes 2022). When interviewed by *the Global Times*, Manasseh Sogavare, former Prime Minister of the Solomon Islands, said that his country has an urgent need to improve mobile communication services and to provide service guarantees for the 2023 Pacific Games (Shen et al 2023). The primary objective of this project is to bridge the digital divide by providing rural communities with improved access to connectivity, thereby linking them with the central hubs. The communication project contract period is 36 months long and it will be completed in three phases. The first phase was to complete 30 base stations in 2023 to provide network guarantees for the South Pacific Games; the second phase was to complete 68 base stations in 2024, and the third phase will be in 2025 to complete the remaining base stations.

In the viewpoints of Manasseh Sogavare, former Prime Minister, the BRI is a transformative force in infrastructure development, which aligns with the infrastructure needs and development goals of the country. Manasseh Sogavare expressed his wishes to further the country's cooperation with China: the integration of the Solomon Islands into the BRI will mean closer political and economic cooperation with China that will benefit the Solomon Islands (Chi 2022). Barrett Salato, Ambassador of the Solomon Islands to China, notes that China has been a very important builder of the infrastructure in his country. In his opinions, China is constructing a comprehensive health facility in the Solomon Islands for the benefit of the people, and the construction is already well underway. This is what the Solomon Islands appreciates about China - its ability to build infrastructure projects efficiently: "When the Chinese companies are involved, you can see the progress and the actual changes they bring to our country" (Global Times 2024). The Solomon Islands remains one of the United Nations-listed world's least developed countries decades after it gained independence and wishes to embark upon the track to economic prosperity. This explains why the Solomon Islands is collaborating closely with China in the framework of the BRI and wishes the BRI to play a crucial role in the country's infrastructural progress. In addition to the infrastructure development projects, the Solomon Islands has been viewed by the Chinese authorities as a key partner in terms of economic cooperation and trade in the South Pacific.

The Chinese entrepreneurs have been encouraged by the Chinese government to invest in the country to help intensify the economic cooperation and trade between the two countries. Some Chinese companies have shown enthusiasm in setting up economic zones in the Solomon Islands to attract enterprises across the world to invest in the country. Sam Group, a Chinese state conglomerate, signed a controversial pact with the government of the Central Province, to transform the whole island of Tulagi into an economic development zone similar to those established in China in the late 1970s, which kick-started China's industrialization (Fanasia 2019). Projects that are planned to be implemented in the economic zone cover tourism, agriculture, petroleum, fishery and marine, mining and infrastructural development. In the view of Chen Hong, director of the Australian Studies Center of East China Normal University, there is enormous potential for further cooperation between the two countries, such as strengthening cooperation in agriculture, fisheries, infrastructure, and software improvements, as well as in tourism development.

When interviewed, Barrett Salato, Ambassador of the Solomon Islands to China, expresses his welcome to the Chinese companies to explore business opportunities in his country (Global Times 2024). He said that the government of the Solomon Islands is prioritizing the development of the tourism sector, fisheries, and agriculture, and pursuing a green energy transformation, which widely open the door to foreign investment in sectors from agriculture to green economy. Salato highlights that renewable energy is the way forward for his country as the Solomon Islands is a tropical country with a lot of sunshine and wind. The government of the Solomon Islands invites business investors from China and other countries to explore these opportunities as the country needs the Chinese advanced technology in the areas of renewable energy to tap into these potentials. Salato specifically wishes to have more electric vehicles from China, since it is the symbol of future transportation and is something that the Solomon Islands looks forward to expanding in the future.

As intimated, the economic interest is among the motivations behind China's vigorous involvement in the developing world, including the PICs. At the invitation of the Chinese authorities, the Solomon Islands made its debut at the 6th China International Import Expo (CIIE) held in Shanghai, showcasing the Chinese consumers the country's unique commodities, such as the Solomon Tuna, KOSI, honey and artisan crafts (Solomon Islands Broadcasting Corporation 2023). As a result of their intensified cooperation, China has now risen as one of the largest trading partners of the Solomon Islands, and the primary destination for its exports. The bilateral trade volume between the two countries reached US$498 million in 2022 and the exports of the Solomon Islands to China account for two-thirds of the Solomon Islands' total exports (see Table 3). Data released by the Ministry of Commerce of China in 2022 show that China's FDI in the Solomon Islands in 2020 was US$2.26 million and its cumulative FDI in 2020 reached US$6.86 million (Ministry of Commerce of China 2022c).

Table 3: China's trade with the Solomon Islands (US$ million)

years	aggregate volumes	growth rate%	China's exports	China's imports
2017	463	-14.4	87	376
2018	748	15.5	118	630
2019	559	-25.2	98	461
2020	472	-15.6	117	355
2021	488	29.2	167	321

Sources: Ministry of Commerce of China 2022, *China's Outbound Investment and Cooperation (the Solomon Islands)*, Beijing.

Economic cooperation and trade between China and Vanuatu have seen a rapid growth since the onset of the 21st century. Vanuatu signed a BRI cooperation plan with China in 2019, making it one of the first countries in the South Pacific region to join the BRI (Ministry of Foreign Affairs of the PRC 2019). The two countries agree in the plan to advance their cooperation in a wide range of areas, including trade and investment, infrastructure construction, transportation, communications, agriculture and fishery, tourism, culture, education and health, and climate change. China promises to make their cooperation under the framework of the BRI a win-win arrangement, and the BRI align with Vanuatu 2030, the National Sustainable Development Plan for the period 2016 to 2030 (Chi 2022). The BRI cooperation plan draws up a blueprint for all-round cooperation between the two countries, and promotes the sustained, sound and stable development of China-Vanuatu relations. Moreover, the two governments concluded over 10 cooperation documents to supplement and materialize the BRI cooperation plan. The 10 documents cover fishery, maritime affairs, technology, civil aviation transportation, infrastructure and police exchanges and cooperation, making every effort to promote practical exchanges and cooperation across the board.

Of the BRI projects in the country, Baurefield International Airport in Port Vila, which had recently undergone major works, is a project for the country's immediate future. The project is funded by the World Bank with US$73.9 million and contracted by the China Civil Engineering Construction Corporation (CCECC), which is one of the mega Chinese companies involving in infrastructural development inside and outside China (World Bank 2019). The works were aimed to upgrade the airport, including runway rehabilitation, new lighting, and a new domestic terminal. The airport serves the country as a gateway for and to the world, and was formally re-opened in the end of 2019. Inside Vanuatu, airports help a flow of exchange between people in the islands and the city. In a region as dispersed as the Pacific Islands, airports represent much more than a simple travel hub: they are links to the world, jobs, specialized health care, and a vital connection to markets for many businesses. Charlot Salwai, Vanuatu's Prime Minister, was quoted that "airports have a great impact in terms of tourism; they are important for access to markets; and air transport is also important for health care; or if there is a cyclone, air travel can be the only link." (Cullwick 2017). Tourism is central to the island nation's economy, providing roughly a quarter of Vanuatu's GDP and employing thousands of people across the country.

In addition to the airport, the construction projects that were built by the Chinese companies under the framework of the BRI can be seen everywhere in the country, including the Parliament Building, the National Stadium, the Malakula highway, the Tanna Roads and Malekula Ring Road Project and the project of Malapoa College. The authors had undertaken fieldwork in Vanuatu over the last decade and find that some of the projects have become landmark projects in Vanuatu and even in the South Pacific Islands. In their last fieldwork in Vanuatu in 2024, Zhao Shaofeng and Ni Peng note that these infrastructure projects funded or built by the Chinese companies in the banner of BRI have, to an extent, boosted the economic development of Vanuatu, and particularly its rural areas, and contributed to the better life of the local people. To advance their disaster-reduction cooperation, China National Marine Technology Center constructed a marine observation station in Vanuatu in 2018 in collaboration with the Vanuatu Meteorology and Geo-Hazards Department (VMGD) and the Public Works Department (PWD) (China National Ocean Technology Center 2018). The station displays the collaborative efforts made by both sides in ocean observation and disaster risk reduction. The designs of the joint observation station have been completed, and progress is being made in the construction of meteorological infrastructure. The two countries are planning the construction of Phase II of the joint observation station, including a meteorological station.

In view of the rapid intensification of China-Vanuatu relations, China ensures the government of Vanuatu that China will support Vanuatu's national development and sustainable development by encouraging the Chinese enterprises to invest in Vanuatu. As a result, the Chinese investment in Vanuatu has increased rapidly over the past five years particularly in fishery processing, concurrent with its infrastructural cooperation with Vanuatu. The Sino-Van Fisheries, a joint venture fishery processing plant, was put into operation in 2019, making Vanuatu tuna export a reality and creating more jobs and income for Vanuatuan (Ministry of Commerce of the PRC 2016). It is no denial that the BRI and China's growing investment provide new opportunities for China-Vanuatu economic cooperation and for Vanuatu's economic growth. As a win-win arrangement for their cooperation and assistance to Vanuatu, China has granted the zero-tariff treatment for 98 percent of Vanuatu's commodities to the Chinese market after it joined the BRI (Ati & Zhou 2022).

At the invitation of the China International Import Expo, the government of Vanuatu and some enterprises from Vanuatu have participated in the Expo over the last years, which provides a platform and opportunity for Vanuatu to introduce its commodities and tourism resources to the Chinese consumers and importers (Embassy of China in Vanuatu 2021). The Expo is aimed to helps Vanuatu and other PICs increase its exports to China and be integrated into the global supply, industrial and value chains. The data released by the Ministry of Commerce of China show that the two-way trade between Vanuatu and China in 2022 rose to US$107 million with China's exports standing at US$96 million and imports, US$11 million, and China's cumulative FDI in Vanuatu in 2020 rose to US$130 million (Ministry of Commerce of China 2022) (see Table 4).

Table 4: China's trade with Vanuatu (US$ million)

years	aggregate volumes	growth rate%	China's exports	China's imports
2016	68.7	-16.5	63.7	5.0
2017	79.8	16.0	65.6	14.2
2018	79.0	-1.0	63.3	15.7
2019	91.8	16.1	77.2	14.6
2020	80.4	12.4	72.6	7.8
2021	99.5	23.7	87.6	11.8

Sources: Ministry of Commerce of China 2022, *China's Outbound Investment and Cooperation (Vanuatu)*, Beijing.

Tonga has recently shown willingness to intensify its relations of cooperation with China, which drives it to be a partner of China in terms of the BRI in the South Pacific after the government of Tonga signed a memorandum with China to join the BRI in 2018. Kang Jian, an associate professor at Liaocheng University, had worked in Tonga for three years (2016-2019) as a volunteering teacher. When interviewed by the authors in Tonga in 2019 (personal communication, August 17, 2019), he notes that the Chinese enterprises have invested much in the country's infrastructure projects that boost the economic growth of Tonga and the wellbeing of the local people. Kang refers to a water supply project to justify his argument. According to him, the China Civil Engineering Construction Corp (CCECC) built a key water supply project for Nuku'alofa, Tonga's capital, and neighboring areas, which relieved the local residents from drinking water shortage. When interviewed, the spokesperson of the company said that Tonga needs better infrastructure to serve the country's economic growth and the well-beings of her people, and that the CCECC will be pleased to help advance local infrastructural development as it does in China.

According to the spokesman, the CCECC has undertaken half a dozen key projects in terms of infrastructural development in Tonga since the BRI was proposed in 2013. In his view, these projects have played a significant role in boosting local economic growth and employment as well as a better livelihood. The spokesman recalled that immediately after a volcano erupted in January 2022, the CCECC mobilized her staff in Fiji, Vanuatu and other countries in the region to purchase a large quantity of relief supplies and delivered them to local governments and communities in Tonga to help those who suffered from the disaster. Kang notes that other Chinese companies located in Tonga also provided emergency aids to the local governments and communities to help the victims. As a researcher in the China-PICs Climate Change Cooperation Action Center, Kang pays attention to the efforts made by the PICs to address the climate change. He told the authors that the CCECC and other Chinese companies in Tonga have implemented some small-scale climate aid projects to help combat the challenges arising from the climate change.

The Research Center for the Pacific Island Countries (China-PICs Climate Action Cooperation Center) based at the Liaocheng University is undertaking a 2 million yuan ($280,000) agricultural planting technology project in Tonga. In 2018, the Education Ministries of China and Tonga signed the Memorandum on Communication and Cooperation in Education to support the creation of the Tonga College of Liaocheng University (Li 2022). Chen Dezheng who has pushed for the creation of the College note that the College has helped Tonga cultivate high-level talents in applied science and conduct joint research in marine studies. China's BRI also extended to such small island countries as Niue and the Cooks Islands, both of which signed the Memorandum of Understanding on Cooperation within the Framework of BRI in July 2018 (see Table 5). China has recently completed the construction of a 64 km expressway around Niue and upgraded the wharves and ports there. China has promised to construct a deep-water port on the Penrhyn Island in the Cooks Islands (China Railway Group 2023).

Table 5: Some infrastructural projects in Tonga under the BRI

	2014	government office building	Completed
CCECC	2015	water supplies project (phase one)	completed
	2019	New Ha'apai Hospital	Completed
	2021	Water supplies project	In progress
	2021	Police office building, solar farm, highway project, causeway construction	In progress
Shanghai Construction Group	2017	Government office building	Completed
Gezhouba Group	2020	Wind farm	completed
China Shuifaxingye Energy Company	2016	20mw solar farm	completed

Compiled by the authors based on the data provided by the Research Center for PICs, Liaocheng University.

As intimated, the BRI in the Pacific islands is literally an umbrella initiative that is aimed to bolster "connectivity", and economic cooperation and trade between

China and the PICs. Zhao Shaofeng and Ni Peng at Liaocheng University conclude that the BRI in the South Pacific is primarily aimed to improve local conditions and create conditions for further strengthening economic and trade cooperation given that the Pacific Island countries have long been plagued by poverty, limited economic levels, infrastructure constraints, and underdeveloped living standards. Not surprisingly, increasing Chinese enterprises and individuals have come to the Pacific Islands countries, bringing development through their interactions under the framework of the BRI. Some Chinese enterprises have rooted in the local markets and promoted project localization and local procurement, boosting local economic growth and providing job opportunities for the local people. Data released by the Chinese Ministry of Foreign Affairs, the Chinese government and the Chinese enterprises have to date implemented more than 100 aid projects, delivered more than 200 batches of in-kind assistance, and trained about 10,000 experts in various fields (Ministry of Foreign Affairs of China 2022b).

The BRI and the intensified economic cooperation and trade between China and the PICs also bring benefits for China and the Chinese consumers. China imports the PICs raw materials, minerals, primary industry produces and other commodities. The Chinese fishing fleets work closely with the Pacific Island countries to increase the exports of seafood to China, satisfying the fast-growing need of the Chinese consumers. Notably, the local governments and businesses of the PICs have particularly been invited by their counterparts in China to participate in the China International Import Expo that is held each year in Shanghai to publicize the PICs' products and increase their exports to China[16]. Partially thanks to the BRI, the two-way trade between China and the PICs has grown rapidly over the last decades. According to statistics released by the Chinese authorities, bilateral trade between China and PICs having diplomatic relations with China had grown to US$5.3 billion in 2021 from US$153 million in 1992, an average annual increase of 13 percent and expanding by more than 30 times in 30 years (Wang 2021). The two-way investment has also seen steady

16 Xi Jinping, Chinese President, announced in May 2017 at the Belt and Road Forum for International Cooperation that China will hold China International Import Expo (CIIE) starting from 2018 in support of trade liberalization and economic globalization by opening the Chinese market to the world. It is designed by the Chinese government to enhance economic cooperation and trade between China and the rest of the world, and to promote global trade by making the world economy more open.

progress. China's direct investment in the PICs that have diplomatic relations with China had risen to US$2.72 billion by the end of 2021. By the end of 2020, China has signed engineering contracts worth US$18.48 billion in the Pacific Island countries and completed transactions totaling US$12.75 billion.

In addition to the infrastructural and economic cooperation, medical cooperation between China and the PICs is increasingly becoming a significant part of the BRI. China has to date dispatched more than 600 medical workers to the Pacific Island Countries, according to *the Fact Sheet on Cooperation between China and the PICs* released by the Chinese Ministry of Foreign Affairs in May 2022 (Ministry of Foreign Affairs of China 2022b). The Chinese medical workers have treated about 260,000 local patients, provided free medical services on over 100 occasions, and donated medical machines and medicines. The authors had conversation with some Chinese medical volunteers working in the PICs, who called for the international society to provide more medical aid to the PICs. The Chinese medical workers in the PICs told the authors that the medical volunteers from China and other countries help improve local residents' health and local medical service capacity with their skill and equipment. For example, the Navua Hospital, one of the hospitals given by China as a gift, has brought benefits to over 30,000 local residents, according to *the Fact Sheet on Cooperation between China and the PICs* released by the Chinese Ministry of Foreign Affairs (2022b).

Yang Honglian, a research fellow in the Center for the Pacific Island Countries, Liaocheng University, has been focused on Fiji over the last decade since the BRI was proposed. He notes that the Navua Hospital has provided local people with convenient access to quality medical service since it was opened to the public in 2014. Zhao Shaofeng and the authors visited the Chinese medical team from Shenzhen that launched a malaria elimination program in the Kirivina Islands of PNG in 2016, and helped reduce the local community's vulnerability to malaria. It is noteworthy that China and Australia have cooperated on malaria prevention in PNG, which provides a paradigm of cooperation between the new and traditional players in the region for the benefits of the local people. The China-Australia-PNG Malaria Prevention Program was officially launched in PNG in early 2016, which effectively enhanced the ability of malaria prevention and treatment (Department of Foreign Affairs and Trade of Australia 2018). This trilateral cooperation has implications for the regional players by showing that it is likely for the traditional and new players to go beyond geopolitical competition and conduct cooperation for the benefit of the local people.

After the start of the COVID-19, the PICs and China held more than 10 bilateral and multilateral public health expert meetings via video link to share experience covering disease prevention, control, treatment and diagnosis. China provided vaccines, medicine and financial assistance to the PICs, helping the latter build quarantine cubicles and other facilities. As of May 2022, China had provided the PICs with 590,000 doses of vaccines and over 100 tons of supplies according to the Chinese Ministry of Foreign Affairs (2022b). Restricted by their geographic location, medical standards across the PICs and the connectivity between the countries in the region remain low, meaning that local residents have difficulty in accessing treatment when faced with serious health issues. Yang Honglian notes that China's medical aid and assistance not only bring medicines and equipment to the PICs, but also advance local medical technology, which have helped improve the development of local medical care. Yang told the authors that the Chinese medical team helped the Solomon Islands organize an emergency medical team for the upcoming 2023 Pacific Games that was held in Honiara, the capital city of the Solomon Islands. As Vanuatu celebrated the 43rd anniversary of its independence in July, Vanuatu President Nikenike Vurobaravu awarded nine members of the Chinese medical team with state medals in recognition of their significant contribution to improving local medical standards and consolidating the China-Vanuatu cooperation in medical treatment and public health (Beijing Shijitan Hospital 2023).

Apart from providing medical services to local residents, the Chinese medical teams help train local medical staff through lectures, clinical practice and training sessions, which serve to enhance local medical capacity. According to the Xinhua News Agency, the Chinese medical teams to Papua New Guinea offered more than 11,000 training courses and at least 70 lectures to local medical workers from 2002 to 2023 (Dong 2023). The Chinese teams also provide training for the use of medical technologies that have never been available in the country. Zhao Shaofeng and Ni Peng in their last fieldwork in the Solomon Islands find that the Chinese medical teams in the Solomon Islands are delivering similar outcomes, who have been active in the country for a couple of years. In the last fieldwork in Tonga, the authors visited some Chinese volunteering doctors and medical workers in the local hospitals and had long conversations with them. The authors were impressed by their skill and service, and by their contribution to the local medical service.

The Affiliated Hospital of Guizhou Medical University, China (AHGMU) and the Ministry of Health and Medical Services of the Solomon Islands signed an MOU on medical cooperation in 2021. The two sides agreed on the Chinese assistance in upgrading tertiary hospital care at the National Referral Hospital (NRH) in the Solomon Islands as the center of teaching, treatment of complicated cases and major referral center. According to the MOU, the AHGMU will select senior doctors to be part of the China Medical Team in the Solomon Islands and provide more medical services to local communities. Xiao is a urologist from the AHGMU and a member of the second group of Chinese medical workers dispatched to the Solomon Islands. The local doctors conducted the first laparoscopic surgery under the guidance of Xiao and his colleagues. After the surgery, Xiao was pleased to say:

> In the past, local doctors had to make an opening of 15-20 centimeters on the patient's torso when they conducted the surgery. The patient would lose a large amount of blood and have to be hospitalized for about one week before leaving the hospital. But now, they can leave the hospital two days after the surgery is completed. The laparoscope machines helped us save at least 4 million yuan ($548,320) (Guo et al 2023).

The Traditional Chinese Medicine and Acupuncture Center and Minimally Invasive Urological Surgery Center is set up at the National Referral Hospital (NRH), in which both sides work closely on medical equipment and instruments donated to NRH. Doctors, nurses, and administrative personnel have opportunities to receive training and postgraduate education at AHGMU, and related medical technology supports are provided to the centers to assist NRH medical staff master specialized skills. Doctor Lei is an expert in the traditional Chinese medicine and acupuncture from the medical team, and he has changed the local people's attitude towards acupuncture from "never heard of" to "pure magic" in less than half a year (Guo et al. 2023). Lei is now teaching the accupuncture skills to local doctors and nurses while his colleagues are teaching them other TCM knowledge. The medical team are considering inviting some local doctors to China to further study acupuncture.

China has intensified cooperation with the PICs under the framework of the BRI to combat the challenges of climate change in response to the concerns voiced by the Pacific Islands countries. Most recently, the PICs have endorsed the *2050 Strategy for the Blue Pacific Continent* to maintain environmental integrity and drive sustainable economic prosperity and development' (Pacific Islands Forum 2022). The PICs have long been aware of the threat of climate change as stated by the Pacific Islands Forum (PIF) Secretariat (2014): "Climate change is an immediate and serious threat to sustainable development and poverty eradication in many Pacific Island Countries, and for some their very survival. By their geography and mid-ocean location they are at the 'frontline'. The PICs and regional organizations, such as Pacific Islands Forum, Pacific Community, Melanesian Spearhead Group, and Pacific Regional Environment Program, have long been active in advancing international cooperation on climate change. The Majuro Declaration signals a united position to the Conferences of the Parties (COPs), and to the UN Framework Convention on Climate Change (UNFCCC) to seek an effective global agreement on greenhouse gas emissions (Pacific Islands Forum 2013).

Based on *the Strategy for the Blue Pacific Continent*, the PICs have been seeking international cooperation for advice, financial and technological support for adaptation and mitigation efforts given their incapacity in terms of capitals, technology and knowledge to address climate change. Over the last couple of decades, the PICs have been in cooperation with some regional players (e.g., China and Australia) and international organizations (e.g., the World Bank and the Asian Development Bank) to carry out vulnerability assessments as components of technical assistance or grant projects (UNDP 2017). The cooperation also includes education and communication campaigns directed at policy makers and the general public to ensure their involvement in climate change–related activities, and dissemination of knowledge products, such as tools and methods for climate risk assessment. Specifically, the cooperation focuses on a comprehensive analysis of climate change impacts, and the economic costs and benefits of climate change adaptation and mitigation initiatives.

The adaptation and mitigation efforts made by the PICs in cooperation with regional players and international organizations are being directed at developing renewable energy (e.g., wind and solar power) and reducing emissions. The PICs have sought cooperation with the United Nations to combat climate change, which has provided support to the PICs to plan for climate adaptation, and established a fund to support the preparation and implementation of national adaptation plans of action. Some PICs, such as Kiribati, Samoa, the Solomon Islands, Tuvalu, and Vanuatu, have completed national adaptation plans of action and received support from the Least Developed Countries Fund (UN Climate Change 2024). The PICs undertake a variety of programs in adaptation, mitigation and policy development, including the Pacific Adaptation to Climate Change Project in partnership with UNDP, which coordinates the PICs' policies and activities (Secretariat of the Pacific Regional Environment Programme 2024). The PICs have positively participated in international agreements, such as the United Nations Framework Convention on Climate Change (UNFCCC), the Kyoto Protocol, and the Paris Agreement, displaying the PICs' dedication to global cooperation in combating climate change.

The Pacific islands region is actually one of the most severely affected areas by climate change, characterized by significant environmental sensitivity and vulnerability. Global climate change profoundly affects the survival, economic growth and social development of the Pacific islands. Climate change has led to various natural disasters such as high temperatures, floods, droughts and storms, causing economic losses to the PICs and affecting the livelihoods of local residents significantly. The PICs face challenges in climate governance: lack of sufficient international discourse power, limited economic capacity and insufficient funding for climate change adaptation, lack of infrastructure development for climate change adaptation, and lack of core climate change technologies. In this context, the global climate governance is crucial for the sustainable development of the PICs, and an important part of China's diplomatic statecraft. China responds to the concerns voiced by the Pacific islands countries with climate change and makes efforts in addressing climate change by providing targeted climate governance assistance.

The PICs have cooperated with the ADB and the World Bank on a number of climate change initiatives, such as funding climate adaptation projects, providing preparation of guidelines for climate proofing of infrastructure projects and assessing the feasibility of catastrophe risk financing (World Bank 2013, Asian Development Bank 2012). Multilateral aid has flown to the PICs from the UNFCCC Adaptation Fund and other international agencies, such as the World Bank and the Asian Development Bank, which consider climate change, deterioration of the environment and natural hazards as PICs' major threats. The PICs perceive blue economy and sustainable growth as the pillar of its development agenda with climate change adaptation and mitigation as drivers of the blue economy. The PICs have started the Pacific Climate Change Program (PCCP) under ADB's Regional Capacity Development Technical Assistance that is aimed to enhance the PICs' capacity to address climate change. The PCCP will address climate change–related technical and financing needs and support the planning and implementation of the climate-responsive national development plans.

The PICs set up Regional Partnerships for Climate Change Adaptation and Disaster Preparedness Technical Assistance, which covers eight countries (the Cook Islands, Fiji Islands, PNG, Samoa, Solomon Islands, Tonga, Tuvalu, and Vanuatu). The main objective is to ensure the continued economic growth of the PICs in the face of global climate change, by reducing their vulnerability to its risks and impacts. The Partnership helps the PICs to mitigate risks from the effects of natural disasters, including those exacerbated by climate change by improving the geophysical information system (GIS) that provides information to decision makers on hazard exposure and risk minimization. Specifically, the partnership supports the development of up to eight national databases, and a consolidated regional database, that includes risk, hazard, and vulnerability data, critical to the future development of a Pacific regional catastrophe insurance scheme and vital to informing governments regarding adaptation to natural catastrophes. The PICs are promoting and exploiting opportunities for regional collaboration to better manage mitigation, adaptation and response to climate change, and to develop and disseminate better knowledge in support of those activities. These international collaborations provide a platform for knowledge exchange, technology transfer, and financial support, bolstering the PICs capacity to implement effective climate action strategies.

The authors and some colleagues from the Research Center for Pacific Islands Countries (the China-Pacific Island Countries Climate Change Cooperation Center) had done fieldwork in the Pacific islands over the last decade since the Center was founded in early 2012. The authors note in the fieldwork that the interlocutors from the local governments, universities, NGOs, and communities in the Pacific Islands countries acknowledge the effects of global warming, arguing that the intensity and frequency of natural disasters have markedly increased over the decades. The interlocutors (e.g., Latu Silanka and Pratap) stressed that their voices of concerns with the climate change need to be heard, and that the developed states need to provide the Pacific islands with funds and technology to combat the challenges arising from the climate change[17]. A large number of interlocutors suggested enhancing vocational training, disaster relief supplies, and climate change when asked what areas of cooperation and assistance should be strengthened in the China-PICs relations.

Zhao Shaofeng, Chen Dezheng and other scholars in the Research Center for the Pacific Island Countries have long suggest the Chinese government to align the BRI with the PICs' strategic goals, including practical infrastructure cooperation related to addressing the disasters of climate change, such as storm surge protection. When interviewed, Xu Xiujun, a professorial researcher at the China Academy of Social Sciences, envisions the challenges arising from the climate change as shared challenges faced by all the countries in the world. In his opinions, climate change should be given significant attention by countries across the world, and should be an integral part of the BRI. The Chinese government

17 Latu, Fa'ainuse'iamalie alumalemana, is a lecturer and head of the Science Department, the National University of Samoa. Silanka is a lecturer at the University of South Pacific. Arti Pratap is an Assistant Lecturer in Geospatial Science, the University of the South Pacific (Fiji).

has allocated approximately 1.1 billion yuan (around US$170 million) in recent years to provide the developing countries with energy-efficient and new energy products, and equipment under the framework of the South-South cooperation on climate change. As far as the PICs are concerned, Zhao and Chen note that China has advanced cooperation with the PICs to combat climate change challenges and enhance disaster protection infrastructure in the region. Specifically, China and the PICs are working together to enhance disaster resilience in the region, including the planning and construction of disaster-resistant infrastructure like storm surge barriers and monitoring stations, water storage facilities to combat drought, and improved building standards (Zhang 2019, p. 98).

China places a significant focus on enhancing their cooperation with the PICs in the field of renewable energy and supporting the PICs to develop new energy sources. The Chinese government encourages the Chinese enterprises in the solar power and wind power sectors to "go global" and promotes the development of exemplary green energy projects overseas. In this vein, the Chinese government provides assistance to the Chinese enterprises to participate in projects related to the construction of hydropower plants and solar power farms in the PICs. The Chinese companies possess technical expertise and operational experience in photovoltaic, tidal, and wave energy generation, as well as small-scale integrated energy solutions. The Chinese government aims to help the developing countries address their energy needs by encouraging the Chinese enterprises to assist the PICs in assessing their suitability for solar, wind, and marine energy sources and tailor assistance projects accordingly to their natural conditions and development needs.

Moreover, China has established marine spatial planning technology system and domestically developed green and low-carbon marine economy. The Chinese companies employ the expertise in seawater aquaculture and marine ranch construction to achieve sustainable development, which is comparatively low-carbon and environmentally friendly. In the viewpoints of Xu Xiujun, China has made remarkable progress in green technology and thus can provide support for the Pacific Island nations and help them cope with climate change and build their green economy. The Chinese government also encourages the Chinese enterprises to cooperate with the developing countries, including the PICs, to promote the green and low-carbon marine economy in the developing world (Zhao & Lei 2023, p. 217).

China set up an academic institution in 2022, specializing in the studies on the climate change challenges in the PICs and on the cooperation on climate change with the PICs. The newly founded institution, the China-Pacific Island

Countries Climate Change Cooperation Center (previously known as the Center for Pacific Islands Countries Studies founded in 2012) is based at the Liaocheng University, Shandong Province. The Center has since 2016 hosted a dozen of training programs on climate change and green low-carbon development specifically for the PICs. When interviewed by the authors, Chen Dezheng, professor and deputy director of the China-PICs Climate Change Cooperation Action Center, said that China is acutely aware of the impacts of the climate change and supportive of the Paris Agreement on climate change. As the world's most populous country, China is keen to work with the PICs and other countries to address the climate change challenge and particularly in the domains of disaster-mitigation and climate-induced poverty.

Educational cooperation is a significant part of the BRI in the South Pacific. China has provided scholarship opportunities in marine, environmental, and climate-related areas to the PICs through cooperative programs, such as the "The Marine Scholarship of China". These programs align with China's commitment to offer 2,500 government scholarship opportunities to the PICs from 2020 to 2025. Concurrent with these cooperative programs, hundreds of Chinese volunteering teachers from the Chinese high schools and universities have been to the PICs and worked there as teachers. Kang Jian at the Liaocheng University is a research fellow in the Center for the Pacific Island Countries and had been in Tonga for three years as a volunteering teacher. When interviewed by the authors, Kang views the educational program as significant part of the China-PICs cooperation, contributing to the development of local economy, and the employment of local labor force. After years of working in Tonga, Kang is acutely aware that the young people of the PICs need jobs and vocational training in things like carpentry or masonry to address a shortage of skilled labor, and to support themselves and their families.

Concluding remarks

The BRI that was initiated by the Chinese government to promote "connectivity" and "exchanges among people" within the breadth of the "Belt" and "Road" is providing a new opportunity for China and the PICs to intensify their cooperation. The BRI is also providing a new avenue to expanding China's presence and influence in the region. The objectives of the chapter examine China's BRI and China-PICs cooperation under the framework of the BRI in a political economy way. The chapter argues that China's BRI in the Pacific Islands countries has literally developed as a geopolitical initiative beyond a purely economic one as the BRI has gradually changed the geo-economic and geopolitical landscape in the South Pacific. The chapter contributes to scholarly discussion by analyzing China's BRI in the greater picture of China's rise at the sub-systemic (regional) and systemic (global) level. The chapter finds that the BRI helps China intensify its economic and political cooperation with the PICs. With a combination of political, economic and strategic objectives and consequences, China's BRI in the Pacific islands countries contributes to the fulfillment of China's desire to sustain its economic growth by intensifying its economic involvement and infrastructural cooperation with the PICs.

The Chinese political leadership and academics have over the last four decades since Deng Xiaoping launched the market reform in 1978 formulated a consensus that Chinese economic modernization constitutes the basis underpinning China's "hard" and "soft" power, and its re-emergence at the systemic (global) level. This is why Deng Xiaoping identified economic growth and modernization as the most important task for Chinese political leaders in the 100 years starting from the late 1970s. Some Chinese scholars claim that the Chinese people, after more than a century of suffering and humiliation, have a strong aspiration for restoring their country's past glory of *fuqiang* (wealth and power) and this is why to achieve *fuqiang* has now become China's top priority whereas to secure democracy and human rights as the second (Li 2010, p. 87). The BRI also reflects China's geopolitical desire of intensifying China's partnership and cooperation with the PICs by intensifying its presence and influence in the region. The chapter concludes that China is increasingly capable of reaping not only economic but also geopolitical benefits from the BRI by intensifying economic, and by extension, political relations with the PICs.

References

Asian Development Bank 2012, *Climate Change in the Pacific Stepping Up Responses in the Face of Rising Impacts*, August, Manila, https://www.adb.org/sites/default/files/publication/27476/climate-change-pac.pdf.

Asian Development Bank 2019, The Pacific: Urgent Development Needs Remain Despite Stable Debt and Higher Revenues, 18 September, https://www.adb.org/news/features/pacific-urgent-development-needs-remain-despite-stable-debt-and-higher-revenues.

Ati, Marc and Zhou, Haicheng 2022, 'China, Vanuatu embark on new journey together', *China Daily*, 2 March, https://global.chinadaily.com.cn/a/202203/22/WS6239227da310fd2b29e5265d.html.

Bainimarama, Voreqe 2016, Road is an important symbol of government's commitment, Press Reader, 12 January, https://www.pressreader.com/fiji/fiji-sun/20160112/282097750698974

Baniya, Suprabha, Rocha, Nadia and Ruta, Michele 2019, *Trade Effects of the New Silk Road A Gravity Analysis*, The World Bank, January, https://documents1.worldbank.org/curated/en/623141547127268639/pdf/Trade-Effects-of-the-New-Silk-Road-A-Gravity-Analysis.pdf.

Beijing Shijitan Hospital 2023, *the Chinese medical team are awarded with state medals*, 2 August, https://www.bjsjth.cn/Html/News/Articles/24799.html

Cau, Enrico 2018, 'Geopolitical Implications of the Belt and Road Initiative: The Backbone for a New World Order?', *Contemporary Chinese Political Economy and Strategic Relations: An International Journal*, Vol. 4, No. 1, pp. 39-107.

Central government of the PRC 2023, *China's investment in, cooperation with B&R countries in 2023*, Belt and Road Portal, 7 February, https://eng.yidaiyilu.gov.cn/p/00LMPGLD.html.

Chan, Yolinda 2022, Expo brings China, Fiji closer, China International Import Expo Bureau, 3 November, https://www.ciie.org/zbh/en/news/exhibition/official/20221103/35111.html.

Chi, Jingyi 2022, 'China-Vanuatu relations a model of mutual respect, solidarity and coordination: Chinese ambassador', *The Global Times*, 25 May, https://www.globaltimes.cn/page/202205/1266545.shtml.

China Civil Engineering Construction Corporation 2023, *China-aided Solomon Islands Sports Venue Project Held a Handover Ceremony*, 23 May, http://ccecc.crcc.cn/art/2022/5/23/art_7753_3757546.html.

China National Development and Reform Commission 2020, The KSCNP is completed, 21 August, https://www.ndrc.gov.cn/fggz/gjhz/zywj/202008/t20200821_1236458.html.

China National Ocean Technology Center 2018, China-Vanuatu joint marine observation station is in progress, 19 July, http://www.notcsoa.org.cn/cn/index/gnwhz/show/1944.

China Railway Group 2023, China railway group starts the highway project in Niue, 25 April, http://www.crecg.com/web/10089492/10091148/10248601/index.html

China State Construction Engineering Corporation 2022, The Butuka Academy, 5 August, https://www.cscec.com/ztzl_new/xy20d/jzmhsd/202208/3559950.html

Chinese Embassy in PNG 2018, *The PNG National Power Grid Phase One Project is in progress*, 12 June, http://pg.mofcom.gov.cn/article/sqfb/nky/201806/20180602754505.shtml.

Clare, Angela 2022, *Pacific Islands – key issues*, Parliament of Australia, Canberra.

Cottrell, Christopher 2023, 'Fiji may partner with China to upgrade ports and shipyards, PM Rabuka says', *South China Morning Post*, 29 November, https://www.scmp.com/week-asia/economics/article/3243118/fiji-woos-china-upgrade-strategically-important-ports-even-debt-concerns-mount.

Cullwick, Jonas 2017, Baurefield Airport Runway Rehabilitation Work Starts With Groundbreaking, 31 October, https://southpacificislands.travel/baurefield-airport-runway-rehabilitation-work-starts-with-groundbreaking/.

Das, Shaheli 2016, 'How Important Is Latin America on China's Foreign Policy Agenda?', *Diplomat*, 16 November, https://thediplomat.com/2016/11/how-important-is-latin-america-on-chinas-foreign-policy-agenda/.

Deng, Xiaoping 1993, *Selected works of Deng Xiaoping*, vol. 3, People's Press: Beijing, pp. 370-371.

Department of Foreign Affairs and Trade of Australia 2018, Mid-Term Review of the Australia China Papua New Guinea Pilot Cooperation on Malaria Control, June, https://www.dfat.gov.au/sites/default/files/australia-china-png-pilot-cooperation-on-the-trilateral-malaria-project-independent-mid-term-review.pdf.

Dong, Jianghui 2023, 'Chinese medical team provides medical services at Maputo Central Hospital in Mozambique', Xinhua News Agency, 28 July, Beijing, https://www.globaltimes.cn/page/202307/1295226.shtml.

Ehizuelen, Michael Mitchell Omoruyi and Abdi, Hodan Osman 2017, 'Sustaining China-Africa relations: Slotting Africa into China's One Belt, One Road initiative makes economic sense', *Asian Journal of Comparative Politics*, Vol. 3, Issue, 4, pp. 285-310.

Embassy of China in Vanuatu 2021, *China-Vanuatu Poverty Alleviation Cooperation Contributes to Vanuatu's Economic and Social Development*, 10 May, http://vu.china-embassy.gov.cn/eng/sgdt/202210/t20221021107896l4.htm

Fan, Hesheng and Tang, Huimin 2016, 'zhongguo dui lamei daguo de waijiao zhanlue luoji (the logic of Chinese strategic diplomacy towards the big countries in Latin America)', *Academic Frontier* (People's Forum), No. 8, pp. 42-49.

Fanasia, Andrew 2019, 'Central to lease provincial capital to China group', *Solomon Star*, 9 October, http://www.solomonstarnews.com/index.php/news/national/item/22089-central-to-lease-provincial-capital-to-china-group?fbclid=IwAR31-B3eoae93AJRl2WKa_h8gvK-JRHHCzOnW4TBVKGs7QehsnExa8LqCY8#.XZ1humXo_pE.facebook.

Fildes, Nic 2022, 'China funds Solomon Islands' telecoms deal after signing security pact', *The Financial Times*, 19 August. https://www.ft.com/content/39ca5645-fd50-48a1-9f7f-e58170e0ad1c.

Gao, Fei and Zhang, Jian 2017, 'The strategic triangle of China-US-Russia in the post–Cold War era', Gao, Fei. & Li., Mingjiang (eds.) *China's neighborhood diplomacy: Peaceful development vs strategic hedging*. Beijing, Global Press, p. 48.

Global Times 2024, 'Exclusive: Solomon Islands wide open for more Chinese investment in sectors from agriculture to green economy: envoy', 8 June, https://www.globaltimes.cn/page/202406/1313800.shtml.

Guo, Chunhai 2017, 'zhonggong shibada yilai zhongguo dui lamei waijiao zhengce yu shijian (Chinese diplomatic policy towards Latin America and its implementation since the 18th Congress of the Chinese Communist Party)', *Journal of Latin American Studies*, Vol. 39, No. 2, pp. 1-16.

Guo, Yuandan, Liu, Yang, Shan, Jie, Leng, Shumei and Shen, Weiduo 2023, 'China's medical assistance boosts healthcare development in South Pacific region', *The Global Times*, 14 September, https://www.globaltimes.cn/page/202309/1298192.shtml?id=11.

Huang, Ge 2018, BRI to help Pacific island nations grow, Belt and Road Portal (Yidaiyilu), 15 November, https://eng.yidaiyilu.gov.cn/p/71706.html.

Jiang, Shixue 2018, 'goujian zhongguo yu lamei mingyungongtongti lujing sikao (an analysis on the creation of China-Latin America community of shared future)', *international studies*, No. 2, pp. 30-42.

Maxine Kamus, 'K650m PNG hydropower project opens after 15 years – end to blackouts?', *Asia Pacific Report*, 24 April, https://asiapacificreport.nz/2023/04/24/k650m-png-hydropower-project-opens-after-15-years-end-to-blackouts/.

Laursen, Finn 2009, *The EU in the Global Political Economy*, P.I.E. PETER LIANG: Brussels, p. 224.

Lee, John 2010, 'Don't rush to back Beijing over Delhi', *Australian*, 13 September, p. 10.

Li, Xuanmin 2022, 'China, Tonga are examples of 'building a community with shared future', long-term Chinese investments dwarf US, Australia', *The Global Times*, 30 May, https://www.globaltimes.cn/page/202205/1266930.shtml.

Li, Yuhai 2018, *Strategy*, Tsinghua University Press: Beijing, p. 284.

Liu, Weidong 2017, Studies on the strategy of the "Belt and Road", The Commercial Press, p. 21.

Löfflmann, Georg 2016, 'The Pivot between Containment, Engagement, and Restraint: President Obama's Conflicted Grand Strategy in Asia', *Asian Security*, Vol. 12, No. 2, pp. 92-110.

Lowry, R. 2011, 'China without illusions', 18 January, *National Review Online*, 18 January, http://www.nationalreview.com/articles/257334/china-without-illusions-rich-lowry.

Lu, Guixia 2022, 'China-PICs cooperation under the framework of BRI and the prospects', *The Academic Frontier-People's Forum*, Vol. 258, No. 17, pp. 70-77.

Ma, Jianying 2016, 'meiguo dui zhongguo yidaiyilu changyi de renzhi yu fanying (the U.S. perception of Chinese BRI and its response)', *World Economics and Politics*, Vol. 358, No. 10, pp. 104-132.

Ministry of Commerce of the PRC 2016, The Sino-Van Fisheries was put in operation, 5 November, http://vu.mofcom.gov.cn/article/jmxw/201611/20161101610395.shtml.

Ministry of Commerce of the PRC 2019, The KSCNP is in progress, 15 March, http://www.mofcom.gov.cn/article/i/jyjl/l/201903/20190302840235.shtml.

Ministry of Commerce of the PRC 2020, Fujian Zhonghong Fishery plans to invest in a fishery park in PNG, 30 November, http://pg.mofcom.gov.cn/article/sqfb/yy/202011/20201103015468.shtml.

Ministry of Commerce of the PRC 2022a, China and PNG concluded an agreement on PNG's exports of seafood to China, 9 February, http://pg.mofcom.gov.cn/article/jmxw/202202/20220203278768.shtml

Ministry of Commerce of the PRC 2022b, China-aided Enga Provincial Hospital is in operation, 27 June, http://pg.mofcom.gov.cn/article/todayheader/202206/20220603322109.shtml.

Ministry of Commerce of the PRC 2022c, *China's Outbound Investment and Cooperation (the Solomon Islands)*, Beijing.

Ministry of Commerce of China 2022d, *China's Outbound Investment and Cooperation (Vanuatu)*, Beijing.

Ministry of Commerce of the PRC 2023a, *Report on outbound investment and economic cooperation: PNG*, March, Beijing, p. 24.

Ministry of Commerce of China 2023b, *China's Outbound Investment and Cooperation (Fiji)*, Beijing.

Ministry of Foreign Affairs of the PRC 2019, China-Vanuatu Joint Communique, 28 May, https://www.mfa.gov.cn/web/ziliao_674904/1179_674909/201905/t20190528_9869100.shtml.

Ministry of Foreign Affairs of the PRC 2022a, Prime Minister of Papua New Guinea James Marape Meets with Wang Yi, 3 June, https://www.mfa.gov.cn/mfa_eng/wjb_663304/wjbz_663308/activities_663312/202206/t20220603_10698499.html.

Ministry of Foreign Affairs of China 2022b, *The fact sheet on China-PICs cooperation*, 24 May, Beijing, http://new.fmprc.gov.cn/web/zyxw/202205/t20220524_10691894.shtml.

Ministry of Foreign Affairs of the PRC 2023, Joint statement by the PRC and PNG, 17 October, https://www.mfa.gov.cn/web/ziliao_674904/1179_674909/202310/t20231018_11162574.shtml.

Nanau, Sharon 2021, 'Work on 2023 Pacific Games Stadiums on Schedule', *The Solomon Islands Broadcasting Corporation*, 14 October, https://www.sibconline.com.sb/work-on-2023-pacific-games-stadiums-on-schedule/.

Nie, Zhangnan and Xia, Liping 2016, 'the U.S. policy in the new century towards South China Sea and China-America disputes over the South China Sea', *Social Science*, No. 10, pp. 28-40.

Oeka, Paul 2023, 'K650-M Edevu hydro power plant launches', *PNG Business News*, 2 May, https://www.pngbusinessnews.com/articles/2023/5/k650-m-edevu-hydro-power-plant-launches.

O'Neill, Peter 2023, *Cooperation for a Sustainable 21st Century*, Center for China and Globalization (CCG), http://en.ccg.org.cn/archives/79727.

Paal, Douglas H. 2015, 'China's Counterbalance to the American Rebalance', Carnegie Endowment for International Peace, November, https://carnegieendowment.org/2015/11/01/china-s-counterbalance-to-american-rebalance-pub-61857.

Paal, Douglas H., Zhao, Tong, Haenle, Paul and Chen, Qi 2019, China-America relations at the tipping point of the 40th anniversary of the exchanges of diplomatic recognition, Tsinghua-Carnegie Center for Global Policy, 29 January, https://carnegietsinghua.org/2019/02/03/zh-pub-78275.

Pacific Islands Forum 2013, *Majuro Declaration for Climate Leadership*, July, http://www.majuro-declaration.org/the_declaration.

Pacific Islands Forum 2022, *2050 Strategy for the Blue Pacific Continent*, Pacific Islands Forum Secretariat, Suva, Fiji.

Pacific Islands Forum Secretariat 2014, 'The role of PIFS in climate change', Pacific Islands Forum Secretariat, September, http://www.forumsec.org/pages.cfm/strategic-partnerships-coordination/climate-change/.

Power China 2023, PowerChina signs Fiji water supply pipeline contract, 31 January, https://en.powerchina.cn/2023-01/31/c_828237.htm.

Ratuva, Steven 2014, 'A New Regional Cold War? American and Chinese Posturing in the Pacific', *Asia & the Pacific Policy Studies*, Vol. 1, No. 2, pp. 409-422.

Ren, Feifan 2020, Juncao has rooted in Fiji, Ministry of Commerce of the PRC, http://www.mofcom.gov.cn/article/beltandroad/fj/chnindex.shtml.

Ruta, Michele, Dappe, Matias Herrera, Lall, Somik, Zhang, Chunlin, Constantinescu, Cristina, Lebrand, Mathilde, Mulabdic, Alen, and Churchill, Erick 2019, *Belt and Road Economics: opportunities and risks of transport corridors*, World Bank: Washington D.C.

Secretariat of the Pacific Regional Environment Programme 2024, *Climate Change Resilience*, https://www.sprep.org/programme/climate-change-resilience.

Shambaugh, D. (2023, February 22). U.S.-China Relations at a Tipping Point. China-US Focus, https://www.chinausfocus.com/foreign-policy/us-china-relations-at-a-tipping-point#:~:text=U.S.-China%20relations%20have%20been%20very%20volatile%20 and%20very.

Shen, Weiduo, Shan, Jie and Leng, Shumei 2023, 'Chinese projects in South Pacific islands boost development, stabilize economy, debunking 'military influence', 'debt trap' hype', *The Global Times*, 14 September, https://www.globaltimes.cn/page/202309/1298184.shtml.

Sihaloho, Rezya Agnesica Helena; Prabowo, Tri Bagus and Pamungkas, Cahyo 2024, 'China's Belt and Road Initiative Implementation Maneuvers in the South Pacific Region', *Nation State: Journal of International Studies*, Vol. 7, No. 1, pp. 53 – 70.

Solomon Islands Broadcasting Corporation 2023, *Mesepitu: We will return to China International Import Expo (CIIE) 2024 on a bigger scale*, 11 November, https://www.sibconline.com.sb/mesepitu-we-will-return-to-china-international-import-expo-ciie-2024-on-a-bigger-scale/.

State Council of The PRC 2018, *Belt and Road Initiative paves way for cooperation between China, Pacific island countries*, Xinhua News Agency, 19 November, http://english.scio.gov.cn/beltandroad/2018-11/19/content_73622892.htm.

Sui, Sophia and Yu, Le 2020, 'Sino-Russian military cooperation in the context of strategic partnership', *Asia-Europe Journal*, Asia Europe Journal, Vol. 18, No. 3, pp. 325-345.

Sui, Sophia and Yu, Lei 2024, 'Ontological Security in China–Pacific Islands Countries (PICs) Geopolitics', *Journal of Island and Marine*, Vol. 1, No. 1, pp. 1-23.

Szadziewski, Henryk 2021, 'A Search for Coherence: The Belt and Road Initiative in the Pacific Islands', *The China Alternative: Changing Regional Order in the Pacific Islands*, Australia National University Press.

Tow, W. and Loke, B. 2009, 'Rules of engagement: America's Asia-Pacific security policy under an Obama administration', *Australian Journal of International Affairs*, Vol. 63, No. 4, pp. 442-457.

Trankmann, Beate 2019, *What changes after China defeats poverty?* United Nations Development Programme, 23 December, https://www.undp.org/china/blog/what-changes-after-china-defeats-poverty.

UN Climate Change 2024, *National Adaptation Programmes of Action*, August, https://unfccc.int/topics/resilience/workstreams/national-adaptation-programmes-of-action/napas-received.

UNDP 2017, *China's South-South Cooperation with Pacific Island Countries in the context of the 2030 Agenda for Sustainable Development, Series Report: Climate Change Adaptation*, 10 April, https://www.undp.org/china/publications/chinas-south-south-cooperation-pacific-island-countries-context-2030-agenda-sustainable-development-series-report-climate-change.

Vice, Margaret 2017, 'In global popularity contest, U.S. and China – not Russia – vie for first', Pew Research Center, 23 August, http://www.pewresearch.org/fact-tank/2017/08/23/in-global-popularity-contest-u-s-and-china-not-russia-vie-for-first/.

Wang, Yiming 2018, 'America's trade war cannot alter China's strategic opportunity', *Qiushi*, No. 19, pp. 57-59.

Wilson, Karl 2021, 'Papua New Guinea's seafood gets MOU lift', *China Daily*, 2 February, https://epaper.chinadaily.com.cn/a/202102/02/WS601886dea31099a234353b2b.html.

World Bank 2013, 'Acting on Climate Change & Disaster Risk for the Pacific', 20 November, http://documents.worldbank.org/curated/en/2013/01/18530985/acting-climate-change-disaster-risk-pacific.

World Bank 2019, *Rebuilding Vanuatu's Gateway to the World*, 6 December, https://www.worldbank.org/en/news/feature/2019/12/06/rebuilding-vanuatus-gateway-to-the-world.

Pacific island countries, the Central Government of the PRC, https://www.gov.cn/xinwen/2014-11/22/content_2782299.htm.

Xia, Liping and Zhong, Qi 2018, 'an analysis on Trump Administration's "Indo-Pacific" strategy', *Contemporary International Relations*, No. 1, pp. 22-28.

Xinhua 2018, 'Spotlight: Belt and Road Initiative paves way for cooperation between China, Pacific island countries, 18 November, http://www.xinhuanet.com/english/2018-11/19/c_137617032.htm#:~:text=PORT%20MORESBY,%20Nov.%2018%20(Xinhua)%20--%20The%20China-proposed

Yu, Le 2015, 'China-Latin America Strategic Partnership: a fulcrum in China's rise', *International Affairs*, Vol. 91, No. 5, pp. 1047-1068.

Yu, Lei 2021, 'China-Pacific Island Countries Strategic Partnership: China's strategy to reshape regional order', *East Asia: An International Quarterly*, 2021, Vol. 39, Issue 1, pp. 81-96.

Yu, Lei and Zhao, Shaofeng 2019, 'An analysis on the geopolitical development of China-South Pacific relations', *The Contemporary World*, Vol. 357, No. 2, pp. 26-42.

Zeng, Fanhua 2023, 'BRI projects facilitate social economic development in PNG as bilateral ties remain steadfast: Chinese ambassador', *The Global Times*, 8 October, https://www.globaltimes.cn/page/202310/1299426.shtml.

Zhang, Min 2019, 'Gezhouba Group signed a contract on the Edevu Power Project', Gezhouba Group. 19 August, http://www.cggc.ceec.net.cn/art/2019/8/19/art_7369_1960202.html.

Zhang, Ming 2019, 'Gezhouba Group concludes contract to construct the Edevu powerhouse', *China Energy*, 2 September, http://paper.people.com.cn/zgnyb/html/2019-09/02/content_1944905.htm#:~:text=%E6%9C%AC%E6%8A%A5%E8%AE%AF%208%E6%9C%8815.

Zhang, Ying 2019, 'The Belt and Road Initiative in South Pacific Island Countries', *The Pacific Journal*, Vol. 27, No. 1, pp. 93-104.

Zhang, Yongxing 2018, *China helps build roads in Fiji to common development*, Xinhua News Agency, 9 May, http://xinhuanet.com/english/2018-05/09/c137166911.htm

Zhao, Shaofeng and Yu, Lei 2023, *zhongguo zaitaipingyang daoyu diqu de shenfeng jiangou (China in the Pacific islands)*, China Social Sciences Press: Beijing, p. 27.

Zheng, Yongnian 2016, 'yidaiyilu yu zhongguo dawaijiao (the BRI and grand Chinese diplomacy)', *The Contemporary World*, Vol. 266, No. 2, pp. 8-11.

ZiroMwatela, Raphael and Zhao, Changfeng 2016, 'Africa in China's'One Belt, One Road'Initiative: A Critical Analysis', *Journal Of Humanities And Social Science*, Vol. 21, Issue12, pp. 10-21.

3

China-PICs Strategic Partnership in the Context of the BRI

Introduction

China has since the beginning of the 21st century been committed to creating a close relationship of cooperation, and a strategic partnership with the Pacific Island Countries (PICs) by persistently providing them with economic assistance and, more importantly, by extending its economic and political involvement there. China's rapidly increasing presence and influence in the South Pacific display its desire for intensifying economic cooperation and political relations with the PICs and its strategic goal of creating a "sphere of influence" in the South Pacific in the form of "a community of shared future" (Zhao & Yu 2023, p. 52). By pursuing its traditional strategy of "non-interference", China satisfies the PICs' demands for self-determination and independence, helping cement its relationship and the creation of a strategic partnership with the PICs. China reaps not only economic but also geopolitical benefit from its intensified economic, and by extension, political and strategic relations with the PICs, which assists China's rise at the systemic (global) and sub-systemic (regional) levels.

The Chinese foreign policy makers proposed a new diplomatic strategy at a time when it rose as the second largest economy around the end of the first decade of the 21st century to guide its relationships with countries across the world.

The strategy specifically identifies China's ties with the developing countries as the "basis" underpinning its external relations (*fazhanzhong guojia shi jichu*) (Zhang 2009, p. 33, Yu 2015, p. 1047). This definition accentuates the magnitude of the developing states in China's international relations when it is re-emerging at the systemic (global) level as a superpower. It indicates that China perceives the developing states as its allies in the international political arena and makes common cause with them a significant element in its global power and influence. Nevertheless, China's ties with the PICs have to date failed to go beyond the commercial and trading levels particularly in contrast to its relationships with African states, which have frequently been described as 'all weather' by both African and Chinese political leaderships (Taylor 2011, p. 13, Yu 2018, p. 489). The intimacy of China-Africa relations provides a demonstration that the geographical distance between China and the PICs is essentially irrelevant to their lack of intimacy.

Apart from the comparative marginalization of the PICs in the global system of politics and economics, the lack of intimacy is partially attributable to China's strategy of avoiding offending the U.S.-headed West (or the "traditional donors") by intruding into the U.S. "sphere of influence", or "backyard". One strategic consensus has been kept in the Chinese foreign policy making and IR circles ever since Deng Xiaoping launched the market reform in the late 1970s that China's relationship with the West, and especially with the United States remains at the core of its external relations (Wang 2005, p. 41, Zhang 2004, p. 49). This is because the Chinese political leaders come to the realization that China's economic modernization would be impossible without Western capital, technology and markets. Deng Xiaoping (1993, p. 370) emphasizes economic growth and modernization as the basis underlying China's overall power and particularly its military capabilities. Hence, anything that is, in his view, detrimental to China-West relations, would have to be sacrificed to this key relationship—unless China's "core interests", such as its territorial integrity and its rise at the systemic (global) level, are under threat of foreign invasion and blockage.

This situation has, however, altered since Xi Jinping's presidency began in 2013 as he seeks not only to extend China-PICs economic cooperation by announcing the South Pacific as the "southern leg" of the "Maritime Silk Road" (Blanchard & Flint, Colin 2017, p. 223) but also to intensify their political relations by creating a strategic partnership. Xi and the political leaders from eight PICs that have exchanged diplomatic recognition with China announced their strategic partnership in 2014 (Ministry of Foreign Affairs of the PRC 2014). Four years later, they promulgated the idea of creating a 'community of shared future', with the stated aim of seeking 'common growth, shared prosperity and collective security'[18]. The intensification of China-PICs partnership has synchronized with such strategies pursued by the United States and its allies in the Pacific as the "pivot to Asia", "Indo-Pacific" strategy, and "Freedom of Navigation Operations (FNP)" in the South China Sea. The Chinese foreign policy makers and IR scholars perceive these strategies as deliberately designed as such by the United States to contain China's rise[19] (Wei 2016, p. 287, Zhao 2018, p. 89) despite the latter's denial (Löfflmann 2016, p. 92). Against this backdrop, it is not surprising that China expedites its presence in the South Pacific and intensifies its strategic partnership with the PICs as a way to counterattack the U.S. containment by opening up "new battlefields" in the South Pacific (Paal 2015, Wang 2018, p. 17).

The argument of this chapter is that the creation of Chinese–PICs strategic partnership and the extension of "Maritime Silk Road" to the South Pacific

---

18 Some Chinese IR scholars believe that the 'community of shared future' is a new strategy proposed by Xi Jinping, reflecting China's concept of its relations with the developing countries: to seek common development, shared prosperity and collective security through regional economic, political and security cooperation. For more details see Zhong, Sheng 2018, 'To work hard for a bright future for the Asia-Pacific community of shared future', *People's Daily*, 13 November, p. 3. Zhao, Shaofeng and Yu, Le 2019, 'An analysis on the geopolitical development of China-South Pacific relations', *Contemporary World*, Vol. 447, No. 2, pp. 26-42.

19 Some in Australia and elsewhere hold the view that China's assertiveness in the South China Sea contributes to Australia's sense of security. This is a controversial argument if the mainstream Chinese literature of international relations were taken into consideration. The "9 dash-line" on the official Chinese map is actually inherited from that of the Republic of China (ROC) that was founded by Dr. Sun Yat-sun in 1911 after a military uprising overthrew the Qing regime. The regime of the ROC retreated to Taiwan in 1949 after its defeat in the Chinese civil war. The Chinese foreign policy elites and scholars claim that the "11 dash-line" on the official map of the ROC had never ever been challenged by the United States and its allies as well as other states before and after the Second World War. They attribute the growing tension in the South China Sea as a result of the US containment of China's rise as evidenced by the "pivot to Asia", the "Indo-Pacific strategy" and the most recent AUKUS alliance. For more details see Shi, Yubin 2021, 'The South China Sea arbitration and an analysis on the legitimacy of China's activities in the South China Sea', *China Oceans Law Review*, Vol. 16, No. 4, pp. 138-181. Chang, Na 2022, 'The current situation and challenges to China's maritime security', *The Asia-Pacific Security and Maritime Affairs*, Vol. 29, No. 1, pp. 51-60.

accentuate the Chinese economic and geopolitical orientation towards the PICs. China's move in the South Pacific reveals China's desire not only to intensify its economic cooperation and trade with the PICs, but also to create a 'community of shared future' in the traditional 'backyards' of the United States and its major ally, Australia, as a counterbalance to their containment and encirclement. By advancing economic cooperation, China attempts to gain access to the (land and maritime) resources and investment destinations of the PICs to help sustain its economic growth that is considered by the Chinese political leaders as the basis for China's "hard" and "soft" power, including its military strength. Politically, China aspires to reinforce its partnership with the PICs in the hopes of acquiring their diplomatic backing particularly in such global and regional organizations as the UN and the Pacific Islands Forum (PIF), and competing with Taiwan for diplomatic recognition. Geo-strategically, China wishes to counterbalance the United States and its allies in the Pacific to ensure its rise at the systemic (global) level in tandem with its growing strength and prowess.

The political leaderships of the PICs and China announced at the third China-PICs Economic Development and Cooperation Forum held in Samoa in 2019 to upgrade ties to "a strategic partnership" (Ministry of Foreign Affairs of the PRC 2019). Some scholars of international relations (IR) and policy analysts conceive the partnership as a signal for both sides to intensify economic, and, by extension, political and security collaboration amidst a regional backdrop of intensified geopolitical competition between the emerging and established powers (Grieken & Kantorowicz 2021, p. 861).

The partnership is designed as such to be within the ambit of "South-South cooperation"[20], at the heart of which lies the intent to achieve a "win-win" outcome of economic prosperity and mutually political backing in the region and beyond.

20 The "South-South Cooperation" is a process whereby two or more developing countries pursue their individual and/or shared national capacity development objectives through exchanges of knowledge, skills, resources, and technical know-how, and through regional and interregional collective actions, including partnerships with involvement from governments, regional organizations, civil society, academia, and the private sector, for their individual and/or mutual benefit within and across regions. For more details, see Besada, H.; Tok, M.E.; Polonenko, L.M. 2019, *Innovating South-South Cooperation: Policies, Challenges and Prospects; Studies in international development and globalization*, University of Ottawa Press: Ottawa.

The rapid extension of China's presence in the South Pacific and the intensification of China-PICs strategic partnership comes against the backdrop of China's rise in the new century to the juncture of power shift, where the United State has shown reluctance to accommodate China's continued rise. Some IR academics home and abroad warn China of the increasing containment and strategic pressure imposed on it by the United States (Huang 2018, p. 72, Xu 2018, p. 71). Some international academics argue that the primary strategy of the United States is to preclude any emerging powers capable of challenging the latter's hegemony, particularly in the Asia–Pacific region (Tow & Loke 2009, p. 443). The Chinese academics justify their argument with the disintegration of the former Soviet Union and the "lost decades" of Japan: it is the U.S. strategy of 'containment' and 'sabotage' that terminated the Soviet and Japanese rise in the late 20th century in that they both qualitatively challenged America's hegemony. In the same vein, they stick to the belief that a similar U.S. "containment" will most likely befall China and the U.S. strategies of the "pivot to Asia", the "Indo-Pacific" strategy and the "Freedom of Navigation Operations" in the South China Sea as containment of this kind (Sui & Yu 2023, p. 43; Gao & Zhang 2017, p. 56).

Not surprisingly, this perception is dramatically reinforced after the Trump administration of the United States launched a trade war against China. In response, the Chinese scholars suggest that China strategically prioritize economic growth in support of its high-technology progress and military modernization to narrow its distance from those of the United States and ultimately avoid a doom similar to that which befell the former Soviet Union and Japan (Wang 2017, p. 7, Fu 2016, p. 9). Technically, China may counterattack the U.S. containment and especially its aggressive "FNO" in the South China Sea by enhancing its presence in the South Pacific, and intensifying its strategic partnership with the PICs. In this way, China penetrates the 'backyards' of the United States and Australia, the U.S. southern "anchor" in the Pacific (China describes the United States as a "crab" in the Pacific and its two close allies, Australia and Japan, the "claws" of the "crab") (Dwyer 1996, p. 12, Yu 2016, p. 743).

China's strategies

A bipolar system was established after the Second World War within which nations across the world were generally categorized as 'superpowers, middle powers and bottom-layer states' according to the levels of 'hard' and 'soft' power at their disposal (Khan 2012, p. 52). At the top of the global power hierarchy sat the United States and the Soviet Union, the two superpowers by virtue of their enormous economic and formidable military capabilities as well as their cultural and ideological influence on the rest of the world. In the face of the two starkly opposed camps headed respectively by the two superpowers, Mao Zedong, Chairman of the Chinese Communist Party (CCP), had to ponder a question that would have a decisive impact on the fate of his new administration: with whom should the 'new China' side in the bipolar system—the United States or the Soviet Union? Mao eventually decided to side with the Soviet Union, even though some veteran Chinese politicians and IR scholars suggested that a balanced strategy between the two superpowers would most benefit the interests of Beijing.

Many Chinese IR scholars, indeed, argue that the pursuit of national interest played a much more important role than communist ideology in Mao's decision to side with the Soviet Union (Hui 2011, p. 9, Guan 2009, p. 32). In Mao's view, the new China had no chance of adopting a balanced strategy in the face of the intense confrontation between the two superpowers (Mao 1991, p. 1478). More importantly, Mao worried that the 'imperialist powers', headed by the United States, might at any time intervene in the Chinese civil war to nip the new republic in the bud. It is in this context that Mao believed the best policy option for the new government was to adopt the strategy of 'leaning to one side'—more specifically, siding with the Soviet Union[21]. In so doing, the new China would reap many benefits: preventing a possible western military intervention, avoiding diplomatic isolation by obtaining diplomatic recognition from the Soviet bloc,

21 In the spring and summer of 1949 Mao Zedong propounded the principle of 'leaning to one side'. The official Chinese IR literature presents this as a major decision made in the light of China's historical and actual situation and in accordance with the international environment existing at that time. The strategy of 'leaning to one side' indicated that China would incline towards socialism as during the Chinese civil war the United States had aligned itself against the Chinese Communist Party and supported the Kuomintang, and so after the birth of the new China, it might carry out armed intervention against the PRC. In these circumstances, it was necessary for China to ally itself with the socialist countries. For more details, see Ministry of Foreign Affairs of the PRC, Formulation of foreign policy of new China on the eve of its birth, http://www.fmprc.gov.cn/mfa_eng/ziliao_665539/3602_665543/3604_665547/t18057.shtml, accessed 6 Aug. 2015.

acquiring Soviet assistance to restore its war-scarred economy, and keeping its status as a middle power in the global hierarchy.

As Mao anticipated, the Soviet Union diplomatically recognized the PRC promptly, just one hour after Mao announced the founding of the PRC, and other states in the Soviet bloc soon followed suit, notwithstanding the refusal of the majority of western states to do so (Wang 2011, p. 37). Over the next decade, from late 1949 to the early 1960s, the Soviet Union provided China with large quantities of economic assistance, helped it establish a system of modern industry, and assisted the People's Liberation Army (PLA) in creating its naval and air forces (Ji 2008, p. 140, Yang 2012, p. 80). By 'leaning to one side' with the Soviet Union, the new China not only survived the Korean War, in which it fought face-to-face with formidable U.S.-headed UN forces[22], but also reinforced its status as a middle power at the systemic level (Department of Military History, Academy of Military Science of the PLA 2000, p. 452). In view of the enormous stakes, some Chinese IR scholars (e.g., Huamin Yu) defend Mao's strategy of 'leaning to one side', arguing that had China not taken this route it might have been unable to secure diplomatic recognition, political espousal and economic assistance from either of the superpowers, potentially putting the new China in grave jeopardy (Yu 2007, p. 82).

However, other Chinese scholars, such as Xiuhua Zhang (2000, p. 48), contend that, having cast its vote in favor of the Soviet Union, China had to subordinate its interest in seeking an independent foreign policy to the interests

22 The mainstream perceptions of Chinese academics on China's involvement in the Korean War are radically different from those of the West. Many Chinese scholars characterize China's involvement in the war as inevitable. They argue that China's involvement was not merely a logical outcome of the communist ideology that Mao Zedong upheld, but was strongly related to China's geopolitical interests, territorial security and economic rehabilitation from its long-term wars. In their view, after the U.S.-headed UN forces crossed the 38th parallel into North Korea and quickly pushed forward towards the Chinese border, Mao Zedong was left with only one option: to roll back the UN forces to the 38th parallel by sending troops to North Korea. For more details, see Qin, Xiaofan 2010, 'Mao Zedong yu zhong guo kang mei yuan chao jue ce' [Mao Zedong and China's decision on the war to resist American aggression and aid Korea], *Foreign Affairs Review, Vol.* 27, No. 1, pp. 4-10; Jiansun Sha, 'Kang mei yuan chao zhan zhen ji qi li shi yi yi' [The war of resisting American aggression and aiding Korea and its historic meaning], Journal of Ideological and Theoretical Education 139: 7, 2010, pp. 33-7.

of the Soviet Union, thereby undermining its own sovereignty and status as an independent centre of power. More damagingly still, this strategy led China into comprehensive confrontation with the United States, which lasted for more than two decades from 1949 to 1972, when President Nixon paid his ice-breaking visit to Beijing. In the view of these Chinese scholars, it was that direct confrontation that led the United States to adopt the strategy of encirclement of China, precluding it from integration into the world system (Sui 2004, p. 49). These scholars argue that China's economy might otherwise have taken off in the 1960s and 1970s along with those of its neighbors, such as Japan, South Korea and the 'Asian tigers' of Taiwan, Hong Kong and Singapore. Mao's strategy of 'leaning to one side' lasted throughout the 1950s, but in the early 1960s Sino-Soviet relations began to deteriorate, culminating in violent border clashes in 1969.

Perceiving the Soviet military threat as 'most dangerous and imminent' (Niu 1999, p. 67), Mao had to undertake a strategic volte-face to create a united anti-Soviet front with America and its allies. Some Chinese IR scholars (e.g., Niu) argue that by aligning itself with the West, China mitigated the Soviet threat. Moreover, the normalization of China's relations with the West in the early 1970s paved the way for Deng Xiaoping's market reform and China's modernization drive later that decade—processes that, in the view of these scholars, would have been impossible without western capital, technology and markets. Other Chinese IR scholars (e.g., Liu 1997, p. 3), however, argue that 'leaning' to the other side, this time towards the United States against the Soviet threat, once again precluded China's development of an 'independent' foreign policy and a role as an independent centre of power.

Since his return to the top Chinese leadership in the late 1970s, Deng Xiaoping had been committed to China's re-emergence as an independent 'pole' at the systemic (global) level like the United States and the former Soviet Union to restore the country's past glory of *fuqiang* (wealth and power). To this end, he abandoned Mao Zedong's "proletarian revolution" ideology at home"[23], and prioritized economic growth and modernization. Internationally, Deng restored

23 In 1966, Mao Zedong launched the so-called Great Proletarian Cultural Revolution (Cultural Revolution) in order to purge the "revisionists" of Chinese Communist Party and revive "the spirit of the Chinese Revolution". The Cultural Revolution continued until Mao's death in 1976 and threw China's cities into turmoil. For more details, see Yan, Jiaqi and Gao, Gao 1996, *Turbulent Decade: A History of the Cultural Revolution*, University of Hawaii Press: Honolulu.

the strategy of "Five Principles of Peaceful Co-existence (commonly known as "non-interference" overseas)" that was initiated in the 1950s to guide China's relations with the developing states and win their diplomatic recognition and political endorsement[24]. In accordance with this strategy, Deng proposed that China cultivate a cooperative and mutually beneficial relationship with other states across the world 'in all dimensions and at all levels regardless of their ideologies and political institutions' (Fujita 1993, p. 464, Yu, 2015, p. 1048).

The Tian'anmen Square incident in 1989 and the demise of the former Soviet Union in 1991 terminated the political 'honeymoon' between China and the West, which had come into being since President Nixon's visit to Beijing in 1972 in search for a jointed effort to contain their perceived "most dangerous and imminent Soviet threat" (Sutter 2000, p. 62, Niu 1999, p. 67). In its place, a sense of crisis emerged among the Chinese political leadership following the falls of the Soviet Blocs, suspecting China to be the next target of the West's 'peaceful evolution'[25]. Deng Xiaoping (1993, p. 380) hardly concealed his anxiety and concluded: 'The Western states are staging a Third World War … they want to bring about the peaceful evolution of socialist countries towards capitalism.' In Deng's viewpoints, the motivation behind the western strategy of 'peaceful evolution' was nothing but to bring the communist rule in China to an end.

---

24 The Chinese foreign policy makers and IR scholars have long viewed the "five principles" as the utmost important principles governing its external relations with the rest of the world. The Five Principles are: mutual respect for territorial integrity and sovereignty; mutual non-aggression; mutual non-interference in internal affairs; equality and mutual benefit; and peaceful co-existence. For more details, see Zheng, Ruixiang 2004, 'heping gongchu wuxiang yuanze chansheng de lishi beijing he shidai yiyi (the historical background of the creation of the five principles of peaceful co-existence and its significance for the current time), Contemporary Asia-Pacific Studies, *No. 6, pp. 3-8.*

25 'Peaceful evolution' is a term generally used by Chinese academics to describe an alleged strategy of the United States and its western allies to either overthrow or westernize socialist states, including China, through peaceful means if or when they fail to achieve the same goal through economic embargoes, military interference or outright invasion. For an elaboration of this term, see Zhao, Fuke 2009, 'Mao Zedong Deng Xiaoping fangzhi he fandui heping yanbian de lilun yu shijian shuxi' [On the theories and practices of Mao Zedong and Deng Xiaoping for preventing and combating peaceful evolution], *Journal of Jiangxi Normal University*, Vol. 42, No. 1, pp. 110-14.

Deng Xiaoping insisted on economic growth and modernization to improve the livelihood of the Chinese people and to reinforce the legitimacy of the communist rule of China. Deng Xiaoping refused to accept the perceptions prevailing in the United States that the disintegration of the Soviet Union marked the triumph of America-style democracy over the Soviet authoritarian communism and the universalization of liberal democracy as the final form of human government (Fukuyama 1992, p. 9). Instead, Deng Xiaoping and his communist ideologues theorized the tragedy of the Soviet fall as the corollary of its economic incapacity that failed to buttress the Soviet "imperial over-expansion" and win the political support of the general public by improving their livelihood (Deng 1993, p. 370, Wang 2007, p. 113, Zuo 2001, p. 34). This sheds light on Deng Xiaoping (1993, p. 371)'s belief that the priority should be given to economic modernization and improvement of the Chinese people's livelihood rather than to the pursuit of military hegemony in the next one hundred years.

Deng Xiaoping proposed, among others, two strategies to sustain the Chinese economic growth and modernization. One is the sophisticated and controversial strategy of "*tao guang yang hui*" (韬光养晦, meaning to conceal China's capabilities and biding its time) (Leng & Wang 2004, p. 1078, Narramore 2008, p. 89). The strategy advises China to keep a low profile in the international affairs and eschew any confrontation with the United States, the status quo superpower (unless its core interests, such as the sovereignty over Taiwan and the communist rule of China, are to be threatened). This strategy is specifically designed as such to ensure China's access to the U.S. markets, capitals and technology, which are vital to China's economic growth and modernization, and to avoid an early containment, or strategic pressure imposed on it by the United States to preclude it from rising at the systemic (global) level.

The other is the strategy of 'South–South cooperation' that encompasses various purposes. First, it mitigated China's economic pressure resulting from offering assistance to the "Third World" to woo their diplomatic support in the international arena. Second, it helped China access the resources, markets and investment opportunities of the developing countries to sustain China's economic growth. Third, it helped China intensify economic and, by extension, political cooperation with other developing countries. Deng (1993, p. 371)'s proposal of South-South cooperation has altered the paradigm of China's economic interactions with other developing countries. Economic cooperation and trade on an equal footing have thereafter been a new "shared interest" between China and other developing countries alongside anti-colonialism and anti-imperialism. The South-South Cooperation altered traditional paradigm of the Chinese relations with the developing countries, paving the way for vigorous Chinese economic involvement in the developing World. Coupled with the low-interest loans and economic assistance, intensified economic cooperation and trade between China and the other developing states have thereafter become a new and more enduring "common interest" in lieu of the out-of-mode anti-colonialism and anti-imperialism (Information Office of the State Council of the PRC 2013).

China develops in the new century a geopolitical strategy that combines economic diplomacy and a diplomatic 'charm offensive' to expand its economic involvement and political influence in the developing world[26]. The economic objective of this strategy is to sustain China's economic growth and enhance its overall power (Khan & Yu 2013, p. 89); the geopolitical one, to ensure the country's rise as a new "pole" in the global power system in tandem with its increasing power and wealth as Deng Xiaoping anticipated. It is no denial that China has, indeed, intensified its economic and, by extension, political relationships with other developing states over the past decades in the new millennium through a variety of strategies.

China-PICs Relations

China had been encircled militarily and isolated diplomatically by the U.S.-headed West over the two decades from the birth of the People's Republic of China (PRC) in 1949 to President Nixon's ice-breaking visit to Beijing in 1972. The developing states had over this period balked at recognizing the PRC for a

26 Since then the term 'economic diplomacy' (jingji waijiao) has been part of the Chinese diplomatic vocabulary to describe the employment of both the official (Track 1) and unofficial (Track 2) channels of diplomacy for advancing China's economic development through various means, such as gaining access to foreign markets as well as the use of trade, investment and finance in support of China's diplomatic goals. Currently, the three main objectives of this 'economic diplomacy' are (1) strengthening China's economic relationship with the developing countries, as demonstrated by China's increasing involvement in Africa and South America; (2) attaining China's diplomatic objectives, i.e. China's increasingly proactive role in G20; and (3) diversifying China's export markets and sources of energy and raw materials. More details see Khan, Shamsul and Yu, Le 2013, "Evolving China–ASEAN Relations and CAFTA: Chinese Perspectives on China's Initiatives in Relation to ASEAN Plus 1", *European Journal of East Asia Studies*, Vol. 12, No. 1, p. 81.

combination of factors, such as Beijing's export of revolution, Taiwan's diplomatic competition and the U.S. blockage (Xia 2005, p. 75). It was not until November 1975 that Fiji and Samoa took the lead in diplomatic recognition of China and ten out of the fourteen PICs had exchanged diplomatic recognition with China by the early 1990s. The normalization of relations should, among others, be attributable to Deng Xiaoping's restoration of the Five Principles of Peaceful Co-existence ("non-interference") to guide its relations with the PICs.

In the first visit to the PICs (Samoa, Fiji and Papua New Guinea, PNG) made by a top Chinese political leader in 1985, Hu Yaobang, General Secretary of the Communist Party, promised on behalf of the Chinese government, not to export revolution, or communist ideology to the PICs as it did in Southeast Asia and Africa in the 1960s and 1970s (Xiao 2010, p. 243). Instead, he proposed that relations between China and the PICs be based upon the 'five principles of peaceful co-existence', which prohibits the interference by one sovereign state with the internal affairs of the others (Tsai 2012, p. 56). It is safe to say that China's 'non-interference' strategy worked and was appreciated by the political leaderships of the PICs in contrast to the stance adopted by the United States and Australia, both of which have long pushed for good governance, democracy and transparency in the region.

To further draw close their relations, China signed and ratified in 1987 the South Pacific Nuclear Free Zone (SPNFZ) Treaty, known as the Treaty of Rarotonga, pledging not to use or threaten to use any nuclear explosive device against the PICs and not to test any nuclear explosive device within the zone (O'Neil 2010, p. 568, Ministry of Foreign Affairs of the PRC 2014b). China was admitted two years later to the Pacific Islands Forum (PIF) as a dialogue partner and China has thereafter dispatched each year a delegation headed by a high-ranking envoy to the forum. In October 2000, the China-PIF Cooperation Fund was established with Chinese government donations to promote trade and investment cooperation between the two sides. This forum, together with the China-PICs Economic Development and Cooperation Forum created in 2006 and the Pacific Islands Development Forum (PIDF) founded in 2013, becomes the major regional platforms for China and the PICs to conduct multilateral dialogue and cooperation. The Chinese government has provided financial assistance to the Secretariat of the Pacific Regional Environment Programme (SPREP) every year since 1998, to support PICs in tackling climate change and achieving sustainable development.

China hardly displayed much interest in the PICs throughout the 1990s, which was obviously reflected by their two-way trade: merely $168 million by the end of 1999 and by no formal visit made by Chinese Head of State, or government (Ministry of Foreign Affairs of the PRC 2019b). The reasons could be expressed in two ways. Firstly, China was in the process of industrialization and economic modernization throughout the 1990s, which is in need of markets, capital and technology as well as resources and raw materials. This explains why China has intensified its economic and technological cooperation with the West in the hopes of gaining access to its markets, capital and technology. As well, China has been vigorously involved in resource-abundant Africa, Southeast Asia and Latin America since mid-1990s by pursuing the "going out strategy (China goes global)" that is specifically designed to tap the vast pool of overseas resources and markets in supportive of Chinese industry and manufacturing[27]. Secondly, the Chinese government cautioned against giving an offence to the West, especially the United States and Australia, by intruding into the South Pacific, their traditional "sphere of influence", or "backyards" as China needs their markets, investment and technology. Moreover, China was in the process of re-gaining a membership of the General Agreement on Tariffs and Trade (GATT) and later, the WTO, in both of which, the United States and Australia enjoy significant influence (Xu 1993, p. 41, Shi 2011, p. 65).

Caution notwithstanding, the Chinese engagement with the PICs still created controversies with the traditional players in the South Pacific, and particularly with the United States. China set up in 1997 a satellite tracking station in Kiribati, whose central Pacific position makes it a key space location. The space facilities, however, aroused wide concerns among the Western states with its dual-use capabilities of boosting both the Chinese economy and its military prowess. The United States accused the Chinese government of spying

27 The Going Out Strategy (also known as China goes global) was first proposed by the Chinese government in the *Tenth Five-year Plan* in 2001 to tap the vast pool of overseas resources and markets to sustain the country's economic growth. The strategy was reinforced in the Twelfth Five-year Plan (2011-2015) that encourages Chinese enterprises to expedite their pace in seeking overseas resources, markets and investment destinations. For more details, see Lin, Hongyu 2011, 'An analysis on China's going out strategy: from the perspectives of international political economy', *Contemporary International Relations*, Vol. 24, No. 8, pp. 8-9. Yu, Le 2015, 'China-Latin America Strategic Partnership: a fulcrum in China's rise', *International Affairs*, Vol. 91, No. 5, pp. 1047-1068.

on a U.S. testing station[28] for its missile defense program (that China opposed) in the nearby Marshall Islands despite the fact that the dishes were too small and pointed to intelligence-gathering equipment on the Chinese Yuan Wang tracking ships (Copper 2016, p. 134). China was forced to close down the station in October 2003 after Kiribati suddenly switched its diplomatic recognition to Taiwan, which produced wide speculations that the United States was behind the diplomatic switch (Reuters 2019).

China has impressively expedited its pace in expanding its economic involvement in and political cooperation with the PICs since the onset of the new millennium due to a blend of strategic, diplomatic and economic calculations. First of all, the Bush administration's conceptualization of China in 2001 as a strategic competitor as opposed to President Clinton's definition of China as a strategic partner (Tull 2008, p. 461), together with America's military belligerence reflected in a string of wars in Iraq and Afghanistan kept increasing the Chinese sense of insecurity. This sense was further deepened by the growing voices in the foreign policy making circle and scholarly community in the United States that America and China are likely to engage in 'an intense security competition with considerable potential for war' and that most of American allies 'will join it to contain China's power' (Mearsheimer 2003, p. 143). Not coincidentally, a trilateral security mechanism between the United States and its two military

28 The Ronald Reagan Ballistic Missile Defense Test Site (RTS) of the U.S. Army Space and Missile Defense Command Technical Center is a missile test range in the Marshall Islands (Pacific Ocean). It is commonly referred to as the Reagan Test Site (formerly Kwajalein Missile Range), and primarily functions as a test facility for U.S. missile defense and space research programs. RTS is located at the U.S. Army Garrison-Kwajalein Atoll, Republic of the Marshall Islands in the Central Pacific Ocean. RTS conducts space operations to provide space situational awareness and the protection of key space assets supporting U.S. Central Command, U.S. Pacific Command and U.S. Northern Command. Radar, optical and telemety sensors on the atoll support missile testing, missile launches, space reconnaissance and surveillance operations, and science experiments for the Department of Defense and multiple other government agencies. The instrumentation is strategically situated on the atoll to collect metric and signature data for characterizing missile and satellite systems. In addition, RTS is ideally located for observation of new foreign launches and a variety of low-inclination satellite orbits. For more details, see U.S. Army Space and Missile Defense Command 2024, Ronald Reagan Ballistic Missile Defense Test Site at Kwajalein Atoll (RTS), August, https://www.smdc.army.mil/Portals/38/Documents/Publications/Fact_Sheets/RTS.pdf.

"anchors" in the Pacific, Australia and Japan, was created shortly afterwards, with much likelihood of India's participation.

This security mechanism reveals the attempts of the United States and Australia to 'expand their regular bilateral security talks into an American-led multinational security framework designed first and foremost to guard against China, particularly against possible military actions in Taiwan' (Sui & Yu 2024, p. 73). It therefore drew the attention of international strategists and political observers across the Asia–Pacific region. Many viewed the new "triple alliance" with suspicion, and regional reactions to the mechanism ranged from "concern to outright condemnation". Jain (2006) at the Adelaide University argues that it is not politically sensible for a select group of nations to 'gang up and exclude others — a Cold War-type response'; A cooperative and inclusive framework rather than exclusion and containment would be a better way forward.

Concurrent with the trilateral security mechanism, the Howard government announced to join the American-led missile defense system (New York Times 2003), which extremely enraged the Chinese government. The Chinese authorities and military scholars have long held fast to the belief that the United States intends to neutralize China's limited nuclear forces and secure unilaterally military superiority over China and other countries. President Jiang Zemin and Putin, his Russian counterpart, issued a joint statement, condemning the missile defense system, accusing the United States of sending global arms control out of control' (Yun 2004). The Chinese government also criticized the Australian government for its closely following up the United States. The *People's Daily*, the official newspaper of the Central Committee of the Chinese Communist Party, reminded Australia of its past sufferings by jumping on the U.S. bandwagon in several world-scale wars', warning that 'the [NMD] system would hurt Australia' and that it had better not to serve 'as a cat's paw for the United States' (Schauble 2000, p. 12).

It is in this context that China has thereafter redoubled its efforts in dramatically expanding its involvement in the South Pacific and intensifying its comprehensive cooperation with the PICs. Most noticeably, a new cooperation framework, the China-Pacific Island Countries Economic Development and Cooperation Forum was created, and Wen Jiabao, Chinese Premier (2003-2013), addressed the first ministerial conference held in Fiji in early 2006. The creation of the Forum is broadly viewed by the Chinese IR scholars as a landmark in the China-PICs relations, signaling that cooperation between the two sides has been substantially expanded into the political and strategic realms (Shi 2019, p. 36, Chen 2011, p. 124). Wen announced it a strategic, rather than a makeshift policy adopted by the Chinese government to intensify the friendly relationship of cooperation with the PICs as it serves 'the fundamental and strategic interests of each side' and strengthens peace and prosperity of the South Pacific region. Wen proposed both sides to strengthen coordination and cooperation on major international and regional issues; reinforce mutual support in the international community; and work together for a more rational and fairer system and order globally and regionally (Gao & Yan 2006, p. 1).

China-PICs relations in Xi's time

Xi Jinping, the incumbent Chinese President (2013-), apparently attaches much more strategic significance than his predecessors to the China-PICs relations, as demonstrated by his three visits to the South Pacific and the unprecedented enhancement of economic and political cooperation between China and the PICs. In his visit to Fiji in 2009 as Vice President, Xi Jinping reassured the PICs that China respects their independence and sovereignty, and treats them as equal members of the international community (Yu 2020, p. 83). Xi promised to advance their cooperation by providing more economic aid and technological assistance to the PICs in an endeavor for the birth of more tangible projects in fishery, mining and other areas, and by intensifying their partnership at both regional and global levels. In his visit to the South Pacific in 2014 in the capacity of Presidency, Xi Jinping and his counterparts of eight PICs, namely, Fiji, Papua New Guinea, Tonga, Samoa, Vanuatu, Micronesia, Cook Islands and Niue, announced to create "a strategic partnership of mutual respect and common development" between China and the eight PICs (Zhang 2016).

In Xi's viewpoints, this partnership is aimed to seek common development, shared prosperity and enduring regional peace by intensifying their economic integration, political trust and security cooperation (Xi 2013, He 2018, p. 3). Xi invited the PICs to take a ride on the Chinese "express train" of economic growth and prosperity by announcing a range of initiatives to increase China's engagement with the PICs, such as more Chinese economic and technological assistance to the PICs, zero-tariff on the imports from the PICs and 2000 scholarships for students to study in China (Zhao & Yu 2023, p. 108). In November 2018, Xi Jinping attended the APEC summit that was held in Port Moresby, PNG and paid a state visit to the country. Xi had a group meeting with the leaders of the PICs that have diplomatic ties with China, where the China-PIC relations were elevated to a comprehensive strategic partnership featuring mutual respect and common development. Xi Jinping touted the BRI to his counterparts from the PICs at the group meeting. The BRI was first proposed by Xi in 2013 at the height of former President Obama's adoption of the strategy of "pivot to Asia".

The strategy was widely considered by the Chinese foreign policy makers and IR scholars as specifically designed to contain China's rise (Wei et al 2016, p. 287, Zhao 2018, p. 89) despite Washington's denial (Löfflmann 2016, p. 93).

Against this backdrop, it is not surprising that the BRI was proposed partially as a strategy to counterattack the U.S. containment of China in the name of "pivot to Asia" by substantially intensifying China's economic and infrastructure cooperation with the PICs and opening up a "new battlefield" in the other parts of the world against its perceived U.S. containment (Paal 2015, Wang 2018, p. 17). The BRI is a strategy designed to advance "connectivity and communication" throughout Eurasia, Africa, Oceania and South America (Cambero & Sherwood 2018, Wang 2017, p. 39). China's BRI is mainly composed of the land-based Silk Road Economic Belt (the "Belt") that extends across Central and West Asia to Europe and the sea-based 21st Century Maritime Silk Road (the "Road") that starts from Chinese seaports to those in Europe, Oceania and South America. According to *the New York Times*, more than 140 countries have to date signed on to the BRI to cooperate with China on infrastructural development. The Chinese government typically lends large sums of money to its global partners to help them with the construction of new roads, dams, railways, ports and sports facilities (Cave 2022). The BRI in the PICs is an umbrella initiative, involving a massive amount of infrastructure construction and investment projects and enabling it to alter the built environment and geopolitical landscape.

The BRI in the PICs therein contains a number of geopolitical elements as observed by IR scholars and analysts within and without China (Ehizuelen et al 2017, p. 286, Cau 2018, p. 41). China has to date signed the Belt and Road Cooperation MOUs with all the 10 PICs that have formed diplomatic relations with China, and signed the BRI cooperation plans with PNG and Vanuatu. Progress under the framework of the BRI has been achieved in practical cooperation such as policy, infrastructure, trade, financial and people-to-people connectivity. China has carried out a host of economic and technical cooperation projects in the PICs under the framework of the BRI, such as roads, bridges, wharfs, hospitals, schools, and stadiums. In recent years, China has carried out a series of key infrastructure projects, including the Independence Boulevard in PNG, Malakula island highway in Vanuatu, renovation of Tonga national road, and Pohnpei highway in Micronesia (Zhao & Yu 2023, p. 62). Over the years, more and more Chinese enterprises have been operating in the PICs in tandem with the implementation of the BRI and the construction of the Chinese aided projects. As expected, the Chinese companies have promoted localized management and procurement of projects, boosted economic growth and created a lot of local jobs, helping intensify China's relations with the PICs.

After Xi's visit in 2018, China and the PICs that have exchanged diplomatic recognition with China have maintained frequent exchanges at the top and other levels until the breakout of Covid-19 in early 2020. Multiple leaders of Fiji, Tonga, Samoa, Vanuatu, the Federated States of Micronesia, Solomon Islands, Kiribati, PNG, Cook Islands and Niue have visited China. Exchanges and cooperation between government agencies, legislatures and political parties have since flourished. China reiterated its commitment to increasing its strategic partnership with the PICs in a Five Year plan that covered a wide array of sectors from politico-security, climate change, capacity-building, health, and multilateral cooperation. Wang Yi, Chinese foreign minister, chaired the Second China-PICs Foreign Ministers' Meeting in Fiji in May 2022, and visited the Solomon Islands, Kiribati, Samoa, Fiji, Tonga, Vanuatu, Papua New Guinea and East Timor (Ministry of Foreign Affairs of the PRC 2022). As well, Wang had talks with the political leaders of the Cook Islands and Niue via video links. Wang's trip to the South Pacific came after the U.S. president's visits to South Korea and Japan, which was widely assumed by the Chinese policy analysts (e.g., Yang Xiyu, China Institute of International Studies) as a move to strengthen the containment of China (Zhou et al 2022). Wang's visit to the PICs and the intensified ties between China and the PICs signal that China has the capability of breaking the U.S. containment of China by employing the first and second island chains.

To further intensify China's partnership with the PICs, the much delayed Third Ministerial Conference of the China-PICs Economic Development and Cooperation Forum was convened in Samoa in October 2019 under Xi Jinping's 'personal promotion'. The Forum is the highest-level dialogue mechanism on economy and trade between China and the PICs. Vice Premier Hu Chunhua addressed the conference, stressing to deepen their strategic coordination in international affairs, push forward the BRI in the South Pacific and cement their strategic partnership (Zhang & Zheng 2019). China displayed its intention to further step up its presence and involvement in the South Pacific by concluding with the PICs *the Program of Action on Economic Development and Cooperation*, which suggests both sides to jointly promote the BRI projects and cooperation in such fields as trade, investment, agriculture, fishery and infrastructure construction. China is very much a strong participant in the local economy of the PICs, which has benefitted the region significantly, particularly the small economies of the islands. For instance, a Chinese fishery company concluded a memorandum of understanding with the government of the western province of PNG to build a multifunctional fishery industrial park on the Daru Island. The park is widely expected by the local governmental officials as a major boost to the provincial ambition to establish itself as a significant exporter of seafood to the Chinese market. Yoto, the governor of the province said that the young Solomon Islanders need jobs and vocational training to address a persistent shortage of skilled labor and to put food on the table.

Statistics released by the Chinese Ministry of Commerce shows that the two way-trade between China and the PICs skyrocketed to $9.04 billion in 2020 from $880 million in 2005. China's exports to the PICs reached $5.20 billion and its imports from the PICs stood at US$3.84 billion (Ministry of Commerce 2020b). The PICs invested US$880 million in 129 projects in China in 2020 and their cumulative investment in China stood at US$32.95 billion. China's investment in the PICs rose to US$4.5 billion, up from US$900 million in 2013 (Master 2018). The trade volume between China and the PICs that have diplomatic relations with China grew to US$5.3 billion from US$153 million in 1992, registering an average annual increase of 13 percent and expanding by over 30 times in 30 years. China's direct investment in the PICs that have diplomatic relations with China rose to US$2.72 billion (see Fig 3).

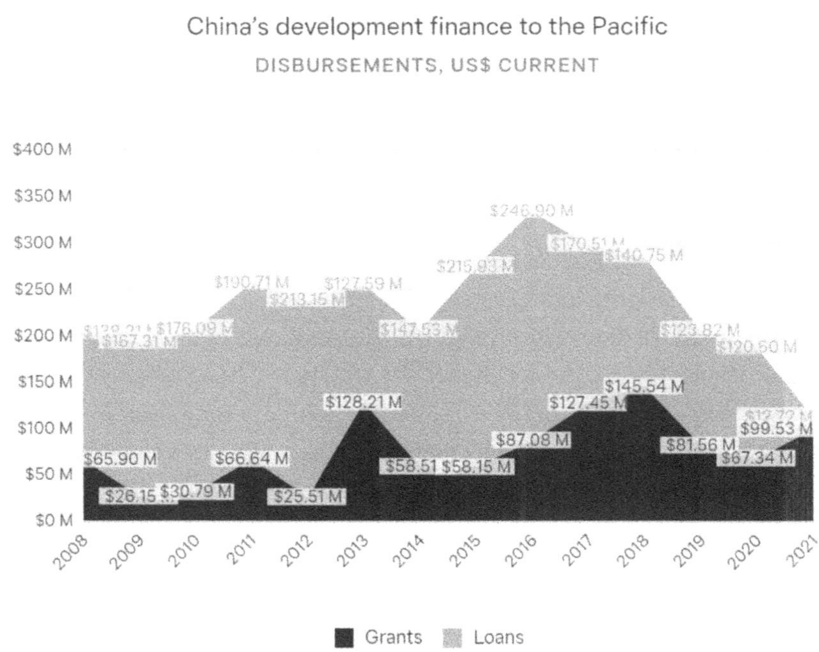

Fig. 3: China's development finance to the Pacific
Sources: Dayant, Alexandre, Keen, Meg and Rajah, Roland 2023, Chinese aid to the Pacific: decreasing, but not disappearing, Lowy Institute, 25 January, https://www.lowyinstitute.org/the-interpreter/chinese-aid-pacific-decreasing-not-disappearing.

When interviewed by the authors, Niu Li, at the Beijing Foreign Studies University, summarizes that "by drawing on my work experiences there", the China-proposed initiatives dovetail the PICs' "Look North policy" and the "2050 Strategy for the Blue Pacific Continent". Niu had been working in the South Pacific around a decade. In her viewpoints, the China-proposed initiatives, such as the BRI, the Global Development Initiative, the Global Security Initiative, and the Global Civilization Initiative, are in line with the needs of regional development. Niu comments that decades after the independence of some PICs, a large population in the region still lives in poverty, and lacks access to drinking water, electricity and health care. Niu notes that China has helped the PICs construct and upgrade roads, ports and other infrastructure that, in turn, facilitate the trade and investment activities in the South Pacific. China has now grown as one of the most important partners of the PICs in the spheres of infrastructure cooperation and economic development. Niu predicts that the people-to-people exchanges, trade and ocean-based investments will play important roles to tap the potential of China's economic cooperation and trade with the PICs".[29]

Niu who had been involved in tourism industry in the South Pacific for eight years foresees that the Chinese in-bound tourism will remain flourishing as the Chinese travelers are looking for new destinations and experiences, and that the Pacific Island countries are still an untapped destination for the Chinese tourists. Niu highlights that the flouring tourism will help promote the cultural and personnel exchanges between China and the PICs. Li Haolin, general manager of the Guangdong Silkroad Ark Investment Company in Fiji, shares Niu. Li is building a beachside hotel in Fiji, whose design represents the merging of cultures. The design is in line with Fiji's local customs and the culture of the ancient Silk Road. Li notes that the PICs attracted a total of 2.1 million visitors in 2019, and of such visitors, an estimated 125,000 plus Chinese visitors visited the South Pacific countries (Cao 2019). Liu concludes that the Chinese investment in the tourism industry of the PICs not only boosts local tourism and the hotel industry, but also provides employment to the local people.

To attract more Chinese tourists, the South Pacific Tourism Organization (SPTO) and China launched "the 2019 year of tourism" in some capitals of the PICs. "The year of tourism" is an outcome of the SPTO's attendance of a

29 Niu Li is executive director of the Research Center for Pacific Studies at Beijing Foreign Studies University. She had been in Samoa for 8 years as General Manager of a four-star hotel.

high-level dialogue of the BRI Forum for International Cooperation that was held in Beijing in 2017. Fiame Naomi Mataafa, Prime Minister of Samoa, expressed her appreciation of the launch of the tourism year: "the China-Pacific Tourism Year 2019 reflects, how we as leaders of the region, have placed value on the thriving Asian outbound tourism markets particularly China with the world's largest outbound market of around 140 million visitors last year". Ms Mataafa viewed the "tourism year" as an opportunity to showcase the Chinese tourists what the Pacific islands have to offer with their stunning natural landscapes, sandy beaches, unique culture and friendly people.

Christopher Cocker, SPTO Chief Executive Officer and Papalii Sonja Hunter, Samoa Tourism Authority Chief Executive Officer, have contributed to the launch of the "tourism year". In their view, the Pacific tourism industry is working on programs to be "China Ready". The focus is to sustainably develop and promote the Pacific to niche the Chinese outbound market segments who wish to experience the region's beautiful islands, unique cultures and the healthy, organic food experience of the region. They both highlight that the launch of tourism year marks an important chapter in the PICs' tourism calendar as it officially marks the PICs' categorization by the Chinese tourism authorities as a tourism destination for the Chinese visitors. Cooker stresses that China is an important target for tourism growth in the region over the coming years given the number and spending power of the Chinese visitors. To draw the ties between the PICs and China, Hunter claims that "We, as Samoans, have DNA connections with China as some Samoans have blood relationship with Chinese. We are ready and welcome the Chinese to visit our beautiful country". Samoa, which has a population of around 190,000, received over 172,000 foreign tourists in 2018. Currently, Samoa has a development blueprint to woo more foreign tourists, including the Chinese tourists who have shown increasing interest in spending their holidays in the South Pacific.

Zhao Shaofeng in the Research Center for the Pacific Island Countries of Liaocheng University edited a 258-page report on the PICs' economic and social development in 2023 (Wang & Zhao 2023). He summarizes that the BRI has played the role in boosting the China-PICs links and regional economic development through infrastructure related investments. In his viewpoints, China and the PICs have made such an ideal partnership in terms of infrastructure construction:

> China has a great export capacity in the global infrastructure construction market, while run-down infrastructures have been holding back the PICs' economic development. The China-backed infrastructure projects help the PICs

> benefit from their improved domestic and international connectivity. Better domestic connectivity facilitates the formation of a unified domestic market and raises their sense of national identity. The improved international connectivity diversifies the PICs' import sources and provides the local people with more affordable basic commodities.

When interviewed by the authors, Zhao Shaofeng predicts that there are many potential areas of cooperation to be tapped, such as the deep-sea mining and offshore wind energy in the South Pacific region. Zhao highlights that the PICs lack in landmass, but they are large in territorial waters. For instance, Kiribati ranks 172nd in the world for its land mass, but ranks 12th for the size of its exclusive economic zone (EEZ), which takes into consideration a country's authority over both land and water. Altogether, the PICs control nearly 12 million square miles of the Pacific Ocean across an area equivalent to around 15 percent of the globe's surface. Zhao notes that some PICs bordering the resource rich Clarion-Clipperton Zone (CCZ), have begun sponsoring mining companies to take out licenses for deep-sea mining in that region (Mcdonald 2019). The CCZ, which borders the territorial waters of the Cook Islands, Kiribati, Nauru, and Tonga, is a deep-sea trench approximately the size of Europe. It is estimated that this area is rich in polymetallic nodules that contain mostly manganese, but also iron, nickel, copper, titanium and cobalt. Such metals are in increasing demand amid a push to develop batteries for electric vehicles and renewable energy. However, a large number of issues, such as environmental damage and infringement of indigenous rights, should be seriously considered before any decision is made. Such consideration is necessary to maintain sustainable development and the political and the social acceptability of the projects.

Yu Changsen, vice director of the Center for Oceanian Studies at the Sun Yatsen University, notes that China encourages the PICs to export more seafood and agricultural products to China. In so doing, the Chinese government wants to let the PICs share the economic dividends of the booming Chinese market, and intensifying their economic cooperation and trade. Yu attributes PICs' fast-growing exports of raw materials, minerals, primary industry produces and other goods to the Chinese markets partially to the "zero tariff" adopted by the Chinese Customs on the PICs' commodities. Yu notes that there is a growing fishery cooperation between the Chinese companies based in Guangdong Province and their counterparts in the PICs, and the Chinese fishing fleets are working closely with the PICs. Yu stresses that both sides need to pay much attention to environmental protection and sustainability when they increase their fishery cooperation.

Shan Yuqiang, General Manager of Fiji International Trade Company, predicts that the China-PICs cooperation potential will be unleashed by the BRI. He foresees that the trade volume between the PICs and China, and particularly the exports from the PICs to China will have a rapid increase. In Shan's eyes, the cosmetics and other world-famous skin-care products of the PICs are lucrative and increasingly exported to the Chinese market. Shen's company has got the dealership for the cosmetics and skin-care products in China, and claims that his business is good as the Chinese people get to know the PICs and their products a lot better after President Xi's visit to Fiji in 2014.

Besides the China-PICs Economic Development and Cooperation Forum, other dialogue and cooperation mechanisms between China and the PICs have been subsequently set up to advance their relations and cooperation. In October 2021, the first China-Pacific Island Countries Foreign Ministers' Meeting was held via video link, and issued the *Joint Statement of China-Pacific Island Countries Foreign Ministers' Meeting*. Since the start of the COVID-19, the two sides have held two special meetings of vice foreign ministers on the COVID response (Ministry of Foreign Affairs of China 2021). The two sides have also established other bilateral and multilateral dialogue mechanisms, including the Joint Economic and Trade Committee, the Agriculture Ministers' Meeting and Forum on Fishery Cooperation and Development. As well, both sides set up a series of cooperation mechanisms, such as the Reserve of Emergency Supplies, the Climate Action Cooperation Center and the Poverty Reduction and Development Cooperation Center. In October 2021, China announced the establishment of the China-Pacific Island Countries Poverty Reduction and Development Cooperation Center on the sidelines of the first China-Pacific Island Countries Foreign Ministers' Meeting. China promised to support the PICs in developing human resources, and help the PICs train talents in various fields, including the public administration and social organization, agriculture, forestry, animal husbandry, fishery, and education.

Agricultural cooperation is one of the significant components of the China-PICs relations of cooperation. The China-Pacific Island Countries Agriculture Cooperation Forum has been convened since 2009, which is designed to promote agricultural policy exchanges and business interactions, and boost economic and trade cooperation in farming, animal husbandry and fishery between the two sides (Xinhua News Agency 2019). In 2019, the First China-Pacific Island Countries Agriculture Ministers Meeting was held in Fiji, which issued the *Nadi Declaration of China and Pacific Island Countries on Agricultural Development*, charting the course for practical agricultural cooperation in the new era. At the request of the PICs, China has launched multiple agricultural technical assistance projects in PNG, Fiji, Tonga, Micronesia, and Samoa where China helps these countries improve agricultural production capacity and food security by sending agricultural experts, building demonstration farms, training model farmers, promoting improved crop varieties, and providing technical support (Jiangsu Academy of Agricultural Sciences 2023).

Some PICs, such as Tonga, Samoa and Fiji, have given importance to the agricultural cooperation with China, and they request China to provide multiple agricultural technical assistance projects. Kang Jian who had been in Tonga as a volunteering teacher for three years, is an agricultural expert from the Liaocheng University. When interviewed by the authors, he said that the PICs, such as Tonga, Samoa and Fiji, need agricultural assistance to ensure their food security. In Kang's view, the PICs welcomed the China-aided agricultural technical assistance projects as they have helped the PICs to boost their economic growth and employment. Liu Zhiwen, head of the China-Samoa Agricultural Technical Aid Project, shares Kang. He notes that agriculture is a key economic pillar in Samoa with over 80 percent of families engaged in different forms of agricultural production.

The agricultural technical aid projects provided by the Chinese government were initiated in 2010, and were divided into five phases, aimed to help the farmers in the PICs enhance their sustainable livelihoods. China has sent scores of agricultural experts to the PICs to help the farmers in the PICs increase their productivity and promote sustainable agriculture by setting up demonstration farms. Liu Zhiwen says that through these projects, modern agricultural technology facilities on greenhouse cultivation, high-yield fruit cultivation, organic fertilizer and soil improvement are set up in Samoa, helping the country raise agricultural productivity. In addition to the demonstration farm near Samoa's capital city of Apia, the Chinese experts have also established nine agricultural stations, cultivated over 100 model farms and provided agricultural training to over 10,000 farmers. Laauli Leuatea Polataivao Fosi, Samoa's Minister of Agriculture and Fisheries, said that his country was pleased to have support from China to help develop the country's agricultural sector, and hoped to expand areas of cooperation that could help Samoa's economic and social development (Zhang 2023).

Besides the demonstration farms, China has set up a Juncao technical demonstration center in Nadi, Fiji, and provided Juncao technical assistance to Fiji, PNG and others. The Juncao technology, which in Chinese means breeding fungi with herbaceous plants, has benefited many rural areas in China by addressing poverty, soil erosion and desertification. The technology has been promoted in 15 languages and seventeen countries in Asia, Africa, and China has established training and demonstration centers of the Juncao technology in Fiji to promote the technology in the South Pacific (Ministry of Agriculture and Rural Affairs of the PRC 2023). China hopes to utilized the Juncao technology to make contribution to poverty alleviation, sustainable development and efforts to fight against climate change in the developing states. China has to date set up a Juncao technical demonstration center in Nadi, Fiji, which has so far trained more than 1,700 Fijians with 39 training workshops conducted throughout the country. In addition, the center has also helped establish two model villages of mushroom cultivation in Fiji, which now has an accumulative number of 600 mushroom farmers across the country.

In 2021, the First China-Pacific Island Countries Forum on Fishery Cooperation and Development was held in Guangzhou, China, producing the *Guangzhou Consensus of the First China-Pacific Island Countries Forum on Fishery Cooperation and Development* that is aimed to deepen fishery cooperation between China and the PICs (Xinhua News Agency 2021). The Chinese government promised to enhance maritime cooperation with the PICs, support the *2050 Strategy for the Blue Pacific Continent*, work for a blue partnership, and jointly promote sustainable marine development. China and the PICs emphasized that ocean environment protection is of vital importance to the people's health and safety as well as the PICs' sustainable economic development. Both sides called on relevant country to prudently handle the issue of discharging Advanced Liquid Processing System (ALPS) treated water into the ocean, and have full consultation with stakeholders and relevant international agencies. At the Forum, both China and the PICs agree to deepen scientific and technological cooperation, carry out cooperation in aquaculture technology, fishery facilities and equipment, aquatic product processing and other fields, and explore the establishment of a Modern Fishery Cooperation and Exchange Center.

China and the PICs also agree to work together to find solutions to problems related to illegal, unreported, and unregulated (IUU) fishing by establishing an "intergovernmental multilateral fishery consultation mechanism". China promised to promote market access and free trade for seafood from the PICs and to carry out investment cooperation in fisheries fishing, aquaculture, fishing boat repair and building, fishing port construction, aquatic product processing and cold-chain logistics, and help improve the level of infrastructure in the PICs (Ministry of Agriculture and Rural Affairs 2023b). When interviewed by the authors, Zhao Shaofeng and Ni Peng at the Liaocheng University who did a lot of fieldwork in the South Pacific, advise China to increase its fisheries presence in the PICs by advancing its cooperation with the PICs in fishing, aquaculture and processing, and making the forum a regular event. Zhao Shaofeng and the authors had a lot of face-to-face conversation with the managers of the Chinese fishing fleet and fishing firms when they did fieldwork there from 2016 to 2024. They note that a number of Chinese fishing fleet have increased their presence in the South Pacific, but they would more often than not bring the seafood from the PICs to their processing facilities in China. Zhao suggests that there is a "great potential" for the two sides to increase their fishery cooperation by launching joint enterprises "on the basis of equality and mutual benefit". In so doing, both sides could maximize their interest by taking advantage of the local fishery resources and the huge Chinese market.

Education cooperation has long been an important domain in the China-PICs relations. China has signed education cooperation MOUs with Fiji, PNG, Samoa, Tonga, Solomon Islands, Vanuatu and Kiribati, and encouraged the students in the PICs to study in China by providing them with increasing government scholarships each year (Ministry of Foreign Affairs of China 2022b). China has to date assisted in the construction of primary schools, secondary schools and universities in PNG, Samoa, Tonga, Micronesia and Vanuatu, and set up a number of Confucius Institutes or Confucius Classrooms in Fiji, PNG, Samoa, Vanuatu and the Cook Islands. China and Vanuatu signed in 2021 the *Memorandum of Understanding on Cooperation in Chinese Education Program in Primary and Secondary School in Vanuatu*, marking the formal inclusion of Chinese language education in Vanuatu's national education system (Xinhua News Agency 2021b).

In 2018, Education Ministries of China and Tonga signed the *Memorandum of Understanding on Communication and Cooperation in Education* to support the establishment of the Tonga College of Liaocheng University, which has helped Tonga cultivate high-level talents in applied science, and conducted joint research in marine science and PIC studies. Zhang Jianfeng was one of the agricultural experts at the Liaocheng University, who had been working in Tonga for more than 4 years since 2018 to provide education and vegetable growing techniques to the students there. Zhang told the authors when interviewed that the Chinese experts teach the local students to grow cucumbers, pumpkins, cowpeas, leeks, bitter melons, loofahs, cabbage and other vegetables. Zhang notes that the PICs are experiencing a high burden of diet-related diseases, and consumption of fat, sugar and salt are important factors contributing to this. He hopes that these vegetables will help optimize the local food regime and boosting local health.

Concurrent with the development of political and economic relations, exchanges and cooperation between China and the PICs are gradually extended to security and other domains. Over the last decade, senior defense and military officials of the PICs have paid multiple visits to China, and participated in events such as the Beijing Xiangshan Forum and the Forum for Senior Defense Officials from Caribbean and South Pacific Countries. The Peace Ark Hospital Ship of the People's Liberation Army Navy (PLAN) visited Fiji, PNG, Tonga and Vanuatu in 2014 and 2018 respectively, and carried out activities such as medical tour and medicine donation (Shan et al 2023). Military delegations of Fiji, PNG, Tonga and Vanuatu were invited to China in September 2015 to attend the military parade to commemorate the 70th anniversary of the victory of the Chinese People's War of Resistance against Japanese Aggression and the World Anti-Fascist War. The two sides have deepened exchanges and cooperation in law enforcement over the last years in response to Xi Jinping's promise of providing police capacity building support to the developing countries at the 86th Interpol General Assembly. The Ministry of Public Security of China has to date held 23 training sessions of capacity building for the PIC law enforcement agencies since 2017, which was attended by a total of 490 law enforcement officers (Ministry of Foreign Affairs of China 2022c).

Thirty-two officers of the Royal Solomon Island Police Force (RSIPF) had recently completed their one-month onsite training in late 2022. The training program was held under the auspicious of *Memorandum of Understanding (MoU) on the Police Cooperation between the Chinese Ministry of Public Security and Solomon Island (SI) Ministry of Police, National Security & Correctional Services* (RSIPF Press 2022). The training was facilitated by the Fujian Police College, which was intensive and covered a wide range of law enforcement constructive subjects from unarmed tactics to the use of weapon techniques, including VIP guard techniques, Police operation Command & Onsite Command, large-scale event planning and control administration, etc. These trainings were scenario based where officers were tested to make plans and decisions to respond to these levels of real and complex situations. As part of the program, the officers were provided opportunities to make onsite visits to police stations and police training sites to see first-hand responses, technologies, operations command, systems, processes and procedures used. The Fujian Police College is actively engaged in various forms of cooperation with other international police forces around the world with their high-level programs. Mr. Ian Vaevaso, Head of the RSIPF delegation and Deputy Commissioner (DC), said that the training was significant for the ongoing building of the RSIPF capacity and its capability for the maintenance of stability, peace and security in the Solomon Islands.

China has intensified medical cooperation with the PICs under the framework of the BRI to enhance the country's "soft" power in the South Pacific and draw close the relations between the peoples. There have to date been more than 600 volunteering medical workers from China working in the PICs, who have treated 260,000 local patients, and provided free medical services for the local patients over 100 times. Moreover, the Chinese government has donated a number of medical equipment and medicines to the PICs (Ministry of Foreign Affairs of China 2022c). The Navua Hospital that is assisted by China started operation in Fiji in 2014, providing better medical service to more than 30,000 local residents. In January 2016, the China-Australia-PNG Malaria Prevention Programme was officially launched in PNG, which was aimed to enhance the ability of malaria prevention and treatment of PNG (Ministry of Foreign Affairs of China 2022c).

The Trilateral Malaria Project supports a number of hospitals and institutions to improve the quality of malaria testing, and diagnosis, sentinel surveillance and operational research to inform malaria policy and programming in PNG. The Trilateral Malaria Project has provided support to the PNG Central Public Health Laboratory (CPHL), PNG Institute of Medical Research (PNGIMR), UPNG School of Medicine and Health Sciences (SMHS), the National Malarial Control Program and the West Sepik Provincial Health Authority (WSPHA). In October 2017, the Shenzhen municipal government of China helped launch malaria elimination programme in Kirivina Islands of PNG, freeing the local residents from infection of malaria. After the start of the COVID-19, China has held more than 10 bilateral or multilateral public health expert meetings via video link with the PICs that have diplomatic relations with China, to share experience of disease prevention, control, treatment and diagnosis. China had provided vaccines, over 100 tons of supplies and cash assistance to PICs, and helped the latter build quarantine cubicles and other facilities (Ministry of Foreign Affairs of China 2022c).

Moreover, China and the PICs have intensified their cooperation in the field of ocean affairs and climate change. China hosted the China-Small Island States Ocean-related Ministerial Round Table in 2017 with the theme of "Blue Economy and Ecological Islands". Senior representatives from Samoa, Fiji, Vanuatu and Niue were invited to address the conference, which adopted and published the *Pingtan Declaration* (Information Office of the State Council of China 2017). China shared its environmental protection experience with the PICs and promised to help the PICs improve environmental management capacity. China has over the years hosted multiple seminars for the PICs' officials on such topics as environmental protection and management, water pollution treatment, and water resource protection. China has carried out earthquake mitigation cooperation with PICs since 2006 and helped Samoa, Vanuatu and Fiji to build seismic networks and enhance earthquake monitoring capacity. The China-Pacific Island Countries Reserve for Emergency Supplies was officially launched in Guangdong Province of China in late 2021 (Ministry of Foreign Affairs of China 2021). China provided immediate humanitarian aids to Tonga immediately after a large-scale volcanic eruption struck Tonga in January 2022, which triggered disasters such as tsunami and ash fallout.

It is worth noting that China shares the viewpoints of the PICs that climate change is a major challenge facing humanity, and particularly the South Pacific. The Chinese authorities hence promise to be committed to jointly promoting the full and effective implementation of the Paris Agreement and a fair and equitable system of global climate governance for win-win cooperation (Ministry of Foreign Affairs of China 2021b). The PICs are facing compounding challenges arising from climate change as exemplified by rising sea levels, floods, cyclones, erosion, tsunami and water-scarcity, which are becoming more frequent and widespread (Almulhim 2024, p. 1). In Kiribati, for example, 94 percent of households reported being affected by natural hazards in the past decade (Oakes et al 2016). The PICs are committing themselves to enhancing the sustainability of Pacific coastal and marine systems through strengthening the management of coastal and marine resources, thus preventing environmental degradation and preparing for the challenges posed by climate change impacts.

China has responded positively to the calls made by the PICs to intensify cooperation to combat the climate change challenges, and has been committed to helping the PICs strengthen their capacity to tackle climate change (Ministry of Ecology and Environment 2022). A report released by the Asian Development Bank (2019) estimates that the PICs need US$300 million a year for climate mitigation and adaptation. The Chinese government sets up a climate fund with around US$3 billion to help the developing states, including the PICs to address the climate challenges. Since 2019, China has held three South-South cooperation training sessions for officials and scholars from the PICs under the theme of "Tackling Climate Change for Green and Low-carbon Development". The authors have been invited to lecture on green energy cooperation between China and the PICs as the authors have practical experience in this regard gained from fieldwork in China and the PICs.

Apart from providing batches of supplies to the PICs to tackle climate change, China has strengthened renewable energy cooperation with the PICs, and supported the Chinese enterprises in joining the construction of hydropower stations in such PICs as PNG and Fiji (Economic and Commercial Office of the Embassy of the People's Republic of China in Fiji 2017). The Chinese government understands the difficulties of PICs in tackling climate change and sets up the China-Pacific Island Countries Climate Change Action Cooperation Center (CCACC) in April 2022, which is based at the Liaocheng University in Shandong (Xie 2022). Chen Dezheng, professor and vice director of the CCACC, said that the PICs are prone to earthquakes, tsunamis and cyclones and they are now facing new threats arising from the climate change, such as coral bleaching and rising sea levels. Chen told the authors that the CCACC is aimed to intensify studies on the impacts of climate change on the Pacific islands, enhance academic cooperation with the PICs and assist PICs in enhancing capacity building to tackle climate change under the framework of the BRI. The CCACC has to date provided hundreds of training opportunities to the PICs.

It is not hard to conclude from the discussion to this point that although its claimed purpose in enhancing closer relations with the PICs is for economic gains, China's partnership with the PICs contains geopolitical, strategic and humanitarian consideration; and the China-PICs Economic Development and Cooperation Forum marks a significant step in this regard. The Chinese foreign policy makers expect the Forum, together with others, to substantially advance not only economic cooperation and trade between China and the PICs, but also their strategic cooperation of creating "a community of shared future" in the region. However, the China-PICs partnership can be said to be built on a great asymmetry arising from their divergence in the size of population, territory, economics, etc. Nevertheless, an analysis on the "asymmetry" finds that it is essentially different from that in the relationships between the PICs and the former colonial powers (e.g., the United States and Australia). As the latter has to date been based on the coloniality of power and characterized by the hierarchical relationships of domination that the Chinese authorities wish to reform by pushing forward the "democratization of the international relations" (Hayward-Jones 2015, p. 67).

China's pursuit of "democratization of international relations", in which, states across the world, shall be treated equally, free from foreign bullying and intervention, is primarily driven by its state identity. As intimated, China's state identity had been primarily created by the country's historical experiences and the memory of being bullied and invaded by colonial and imperialist powers over the "century of humiliation" that started from the first Opium War/Chinese-British Trade War in 1839-1842 to the founding of the PRC in 1949 (Pant 2012, p. 32). The narratives of the "century of humiliation" have played a decisive role in the formation of China's state identity as a "revolutionary" and "challenger" of the hierarchical global order dominated by the West (Malhotra 2020, p. 1047). In the same vein, the founders of the PRC and the present Chinese foreign policy elites alike view the hierarchical global order as a result of colonialism, imperialism, and hegemonism, posing a critical threat to the security, sovereignty, and territorial integrity of the developing states in general and China in particular. The ideological values and worldviews of the founders of the PRC (e.g., Mao Zedong and Deng Xiaoping) and the current Chinese foreign policy makers (e.g., Xi Jinping) alike are profoundly shaped by the "Chinese century of humiliation". The bullying imposed by the imperialist powers on the "Old China" before 1949 spurred Mao Zedong and other Chinese intellectuals, such as Professor Chen Duxiu & Professor Li Dazhao at Peking University, to "shatter the old world" dominated by the imperialist powers and to "create a new one" by accepting Marxist theory and leading to the creation of the Chinese Communist Party (Mao 1991, p. 342).

Mao Zedong later recalled the bullying and humiliation suffered by the "Old China" at the Paris Conference in 1919 as the main incentive for him to accept the Marxist theory and devote his life to "shatter the old world" and create a "new one" (Tang 2009, p. 6). The above narratives of the Chinese revolution could be commonly found in the mainstream literature on Chinese history and politics. It provides insight into how the "Chinese century of humiliation", among others, shaped the ideological values and worldviews of the founders of the PRC and why they aspired to create a "new world" with an equal and fairer order by "shattering the old one" with a hierarchical and unfair order through revolution ("armed struggle") instead of evolution (peaceful reform) (Mao 1991, p. 433).

Mao's "new China" (the People's Republic of China, PRC) had indeed risen in the ashes of a fourteen-year war against the invasion of the Japanese imperialists (1931-1945) followed by a three-year civil war against the Nationalist regime (the Republic of China), which was militarily supported by the "American imperialists" (the United States). Their self-identity as "revolutionaries" and their worldviews prompt the founders of the PRC to be committed to "shattering the old world" dominated by the imperialist powers, and "creating a new one" for the "oppressed peoples" in the "third world", who were living under "oppression" and "exploitation" by the imperialists and their domestic proxies. The identity of "new China", on the one hand, served Mao Zedong's strategy of mobilizing all the resources inside and outside China to frustrate any military intervention launched by imperialist powers. On the other hand, it placed the PRC on a moral high ground in the international community as a "revolutionary", challenging the hierarchical global order dominated by the colonial and imperialists powers (the U.S.-headed West).

Based on their personal experiences of the Chinese "century of humiliation", the founders of the PRC anchored a deep suspicion of the hierarchical world order and conceived it as designed as such by the U.S.-headed imperialist powers to "repress world revolutions" and "exploit" the nations later categorized as the "third world" (Zhou & Zhang 2007, p. 57). The founders of the PRC thereby called for the "oppressed nations and peoples across the world" to revolutionize the global system and order by "creating a new world". This is why the founders of the PRC defined "new China" as "a champion of revolutionary in the world politics" and identified the mission "to promote the world's revolution as one of their major tasks" (Khan & Yu 2013, p. 89, Yu 2020b, p. 207). The PRC had not only acted as a challenger to the post-war hierarchical order and a revolutionary "mentor" of the "third world", but had also been committed to reshaping the post-War order and security arrangements, particularly in East and Southeast Asia where it had the capability of power projection.

It is noteworthy that the military involvement of the PRC in the Korean War[30] and the Vietnam War could hardly be viewed as driven solely by the PRC's national interest but as much as, if not more than, by its state identity, as discussed in the previous paragraphs. These two wars changed the post-war geopolitical landscape in East Asia, exemplifying the significant role of China's state identity

30 The mainstream perceptions of Chinese academics on China's involvement in the Korean War are radically different from those of the West. Many Chinese scholars characterize China's involvement in the war as inevitable, driven not solely by Communist ideology, but also by geopolitical interests, territorial security and economic rehabilitation from its long-term wars. In their eyes, after the U.S.-headed UN forces crossed the 38th parallel into North Korea and quickly pushed forward towards the Chinese border, Mao Zedong was left with only one option: to roll back the UN forces to the 38th parallel by sending troops to North Korea. For more details, see Sha, J. 2010, 'The War of Resisting American Aggression and Aiding Korea and Its Historic Meaning', *Journal of Ideological Theory and Education*, Vol. 139, No. 7, pp. 33-37. Qin, Xiaofan 2010, 'Mao Zedong and China's decision on the war to resist American aggression and aid Korea', *Foreign Affairs Review*, No. 1, pp. 4-10.

in challenging and altering the regional order. This argument is supported by the mainstream Chinese IR literature, where the Chinese scholars expound China's involvement in the Korean and Vietnam wars as a result of various factors, such as the Communist ideology upheld by the founders of the PRC, the state identity of the PRC, and China's security and geopolitical interests (Shen 2013, p. 72, Li 2002, p. 69).

The sufferings of "Old China" of being bullied and invaded by the colonial and imperialist powers in the "Chinese century of humiliation" and the experiences of the PRC of being militarily encircled and diplomatically isolated by the United States and its allies have constituted the basis of China's ontological security. This conception of ontological security results in China's view of the existing hierarchical order dominated by the US-headed West as a threat to its security and prompts it to work together with other developing states to create a new international order that China deems more reasonable and fairer. China's ontological security has posed a critical challenge to the hierarchical order in the South Pacific and the existing hierarchical relationship between the PICs and the former colonial powers that have to date keep the hierarchical relationship as the basis for their ontological security.

Concluding Remarks

The argument of this chapter is that the creation of China–PICs strategic partnership and the extension of the BRI to the PICs accentuate China's economic and geopolitical re-orientation towards the PICs. China's BRI and particularly its strategic partnership with the PICs reveals the country's desire not only to intensify its economic cooperation and trade with the PICs, but also to create a 'community of shared future' in the traditional 'backyards' of the United States and its major ally, Australia, as a counterattack to their containment and encirclement. By advancing economic cooperation, China attempts to gain access to the (land and maritime) resources and investment destinations of the PICs to help sustain its economic growth that is considered by Chinese political leaders as the basis for China's hard, including its military strength.

Politically, China aspires to reinforce its partnership with the PICs in the hopes of acquiring their diplomatic backing particularly in such global and regional organizations as the UN and the Pacific Islands Forum (PIF), and competing with Taiwan for diplomatic recognition. Geo-strategically, China wishes to counterattack the containment of the United States and its military allies in the South Pacific to ensure its rise at the systemic (global) level in tandem with its growing wealth and prowess. A noteworthy point in the discussion above emerges that is China's adoption of economic and infrastructural diplomacy as a means of advancing its economic and strategic partnerships with the PICs. In view of the enormous economic benefits derived from their economic cooperation and trade with China, the PICs would like to see China's expanding presence in the region as an opportunity to gain wealth and prosperity, rather than a threat (at least not a threat to them) (Khan & Yu 2013, p. 105). This is likely to help China gain 'soft' power in the South Pacific and leverage over its economic partners in the region, and thereby help its rise at the systemic (global) and sub-systemic (regional) levels.

References

Almulhim, A.I., Alverio, G.N., Sharifi, A. *et al 2024*, 'Climate-induced migration in the Global South: an in-depth analysis', *npj Climate Action*, Vol. 3, No. 47, pp. 1-12, https://doi.org/10.1038/s44168-024-00133-1.

Asia Development Bank 2019, *The Pacific: Urgent Development Needs Remain Despite Stable Debt and Higher Revenues*, 18 September, https://www.adb.org/news/features/pacific-urgent-development-needs-remain-despite-stable-debt-and-higher-revenues.

Blanchard, Jean-Marc F. and Flint, Colin 2017, 'The Geopolitics of China's Maritime Silk Road Initiative', *Geopolitics*, Vol. 22, No. 2, pp. 223-245.

Cambero, F. and Sherwood, D. 2018, China invites Latin America to take part in One Belt, One Road, Reuters, https://www.reuters.com/article/us-chile-china/china-invites-latin-america-to-take-part-in-one-belt-one-road-idUSKBN1FB2CN.

Cao, Desheng 2019, 'China Pacific Tourism Year 2019 kicks off in Samoa', *China Daily*, 2 April, https://www.chinadaily.com.cn/a/201904/02/WS5ca5667ca3104842260b46a5.html

Cau, E. 2018, 'Geopolitical Implications of the Belt and Road Initiative: The Backbone for a New World Order?', *Contemporary Chinese Political Economy and Strategic Relations: An International Journal*, Vol. 4, No. 1, pp. 39-107.

Cave, Damien 2022, 'Why a Chinese Security Deal in the Pacific Could Ripple Through the World', *New York Times*, 20 April, https://www.nytimes.com/2022/04/20/world/australia/china-solomon-islands-security-pact.html

Chen, Fei 2011, 'China-PICs cooperation: the present, challenge and suggestion', *Socialist Studies*, No. 5, pp. 123-126.

Copper, John F 2016, *China's Foreign Aid and Investment Diplomacy, Volume III: Strategy Beyond Asia and challenges to the United States and the international order*, Palgrave McMillan: London, p. 134.

Deng, Xiaoping 1993, *Selected works of Deng Xiaoping*, vol. 3, People's Press: Beijing, pp. 370-371.

Department of Military History, Academy of Military Science of the PLA 2000, *The history of the war to resist US aggression and aid Korea*, Beijing: Military Science Publishing House.

Dwyer, M. 1996, 'Australia and Japan are the claws US will use to entrap us, says China', *Australian Financial Review*, 8 August, p. 12.

Economic and Commercial Office of the Embassy of the People's Republic of China in the Republic of Fiji 2017, China-aided hydro plant put into operation, Ministry of Commerce of China, 10 March, http://fj.mofcom.gov.cn/article/jmxw/201703/20170302531495.shtml

Ehizuelen, M., Mitchell. O. and Abdi, H. O. 2017, 'Sustaining China-Africa relations: Slotting Africa into China's One Belt, One Road initiative makes economic sense', *Asian Journal of Comparative Politics*, Vol. 3, No. 4, pp. 285-310.

Fu, Ying 2016, 'Are China and Russia partnering to create an axis?', *Contemporary International Relations*, No. 4, pp. 1-10.

Fujita, Kimio 1993, 'China and its Asian neighbors: a Japanese perspective', Kau, Michael Ying-Mao and Marsh, Susan (eds), *China in the era of Deng Xiaoping: a decade of reform*, M.E. Sharp: New York, p. 464.

Fukuyama, F. 1992, *The end of history and the last man*, Hamilton, London.

Gao, Fei and Zhang, Jian 2017, 'China-the US and Russia in the post-Cold War era', Gao, Fei and Li, Mingjiang (eds), *China's neighborhood diplomacy*, Beijing: Global Publishing.

Gao, Hanqing and Yan, Feng 2006, 'Wen Jiabao: it is a strategic decision made by China to develop a friendly relationship with the PICs', *People's Daily*, 5 April, p. 1.

Grieken, B.J.V. and Kantorowicz, J. 2021, 'Debunking Myths about China: The Determinants of China's Official Financing to the Pacific', *Geopolitics*, No. 26, pp. 861-888.

Guan, Jingwei 2009, 'Xinzhongguo chengli chuqi yibiandao zhengce yanjiu zongshu' [An overview of studies on 'leaning to one side' adopted by the new China], *Beijingdangshi*, Vol. 178, No. 5, pp. 30-34.

Hayward-Jones, J. 2015, 'Australia and Security in the Pacific Islands Region, In *Regionalism, Security & cooperation in Oceania*, Asia-Pacific Center for Security Studies: Honolulu, p. 67.

He, Wenping 2018, 'zhongfei mingyun gongtongti yu zhongguo tese daguo waijiao ('China-Africa community of common destiny' and China's 'great country diplomacy with Chinese characteristics')', *Global Review*, Vol. 56, No. 4, pp. 1-15.

Huang, He. 2018, 'the containment thinking in the evolution of American geopolitical strategy: from "selective containment" to "Indo-Pacific" strategy', *Journal of Shenzhen University (Humanities & Social Sciences)*, Vol. 35, No. 1, pp. 72-78.

Hui, Meng 2011, 'Guojia liyi yu yibiandao zhengce de xingcheng' [National interest and the formation of the strategy of 'leaning to one side'], Extensive collection of the Party history (theoretical edn), No. 10, pp. 8-9.

Information Office of the State Council of the PRC 2013, *the White Paper on China-Africa Economic and Trade Cooperation*, IOSC, August, Beijing.

Information Office of the State Council of China 2017, *Pingtan Declaration made by the China-Small Island States Ocean-related Ministerial Round Table*, 22 September, http://www.scio.gov.cn/gxzl/ydyl_26587/zcxx_26600/202207/t20220728_266576.html

Jain, P. 2006, 'A little NATO against China', *Asian Times*, 18 March, viewed 8 August 2012, <http://www.atimes.com/atimes/China/HC18Ad01.html>.

Ji, Wenbo 2008, 'Mao Zedong yu xin zhong guo guo fang xian dai hua jian she de qi bu' [Mao Zedong and the new China's military modernization], *Mao Zedong Thought Studies*, Vol. 25, No. 3, pp. 139-43.

Jiangsu Academy of Agricultural Sciences 2023, China-PICs demonstration farms of agricultural cooperation, 19 May, https://home.jaas.ac.cn/xww/nkyw/art/2023/art_96f73a7f754042e2b8e5345b1ff08bb0.html

Khan, Shamsul, 2012, 'Middle powers and the dynamics of power shift', *Harvard Asian Quarterly*, Vol. 14, No. 3, p. 52.

Khan, Shamsul and Yu, Le 2013, 'Evolving China-ASEAN Relations and CAFTA', *European Journal of East Asian Studies*, Vol. 12, No. 1, pp. 81-107.

Leng, Rong & Wang, Zuoling 2004, *Deng Xiaoping Nian Pu (A chronicle of Deng Xiaoping's life) (1975-1997)*, Central Literature Press, Beijing, p. 1078.

Li, Danhui 2002, 'China-America detente and the war of assisting Vietnam and resisting America', *Literature of Chinese Communist Party*, No. 3, pp. 67-77.

Liu, Huaqiu 1997, 'Zhong guo shi zhong bu yu de feng xing du li zi zhu de he ping wai jiao zheng ce' [China adheres to the independent foreign policy of peace], *Journal of Qiushi*, No. 23, pp. 2-9.

Löfflmann, George 2016, 'The Pivot between Containment, Engagement, and Restraint: President Obama's Conflicted Grand Strategy in Asia', *Asian Security*, Vol. 12, No. 2, pp. 92-110.

Malhotra, I.C 2020, *Red Fear: The China Threat*, Bloomsbury: New Delhi. Yu, L 2015, 'China's strategic partnership with Latin America: a fulcrum in China's rise', International Affairs, Vol. 91, No. 5, pp. 1047-1068.

Mao, Zedong 1991, 'On the people's democratic dictatorship', *Selected works of Mao Zedong*, 2nd edn, vol. 4, Beijing: People's Press, pp. 1478-9.

Mao, Z 1991, 'Mao's Speech at the Second Plenary Session of the Seventh Central Committee of the Chinese Communist Party', In *Selected Work Mao Zedong* (Volume IV), People's Press: Beijing.

Master, Farah 2018, 'Empty hotels, idle boats: What happens when a Pacific', Reuters, 00, April, https://www.reuters.com/article/us-pacific-china-palau-insight-idUSKBN1L4036.

Mcdonald, Joshua 2019, 'Pacific Island Nations Consider Deep-sea Mining, Despite Risks', *Diplomat*, 18 June, https://thediplomat.com/2021/06/pacific-island-nations-consider-deep-sea-mining-despite-risks/

Mearsheimer, J 2003, *the Tragedy of Great Power Politics*, Norton, Inc: New York, p. 143.

Ministry of Foreign Affairs of China 2021a, Xie Feng, vice foreign minister attends the opening ceremony of China-PICs Reserve for Emergency Supplies, 3 December, http://new.fmprc.gov.cn/web/wjbxw_new/202201/t20220113_10492150.shtml.

Ministry of Foreign Affairs of China 2021b, Joint Statement of China-Pacific Island Countries Foreign Ministers' Meeting, 21 October, https://www.fmprc.gov.cn/mfa_eng/wjdt_665385/2649_665393/202110/t20211021_9604831.html.

Ministry of Agriculture and Rural Affairs of the PRC 2023a, To make Juncao for better livelihoods of the people, 1 September, http://www.moa.gov.cn/ztzl/ymksn/gmrbbd/202309/t20230901_6435657.htm.

Ministry of Agriculture and Rural Affairs 2023b, *The First China-Pacific Island Countries Forum on Fishery Cooperation and Development*, 10 May, http://www.moa.gov.cn/xw/gjjl/202305/t20230510_6427290.htm.

Ministry of Commerce of the PRC 2020a, Fujian Zhonghong Fishery plans to invest in a fishery park in PNG, 30 November, http://pg.mofcom.gov.cn/article/sqfb/yy/202011/20201103015468.shtml.

Ministry of Commerce 2020b, Data of trade and investment between China and the PICs, 29 May, http://mds.mofcom.gov.cn/article/Nocategory/200210/20021000042986.shtml.

Ministry of Ecology and Environment 2022, China-PICs Training program on climate change and low-carbon development, 21 June, Beijing, https://www.mee.gov.cn/ywgz/ydqhbh/qhbhlf/202206/t20220621_986270.shtml.

Ministry of Foreign Affairs of the PRC 2014a, Foreign Minister Wang Yi's comments on President Xi Jinping's attendance to the G20 summit and his visit to Australia, New Zealand and Fiji, Xinhua News Agency, November, http://www.xinhuanet.com/world/2014-11/23/c_1113367972.htm.

Ministry of Foreign Affairs of the PRC 2014b, List of Arms Control, Disarmament and Non-Proliferation Treaties that China has Joined, https://www.fmprc.gov.cn/mfa_eng/wjb_663304/zzjg_663340/jks_665232/tyylb_665254/t141338.shtml.

Ministry of Foreign Affairs of the PRC 2019a, *Xi Jinping Sends a Congratulatory Letter to the Third China-Pacific Island Countries Economic Development and Cooperation Forum*, 21 October, https://www.mfa.gov.cn/ce/cenz//eng/zgyw/t1709953.html.

Ministry of Foreign Affairs of the PRC 2019b, *China-Fiji Relations*, 1 March, viewed 7 May 2019, http://fj.chineseembassy.org/chn/zfgx/.

Ministry of Foreign Affairs of China 2021, Joint Statement of China-Pacific Island Countries Foreign Ministers' Meeting, 21 October, https://www.fmprc.gov.cn/mfa_eng/wjdt_665385/2649_665393/202110/t20211021_9604831.html.

Ministry of Foreign Affairs of the PRC 2022a, The Second Foreign Ministers' meeting between China and the PICs, 30 May, http://new.fmprc.gov.cn/wjbzhd/202205/t20220530_10694549.shtml.

Ministry of Foreign Affairs of China 2022b, China's position on mutual respect and common development between China and PICs, 30 May, http://new.fmprc.gov.cn/ziliao_674904/tytj_674911/zcwj_674915/202205/t20220530_10694631.shtml.

Ministry of Foreign Affairs of China 2022c, *The fact sheet on China-PICs cooperation*, 24 May, Beijing, http://new.fmprc.gov.cn/web/zyxw/202205/t20220524_10691894.shtml.

Narramore, T. 2008, China and Europe: engagement, multipolarity and strategy, *Pacific Review*, Vol. 21, No. 1, pp. 87-108.

New York Times 2003, 'Australia to join U.S. Missile-Defense System', 4 December, viewed 6 May 2012, <http://www.nytimes.com/2003/12/04/world/australia-to-join us-missile-defense-system.html>.

Niu, Jun 1999, '1969 nian zhong su bian jie chong tu yu zhong guo wai jiao zhan lue de tiao zheng' [The 1969 China–Soviet border dispute and China's shift in diplomatic strategy], *Contemporary China History Studies*, No. 1, pp. 66-77.

Oakes, R., Milan, A. and Campbell, J. 2016, *Kiribati: Climate Change and Migration*, United Nations University.

O'Neil, Andrew 2010, 'Australia and the South Pacific nuclear free zone treaty: a reinterpretation', *Australian Journal of Political Science*, Vol. 39, Issue 3, pp. 567-583.

Paal, Douglas H. 2015, 'China's Counterbalance to the American Rebalance', Carnegie Endowment for International Peace, November, https://carnegieendowment.org/2015/11/01/china-s-counterbalance-to-american-rebalance-pub-61857.

Pant, H.V. 2012, *China's Rising Global Profile: The Great Power Transition*, Sussex Academic Press: Brighton. Hsü, I.C.Y. 2000, *The Rise of Modern China*, Oxford University Press: New York.

Reuters 2019, 'China sees Kiribati ties soon, no word on space tracking station', 23 September, viewed 7 October 2019, https://www.reuters.com/article/us-china-kiribati-idUSKBN1W80VG.

RSIPF Press 2022, 'RSIPF officers completed training in China', *The Solomon Islands Government*, 8 November, https://solomons.gov.sb/rsipf-officers-completed-training-in-china/.

Schauble, J. 2000, 'Australia a lackey for US, says China', *Sydney Morning Herald*, 26 July, p. 12.

Shan, Jie, Guo, Yuandan, Liu, Yang, Leng, Shumei and Shen, Weiduo 2023, 'Chinese navy floating hospital docks at Solomon Islands for first time, bringing advanced medical services, goodwill gestures', *The Global Times*, 24 August, https://www.globaltimes.cn/page/202308/1296928.shtml.

Shen, Zhihua 2013, *Mao Zedong, Stalin and the Korean War*, Guangdong People's Press: Guangzhou.

Shi, Chunlin 2019, '*Cooperation between China and Pacific Island Countries: Retrospect and Outlook*', *The Contemporary World*, No. 2, pp. 35-39.

Shi, Guangsheng 2011, *A historical review of China's negotiations on its membership of the WTO*, People's Press: Beijing.

Sui, Shuying 2004, 'On the historical limitation of the policy of "standing on one side"', *Qilu Journal*, No. 6, pp. 48-56.

Sui, Sophia and Yu, Le 2023, 'China-Russia Strategic Partnership', *International Journal*, Vol. 79, No. 1, pp. 40-60.

Sui, Sophia and Yu, Le 2024, *Complex Interdependence and China-Australia relations*, Routledge: London.

Sutter, Robert 2000, *Chinese policy priorities and their implications for the United States*, Rowman & Littlefield: Lanham, p. 62.

Tang, Z 2009, 'From Paris Peace Conference to Washington Conference——Mao Zedong's Concept of the United States in Initial Shape', *Journal of the Xiangtan University*, No. 33, pp. 1-6.

Taylor, Ian 2011, *The Forum on China–Africa Cooperation* (FOCAC), Routledge: Abingdon.

Tow, W. and Loke, B. 2009, 'Rules of engagement: America's Asia-Pacific security policy under an Obama administration', *Australian Journal of International Affairs*, Vol. 63, No. 4, pp. 442-457.

Tsai, Yuchen 2012, *Australia's responses to China-US power competition in the South Pacific*, Zhizhi Academic Press: Taibei, p. 56.

Tull, D. 2008, 'the political consequence of China's return to Africa', Alden, C., Large, D. and Oliveira, R.S., ed, *China Returns to Africa: a rising power and a continent embrace*, Columbia University Press: New York, p. 461.

Wang, Enshou 2011, 'Stalin's changed conception of the Chinese Communist Party', *Hongguangjiao*, Vol. 190, No. 7, pp. 36-8.

Wang, G. 2017, China-America competition in the South China Sea and the promotion of "Belt and Road" initiatives in ASEAN. *Around Southeast Asia*, Vol. 12, No. 5, pp. 38-43.

Wang, Haiyun 2017, 'Trend of Russia-US relations after Trump's election to Presidency and its possible influences on China-Russia relaitonship', *Journal of Russia Studies*, No. 1, pp. 5-9.

Wang, Jianwei 2018, 'One Belt and One Road: a geopolitical strategy?', *Twenty-First Century*, Vol. 168, No. 8, pp. 16-26.

Wang, Jisi 2005, 'China's search for stability with America', *Foreign Affairs*, Vol. 84, No. 5, pp. 39-48.

Wang, Xinhua 2007, 'Mei su leng zhan yu su lian jing ji de beng kui (The American-Soviet cold war and the collapse of Soviet economy)', *Journal of Ningxia University*, Vol. 29, No. 6, pp. 112-115.

Wang, Zuocheng and Zhao, Shaofeng 2023, *Annual report on the development of the Pacific Island countries*, Academic Literature Press: Beijing.

Wei, Ming; Zhou, Qiangwu and Wang, Chunsheng 2016, *China-Japan Relations and Asia-Pacific Economic Cooperation*, China Financial & Economic Press: Beijing, p. 287.

Xi, Jinping 2013, *Trustworthy friends and sincere partners forever–speech at the Julius Nyerere International Convention Center*, Foreign Ministry of the PRC, 25 October 2013, <www.fmprc.gov.cn/mfa_eng/wjdt_665385/…/t1027951.shtml>;

Xia, LP 2005, 'The Bandung Conference and China's Efforts to Establish Diplomatic Relations with the Asia and African Countries', *Journal of China Foreign Affairs University*, No. 81, pp. 74-80.

Xiao, Donglian 2010, *60nian guoshi jiyao (major events in China's international relations over the last six decades)*, Hunan People's Press: Changsha, p. 243.

Xie, Feng 2022, 'to create a community of shared future by making concerted efforts in combating climate change', Ministry of Foreign Affairs of China, 28 April, https://www.mfa.gov.cn/wjbxw_new/202204/t20220428_10675213.shtml.

Xinhua News Agency 2019, China, Pacific Island Countries agree to enhance agriculture cooperation, Ministry of Agriculture and Rural Affairs of China, 30 March, http://english.moa.gov.cn/roll/201905/t20190508_299152.html.

Xinhua News Agency 2021a, *The First China-Pacific Island Countries Forum on Fishery Cooperation and Development Held*, Ministry of Agriculture and Rural Affairs of China, 10 December, http://english.moa.gov.cn/news_522/202112/t20211210_300762.html.

Xinhua News Agency 2021b, China, Vanuatu to jointly promote Chinese language education in Vanuatu, The State Council of China, 10 September, https://english.www.gov.cn/news/internationalexchanges/202109/10/content_WS613b558dc6d0df57f98dffee.html

Xu, Dianqing 1993, 'Studies on China's strategy of re-entry into the GATT', *Comparative Economic and Social Systems*, No. 3, pp. 39-44.

Xu, Jinjin 2018, 'Trump Administration's "Indo-Pacific" strategy', *American Studies Quarterly*, Vol. 32, No. 1, pp. 70-82.

Yang, Aihua 2012, 'The manners, characteristics and influences of Soviet Union's technological aid to the Chinese Air Force (1949-1960)', *Studies in Dialectics of Nature*, Vol. 28, No. 8, pp. 79-84.

Yu, Huamin 2007, 'Three major policies and independent new China diplomacy', *Historical Research in Anhui*, No. 5, pp. 81-90.

Yu, Le 2016, 'China-Australia Strategic Partnership in the Context of China's Grand Peripheral Diplomacy', *Cambridge Review of International Affairs*, Vol. 29, No. 2, pp. 740-760.

Yu, Lai 2018, 'China's expanding security involvement in Africa: a pillar for 'China-Africa community of common destiny', *Global Policy*, Vol. 9, Issue 4, pp. 489-500.

Yu, Lei 2015, 'China-Latin America Strategic Partnership: a fulcrum in China's rise', *International Affairs*, Vol. 91, No. 5, pp. 1047-1068.

Yu, Lei 2020a, 'China-Pacific Island Countries Strategic Partnership: China's strategy to reshape regional order', *East Asia: An International Quarterly*, 2021, Vol. 39, Issue 1, pp. 81-96.

Yu, L. 2020b, 'China's Free Trade Area Strategy: An Alternative Avenue to China's "Peaceful" Rise?', *The Journal of Social Science*, Vol. 57, No. 2, pp. 206-218.

Yun, Jiang 2004, Mei guo yao ba dao dan fang yu xi tong tui xiang quan qiu? Yi tu he zai (Will the U.S. Deploy NMD accross the world? What is its attempt?), Xinhua News Agency, 4 August, <http://news.xinhuanet.com/world/ 2004-08/04/content_1711059.htm>.

Zhang, Ping 2016, Chinese Foreign Policy and China-Fiji Relationship, Foreign Ministry of the PRC, 1 June, https://www.fmprc.gov.cn/mfa_eng/wjb_663304/zwjg_665342/zwbd_665378/t1368453.shtml

Zhang, Qingmin 2004, 'Zhongguo de guojia tese, guojia juese he waijiao zhengce sikao' [The character and role of China and a thought on its foreign policy], *Pacific Journal*, Vol, 12, No. 2, 2004, pp. 47-55.

Zhang, Qingmin 2009, 'Diplomatic composition of China in the last 60 years: a text analysis of the political reports to the Chinese Communist Party National Congress', *Foreign Affairs Review*, Vol. 26, No. 4, pp. 32-42.

Zhang, Xiuhua 2000, 'Dui jianguo chuqi yibiandao zhanlue de xinrenshi' [Reconsidering the strategy of 'leaning to one side' adopted at the beginning of the founding of the PRC], *Collected Papers of History Studies*, Vol. 79, No. 2, pp. 47-51.

Zhang, Yongxin 2023, 'Samoa, Fiji welcome China-aided agricultural technical assistance', Xinhua News Agency, 10 March, https://english.news.cn/20230313/018e6fcf31f84676b2877c37c150e897/c.html.

Zhang, Yongxing and Zheng, Xin 2019, 'Hu Chunhua conveys President Xi's letter to the Third ministerial conference of China-PICs Forum', Chinese Central Government, 21 October, http://www.gov.cn/guowuyuan/2019-10/21/content_5442826.htm.

Zhao, Shaofeng and Yu, Lei 2023, *China-PICs relations*, China Social Sciences Press: Beijing.

Zhao, Xiaoyu 2018, 'Why Obama's Rebalance towards Asia-Pacific Was Unsuccessful?', *International Studies*, Vol. 55, No. 2, pp. 87-105.

Zhou, Q.; Zhang, J. 2007, 'The Shift in China's Perceptions of the UN's Peacekeeping Operations: From the Perspectives of National Security', *Contemporary World Socialism*, Vol. 2, No. 3, pp. 56-60.

Zhou Yubo, Shen, Yuhuan and Cao, Xiangyu 2022, 'President Biden started his first Asian trip to co-opt South Korea and Japan', 21 May, the People's Daily, http://world.people.com.cn/n1/2022/0521/c1002-32426926.html.

Zuo, Fengrong 2001, 'The cause leading to the Soviet Union onto the road of arms race and effect', *Helongjiang Social Science*, Vol. 68, No. 5, pp. 33-36.

4

The economic and geopolitical interests for China and the PICs

Introduction

China has intensified its relations of cooperation with the Pacific Island Countries (PICs) since the onset of the 21st century when the United States and Australia, and other traditional players shifted their attention away from the South Pacific, their "backyard", to Iraq, Afghanistan and elsewhere. The shift in attention by the traditional players in the South Pacific leaves the PICs much neglected, particularly in terms of economic growth, infrastructural development and climate change, and causes grievance among the PICs' social elites and general public alike (Morgan 2021, Yu 2020b, p. 81). The Chinese authorities have redoubled its efforts in expanding its presence and influence in the South Pacific since the BRI was first proposed in 2013 after the US pursuit of "pivot to Asia", which leads to a wide assumption that China's BRI is partially aimed to counterattack the US "pivot to Asia" (Szadziewski 2021, p. 295). In hindsight, both China and the PICs have obtained economic and political benefits from the BRI and China's expanding presence and influence in the South Pacific. Otherwise, it is hard to understand how China could expand its involvement and influence in the PICs in such a short time and at such a rapid rate. This chapter examines the economic and geopolitical interests for China and for the PICs arising from the BRI, and the China-PICs intensified relations of cooperation and trade.

The main argument of the chapter is that China's expanding involvement in the South Pacific and its efforts in creating a strategic partnership with the PICs have brought concrete benefits to China and its partners in the region though there have long been diverse responses from the PICs to the BRI. Over the first two decades in the 21st century, China has created close relations of economic cooperation and strategic partnership particularly with the political and commercial elites in the PICs through the BRI and its vigorous economic involvement in South Pacific. In addition to economic benefits, China's increasing involvement in the South Pacific, the traditional "backyard" of the United States and Australia, the "sheriff" and "deputy sheriff" of the region, has served its interest in breaking through the US containment and encirclement of China by virtue of the so-called "second island chain". China has kept in mind two interconnected objectives whilst pursuing its strategic partnership and economic cooperation with the PICs: one is the commitment to China's economic growth that underlies China's "hard" and "soft" power; and the other, China's rise at the systemic (global) level.

The interests of BRI for China

China's economic growth and modernization have long been considered by the Chinese political leadership and academics alike as the basis underlying China's dream of regaining its past glory of *fuqiang* (wealth and power) as a great power and the legitimacy of the communist rule of China (Sui & Yu 2023). Immediately after the disintegration of the former Soviet Union in early 1991, Deng Xiaoping provided some thoughtful consideration of the prominence of the role of sustained economic growth in winning the Cold War, and the hearts and minds of the general public. Deng disagreed upon the prevalent perceptions in the United States that the Soviet demise marked the triumph of America-style democracy over the Soviet authoritarian communism and the universalization of liberal democracy as the final form of human government (Fukuyama 1992, p. 10). Contrarily, Deng theorized the Soviet fall as a consequence of its economic incapability of buttressing the Soviet "imperial over-expansion" and the long-term rivalry with the United States, and of providing a better life for the Soviet people (Wang 2007, 113, Yu 2020a, p. 240).

Deng's conception of the Soviet demise provides insights into Deng's doctrine that China's priority should be given to the country's economic growth and the improvement of the livelihoods of the Chinese people, rather than to the pursuit of regional and global military hegemony in the next 100 years since the late 1970s (Deng 1993, p. 380). As well, it sheds light on Deng Xiaoping's doctrine of prioritizing economic growth and modernization, and his insistence on China's concentration on economic growth for the next 100 years since his market reform began in 1978[31]. The ruling Communist Party has thereafter been focusing on China's economic growth and masterminded the country's industrialization and modernization, which has set China upon the road to its national rejuvenation and re-emergence at the systemic (global) level. China's economic downturn or stagnation will hurt the livelihoods of the Chinese people and much worse, undermine the legitimacy of the communist rule of China. To sustain economic growth has since become the primary motivation behind China's pursuit of an economic diplomacy, which is, among others, aimed to obtain access to overseas resources, markets and investment destinations, including those of the PICs (Yu 2024, p. 12).

The Chinese policy makers and scholars alike hold fast to the belief that their country shall be categorized as a developing country and a rising middle power, rather than a developed country and a superpower (Zhou 2011). This belief contradicts some international arguments that define China as a developed country and a superpower. The belief of the Chinese elites in their country's categorization as a developing country is plausible given the fact that the monthly income of more than 610 million nationals in China is less than 1000 RMB (US$140) (China National Bureau of Statistics 2020). As a developing country, Deng Xiaoping's doctrine that China should focus on economic development and the improvement of her people's livelihoods, and refrain from seeking military hegemony in the 100 years ahead, has remained consensus among the Chinese policy elites over the last 40 years since the late 1970s. In this context, it is safe to conclude that China's increasing involvement, including the BRI, in the rest of the world has to date remained economic-centered and commercially-oriented, and China's expanding involvement in the PICs is no exception.

In the viewpoints of some Chinese policy makers and economists (e.g., Song Xiuju & Ye, Shengxuan 2016, p. 71), China's economic and infrastructural involvement in the PICs under the framework of BRI is aimed to help China gain

31 'The aim of our foreign policy is to maintain world peace. With the precondition of peace, we are able to wholeheartedly devote ourselves to China's modernisation in the hopes of developing our country', see Deng Xiaoping 1993, *Selected Deng Xiaoping Works (III)*, People's Press: Beijing, p. 57.

access to the markets, resources and investment destinations in the region as it does in the other parts of the world. China is eager to expand overseas markets for its manufactured products, and moreover, to find investment destinations for the Chinese businessmen following the country's rise as the second largest economy with a foreign exchange reserve of around $3 trillion (China State Administration of Foreign Exchange 2019). As a newly industrialized country, China is now working hard to upgrade its labor-intensive production system to a capital-intensive and technology-based industrial structure, which it perceives as "vital" to gain a place among the developed countries by the middle of the 21st century. The Chinese government designed in 2015 the 'Blueprint of Manufacturing 2025', which pinpoints the transformation of China into a manufacturing power as the key to sustaining China's economic growth and lifting it up the value chain of global economy (*Economist* 2015, Wang 2015).

China tries to create a close relationship of economic cooperation and trade with the PICs regardless of their divergent ideological values and political systems. Deng Xiaoping insisted that China's relations of cooperation with the rest of the world be based on "mutual respect", "mutual benefits" and non-interference, rather than on shared ideological value and political system (Fujita, Kimio 1993, p. 464, Liu, 1997, p. 3). While trade of many PICs with the United States has remained negligible over the post-Cold War era, China has rapidly risen as the biggest trading partner of a large number of PICs. China has even cultivated a close relationship of economic cooperation and trade with the PICs that have diplomatic relations with Taiwan, instead of China. For example, the bilateral trade volume between China and Palau that has diplomatic relations with Taiwan rose to US$54.32 million in 2022, a year-on-year increase of 49.1 percent with China's exports worth US$54.16 million, a year-on-year increase of 48.98 percent and China's imports worth US$156 thousand, a year-on-year increase of 82.76 percent (Ministry of Foreign Affairs of the PRC 2023). This trade volume has surpassed that between Palau and the United States, the former's close ally in the region, which stood at US$23.28 million in 2021 (Observatory of Economic Complexity (OEC) 2023a).

Take another example. The bilateral trade volume between China and the Marshall Islands that grants diplomatic recognition to Taiwan rose to US$3.465 billion in 2022, a year-on-year increase of 8.63 percent. The two-way trade volume between the Marshall Islands and China, the new comer in the region, markedly outnumbers that between the Marshall Islands and the United States, the traditional player and former colonial power in the region. The two-way trade between the Marshall Islands and the United States stood at around US$460 million in 2021 (Observatory of Economic Complexity (OEC) 2023b). In the viewpoints of Zhao Shaofeng and Ni Peng at the Liaocheng University, China is providing an increasing number of affordable and quality products to Palau, the Marshall Islands and other PICs, which contributes to curbing the price rise there and improving the quality of life of local people. This explains why the PICs, including those without diplomatic ties with China, are actively advancing their economic cooperation and trade with China despite the US warning of the PICs of the risk of China's "economic coercion" (Birnbaum & Pannett 2023). This also explains why the governments of the PICs are generally appreciative of China's involvement in the region and dismiss the "China threat" thesis coined by some traditional players in the region, such as the United States, the "sheriff" in the region, and Australia, the "deputy sheriff". In the viewpoints of some political leaders (e.g., Fiame Naomi Mata'afa, Prime Minister of Samoa) in the PICs, the thesis of the "China threat" is the narratives of the traditional players, rather than the narratives of the Pacific islanders (Yu 2021, p. 82).

The abundance of the South Pacific region in resources, particularly on the seabed, and in investment opportunities attracts the Chinese investors and entrepreneurs alike (Peterson & Tawake 2017, Sui & Yu 2024, p. 8). The pursuit of resources remains one of the most significant motivations behind China's increasing engagement with the PICs. It is reported that there is an abundance of maritime resources in the South Pacific, such as energy resources, fisheries, and critical minerals, which makes the PICs a lucrative strategic investment. The area of the Pacific between Hawaii and Mexico is scattered with rocks called polymetallic nodules and contains more cobalt and nickel (key ingredients in electric batteries) than all known land deposits (McVeigh 2023). This partially explains why the South Pacific is of significant interest of the traditional players in the region, and of the rising countries, including China. China's domestic resources are unlikely to sustain the country's economic growth in the 21st century, which has consumed enormous resources over the last four decades since Deng Xiaoping started China's modernization drive in the late 1970s. China consumed 46 percent of global coal, copper, aluminium, zinc and nickel production. Its oil imports will have reached 13.1 million barrels per day by 2030 and consumed one-fifth of global energy by 2035 (Ferguson 2010, Pan et al 2020, p. 6).

This reveals China's sustained economic growth to be dependent on its capability of gaining access to overseas resources and the pursuit of their assured supplies. Most recently, the government of the Solomon Islands and the China Railway Group Ltd, a state conglomerate, have concluded a deal worth SBD$6.4

billion (about US$800 million) to build and lease infrastructure projects at the Gold Ridge mines on Guadalcanal, which is set to last until March 2034 (Gray 2019, Iroga 2022). To secure access to resources is joined by a growing interest in securing food sources for the Chinese population. It is no denial that China has to date developed economic interests deriving from the region's large economic exclusive zones (EEZ) despite the small population and market of the PICs. However, China needs to adopt a precautionary approach to avoid harm to natural resources and ecosystems starting from the decision-making stage and based on the independent scientific judgment through a transparent process (Xu 2022, p. 406). In this sense, the extent to which China's investments in resources will be regulated by law needs to be made clear after China becomes a major source of capital flows to the PICs over the past decade (Kirkwood & Chaisse 2020, p. 246). The environmental impacts shows the need for China's investment finance to reckon with risks and the fallout from environment and governance issues (Canuto 2019). Fortunately, official guidelines on environment for Chinese companies investing abroad have been issued, signaling the matter has caught the attention of Chinese authorities.

Apart from economic interest, the Chinese foreign policy makers perceive the country's increasing economic and infrastructural engagement with the PICs as a way to advance development cooperation of the global south. Deng Xiaoping (1993, p. 380), the late supreme Chinese political leader, proposed the "South–South Cooperation" in the mid-1980s to intensify the Chinese economic cooperation and trade with the developing nations'. Deng reminded the Chinese leadership that the 'South–South Cooperation is one of the most important issues in international relations and represents the historic trend'. Deng Xiaoping's South–South cooperation encompassed various purposes. First, it alleviated China's economic pressure resulting from providing massive assistance to the developing countries as a means of securing their diplomatic support and enhancing China's international status (Yu 2018, p. 489). Second, it helped China avail itself of its cordial relations with the developing countries to accelerate and sustain its economic growth by gaining access to their abundant raw materials and resources, as well as their huge markets for exporting Chinese products. Third, it enabled China to intensify its economic relationship, and by extension, its political relationship with other developing countries through expanded trade and economic cooperation. It is in this context that China has redoubled its efforts in expanding its engagement with Asia, Africa and Latin America since the early 1990s. Deng's initiatives of the South-South Cooperation altered the traditional Chinese mindset of China's relationship with other developing countries, paving the way for China's economic involvement in the PICs. Coupled with low-interest loans and economic assistance, intensified economic and infrastructural cooperation and trade between China and the PICs have become a new and more enduring "common interest" in lieu of the out-of-mode anti-colonialism and anti-imperialism (Information Office of the State Council of the PRC 2013).

The Chinese foreign policy makers perceive China's increasing economic and infrastructural involvement in the PICs as a way to intensify political cooperation and relations with the PICs, and obtaining their political and diplomatic support at the world arena. The Chinese authorities have long insisted that China's relations with the developing states, including the South Pacific countries, are the "basis of its international relations". There has long been an agreement in the Chinese foreign policy and scholarly circles that the political backing provided to China by the developing states at the international arena is an indispensable component of China's global power and influence (Zhong 2018, p. 22, Yu 2018, p. 490). China has now established itself as one of the most influential states in the developing world where it has enormous strategic, political and economic interests (Carbone 2012, p. 287). The developing states, including the PICs, have often come to defend China amid western criticism of Chinese policies towards Hong Kong, Taiwan and Tibet. The developing states have played a significant role in blocking Taiwan from entering the UN and other international organizations as an independent sovereign state. It is in this context that Chinese foreign policy elites are generally of the view that the vast developing states remain vitally significant for China's international legitimacy and global influence. China is enjoying considerable popularity in the developing world, 'not only among elites but also at street level', which gives China advantages over other competitors in terms of BRI and other economic involvement (Friedrichs 2019, p. 1635, Silver et al 2019).

Looking to the future, it is safe to predict that the developing states are likely to play an even more significant role in the process of China's rise in view of their economic potential, political influence as a whole and strategic significance. This provides a cogent explanation why China has since Xi Jinping's presidency began in early 2013 intensified its involvement in the developing world, including the Pacific islands and endeavored to create with them a "Community of Shared Future (命运共同体)". In Xi's view, "the community of shared future" is aimed to seek common development, shared prosperity and collective security by intensifying their economic integration, political trust and security cooperation. China is now committed to creating a new international order that it deems "more rational and fairer" for itself and for the other developing states (Sui &

Yu 2023b). However, this new order would be less legitimate and representative without the espousal of the vast developing states, including the PICs. This is why China has always preferred to acquire loyal friends in the developing world who would now and in the future back it in international fora everywhere and always (Rotberg 2008, p. 31). This also explains why China perceives its partnerships with the developing states at the highest levels of diplomacy as a significant part of its external relations.

China emphasizes its relations with the PICs as being based on mutual respect for sovereignty, and non-interference in the internal affairs, and mutual benefit. When interviewed by the authors, Zhao Shaofeng at Liaocheng University said that China's cooperation with the PICs is based on mutual respect for sovereignty and self-determination without imposing any political conditions (i.e., the "non-interference" principle). Zhao comments that the Chinese approach is fundamentally different from the US-led partnership that is mainly driven by its hegemonic interests[32]. In the viewpoints of Ni Peng in the Research Center for the Pacific Island Countries, respect for the sovereignty of the PICs and adherence to the mode of mutually beneficial cooperation with the PICs are the major driver for the PICs to get closer to, support and work with China. Ni explains that the PICs had been colonized by the West, suffering great loss in both politics and economy, and they have valued their sovereignty and self-determination ever since they gained independence from the colonial powers.

Niu Li at Beijing Foreign Studies University explains that only when both sides gain benefits could mutual cooperation last … that is the theory that China persistently underscores in dealing with its ties with the developing states, including the PICs. In the view of the Chinese scholars, China's foreign policy approach explains why when they hype the "China threat thesis", the United States and other traditional players in the region find that the political leaders of the PICs refuse to buy their rhetoric. Instead, they are stuck to the belief that China is not a threat, but a partner (Seneviratne 2024). China's foreign policy approach also explains why the United States and other traditional players fail to stop the PICs from boosting their ties with China after they have made a lot of inputs to the PICs.

Moreover, the Chinese foreign policy makers perceive the country's increasing engagement with the PICs as a way to winning their political and

32 Zhao Shaofeng is a professor and academic dean of the Research Center for the PICs/China-PICs Climate Action Cooperation Center, Liaocheng University.

diplomatic backing regionally and globally in relations to the US containment and Taiwan's diplomatic competition. China is in need of the developing states at the international arena in support of its economic, political and diplomatic stance, such as to create a new international order in favor of China and the other developing states. China also needs the developing states to help it block the West's attempt to pass any resolution on China's human rights records and frustrate Taiwan's efforts to re-gain a membership in the United Nations (Friedrichs 2019, p. 1635, Yu 2018, p. 496). China's BRI and economic involvement in the PICs have won support by some political, commercial and social elites in the region despite the prevalent criticism from the traditional players. Dorothy Wickham, a journalist in the Pacific islands wrote in the *New York Times*:

> Forty-four years after independence, we are still struggling to build a nation. Around 80 percent of our citizens still live in hard-to-reach rural areas, subsisting on family-run plots of lands. Many still lack access to running water, basic sanitation and electricity. Jobs are scarce, access to health care is limited, and high numbers of children are stunted by poor diets. We face ominous new threats because of climate change, including coral bleaching and rising sea levels that are slowly washing away islands...... as Western leaders point fingers at China and chide our leader, we'd like to ask: Where have you been? Chinese-run businesses — construction, hardware, fishing, transport and other sectors — have quickly become part of the local economy...... severing longtime relations with China's rival Taiwan, an unpopular move. But minds are slowly changing. Chinese construction companies significantly upgrade our main hospital and a long-overdue stadium that will host the Pacific Games next year. China's profile has been rising across the Pacific (Wickham 2022).

The South Pacific has long been an arena for China and Taiwan to compete for diplomatic recognition by the PICs, among which ten were in recognition of China and the remaining four in recognition of Taiwan prior to 2019. China's infrastructural and economic cooperation with the PICs boost local economic growth, and by extension, the political relations between China and the PICs, which may make further trade and economic cooperation easier for China and the PICs, and make the PICs distance their policy from the "containment" strategy adopted by the United States. China suspended diplomatic competition ("diplomatic truce") with Taiwan to show its good will to the Nationalist regime (in office from 2008 to 2016) that publicly recognized the "One China" principle. During the "diplomatic truce", the Chinese government declined to exchange diplomatic recognition with some states in central America, such as Panama and El Salvador (Panda 2018, Rich & Banerjee 2015, p. 142).

The Chinese government resumed the diplomatic contest and sought to isolate Taiwan by engineering a mass defection of the latter's remaining friends and preclude it from independence from China shortly after Tsai Ing-wen's refusal of the "One China" principle following her presidency began in 2016. Motivated by political and economic interests, the Solomon Islands and Kiribati in the South Pacific are among the states that switched their diplomatic ties from Taiwan to China in 2019. Beijing is pleased with the switch and encourages more states to follow suit, particularly during Tsai's rule of Taiwan from 2016 to 2024. Most recently, Nauru switched its diplomatic recognition from Taiwan to China in early 2024 and Tuvalu is expected to review its ties with Taiwan after its election in early 2024.

The Chinese foreign policy makers are increasingly aware of the significance of China-PICs security cooperation, first and foremost, for the protection of China's growing interest and nationals in the South Pacific region. China's move is also aimed to boost China's "soft" power in the region by providing the PICs public goods of peace and stability as it is doing particularly in Africa. It is well-noted that China contributes the largest number of personnel to the UN peacekeeping operations in Africa (Blasko 2016, Yu 2018, p. 491. It is safe to say that Wang Yi (Chinese foreign minister)'s tour of the South Pacific region in 2022 signaled a move made by China to expand its presence and influence in the region. It is reported that Wang's visit was aimed to convince the PICs to sign up to a sweeping cooperation agenda that spanned economic, infrastructural, public health, cultural and security cooperation, rather than a merely security agreement (Ministry of Foreign Affairs of the PRC 2022). For example, the cybersecurity and the rules for data governance are mentioned in his agenda that reportedly proposes China to train regional police forces and hold China-Pacific Islands Countries ministerial dialogue on law enforcement capacity and police cooperation, the first of its kind in the China-PICs relations.

The Chinese Foreign Ministry confirmed that China and the Solomon Islands have recently signed the intergovernmental framework agreement on security cooperation (Embassy of the PRC in the Solomon Islands 2022). A spokesman of the Ministry explains that the agreement was designed to promote social stability and long-term tranquility in the Solomon Islands and to protect the interest of both countries. The spokesman further explains that the security cooperation between the two states is open, transparent and inclusive, and does not target any third party. As intimated previously, the Chinese political leadership has long viewed the stability and tranquility of a country as the precondition for the country's economic growth and social progress. This is why China holds fast to the belief that the peace and stability in the region conform to the interests of the Solomon Islands in particular, and the PICs in general. Notably, China's conclusion of the bilateral security agreement with the Solomon Islands has aroused suspicions of the traditional players in the region about the drivers behind China's move. Some assume the security agreement as China's desire to seek military hegemony by creating military bases in the region and projecting power within the second island chain (Jones 2023, US Department of Defense 2023). Others conceive the move as China's attempt to protect the fast-growing Chinese assets and citizens in the region (Grossman 2022, Myers 2022). Still some surmise the move as China's emergence as an interventionist power, intending to support the friendly governments in the region (Hammond 2023, Miller 2022).

The realist theory of international relations concludes that the security footprint of a state will be extended to where its interest exists and there is no exception to China in this regard. What are the Chinese interests in the South Pacific specifically? When interviewed by the authors, Lyu Guixia at the Center for the Pacific and Pacific Countries History, China Academy of Social Sciences, highlighted that there are around 50,000 Chinese nationals currently living in the South Pacific, mainly from Fujian and Guangdong provinces. Most of them are in possession of small businesses in the region and are vulnerable to local riots. Lyu told the authors that some of the Chinese nationals had been looted in the riots that had occurred over the last decades and suffered a lot. They appealed to the governments of the Solomon Islands to provide protection for their lives and interest. Danny Philip, former Solomon Islands prime minister, told the press that the Australian security forces deployed in Honiara to quell last November's riots were instructed not to protect the local China town (Wickham 2022b). The lack of law enforcement capability of the Solomon Islands and the refusal by the Australian security forces to protect foreigners, and particularly the Chinese nationals have led to mounting pressure from the overseas Chinese, around 60 million across the world, on the Chinese authorities to provide them with protection for their lives and properties.

According to *the Global Times*, a survey conducted by the Solomon Islands-based Chinese nationals' association reveals the extent of the impact suffered by the Chinese nationals in Honiara from the riots had lasted for several years (Fan & Shan 2021). The survey shows that many Chinese nationals after the riots suffer from "homelessness and loss of income". Manasseh Sogavare, former Prime

Minister of the Solomon Islands, told the press that the riots "are influenced and encouraged by some powers" (McGuirk 2021). According to *the Sydney Morning Herald*, Sogavare indicated that the forces influencing Malaita [the main island of the nation] are those that "don't want ties with the People's Republic of China". In the context of big power competition, Lyu Guixia emphasizes that the protection of the Chinese nationals in the South Pacific and their property have become the most significant driver behind China's efforts in signing security deals with the PICs.

When interviewed by the authors, Guo Chunmei at the Institute of Southeast Asian and Oceanian Studies, China Institutes of Contemporary International Relations, adds that economic cooperation and trade are among the drivers behind China's efforts. In her eyes, China has rapidly grown as one of the most significant economic players in the South Pacific and has shown a strong capacity to grow even further. Statistics released by the Chinese Ministry of Foreign Affairs shows that the two-way trade between China and the PICs skyrocketed to $9 billion in 2022 from $880 million in 2005, and China's FDI reached $4.5 billion in the same year, up from 900 million in 2013 (Ministry of Foreign Affairs of the PRC 2023). Guo Chunmei adds that China views the Pacific Islands as a significant component of its "Belt and Road" initiative, which is an umbrella initiative, involving a massive amount of infrastructure construction and investment projects. China had signed BRI cooperation documents with 10 of the 14 Pacific Islands countries by 2021. The official Chinese data reveal that the Chinese investment in infrastructure projects has become the lion's share of its investment in the region. Moreover, China displays strong interests in local fisheries and aquaculture with scores of Chinese enterprises having invested in the fisheries industry across the region.

Chen Hong at East China Normal University notes that the Pacific islands have long been an arena for China and Taiwan to compete for diplomatic recognition and are the newest battleground in China-US geopolitics. When interviewed by the authors, he believes that to contain Taiwan's split from China and to overcome the US containment of China are one of the drivers behind China's move for a security pact. The Chinese foreign policy elites view Taiwan as an "inseparable" part of China and accuse the United States of abetting Taiwan's split to contain China (Information Office of the State Council of the PRC 2021). China is in need of political support from the vast developing states, including the Pacific Islands states, to block the US-headed West from "interfering with its domestic affairs", such as Taiwan, Hong Kong, Xinjiang, human right, etc. From the above analysis, it is not hard to conclude that China's efforts to increase its security footprint in the South Pacific is primarily driven by its own interests there, as other states have done in that region and elsewhere. China's efforts reflect its sense of vulnerability in terms of protecting its overseas interests. However, it remains to see if this will develop into a part of China's grand strategy though the possibility is slim.

When the authors conducted fieldwork in the PICs in the years from 2016 to 2020, the language of personal and property security of the Chinese nationals and companies pervaded among the Chinese interlocutors, most of whom came to the PICs for business and investment. It is no doubt that China aspires of presenting itself as a security provider by conducting police cooperation to assist the countries where China and her nationals have much interest, to maintain peace and security. This partially explains why China has over the last couple of decades rapidly grown as the largest personnel contributor to the UN's peace-keeping operations particularly in Africa where China and her nationals have fast-growing interest (Coleman & Job 2021, p. 1451, Mabera 2021, p. 136). In the same vein, the security agreement between China and the PICs should be interpreted as China's broader plan for the region, which displays China's increasing willingness to formalize security arrangements with their counterparts of PICs to consolidate the peace and stability in the region. After the sweeping agenda of a region-wide security agreement was refused, China responded with a statement promising its commitment to increasing its partnership in the region through a Five Year plan that covers a wide array of sectors of climate change, capacity-building, health, security, defense and multilateral cooperation.

Overseas security challenge is hardly new for the Chinese authorities who have learned much from China's vigorously economic involvement in Africa where China has been the largest trading partner and investor for a couple of decades since the end of the Cold War. The Chinese foreign policy elites are acutely aware that they should simultaneously enhance commitment to bolstering peace and security in the place where their country have a lot of economic interest although some international analysts view the Chinese commitment to security as primarily to protect its rapidly growing interest (Sheldon-Duplaix 2016, p. 44, Backman 2008, p. 78). The Chinese authorities have long deemed peace and security as the precondition for economic and social progress, which is a lesson learnt by the Chinese authorities in masterminding China's economic growth over the last decades since the late 1970s (Li 2023). This explains why China has intensified its involvement in African peace and security affairs by providing funds to African Union (AU) in support of its peace-keeping efforts, engaging in intervention in the South Sudan conflict and dispatching combat troops to the UN peace-keeping missions (Chun 2018, p. 124, Zhang 2018, p. 125).

Security cooperation has now become a key pillar of the China-Africa relationship concurrent with their rapidly increasing economic cooperation and trade. China and the African states have institutionalized since the onset of the 21st century the China-Africa Defence and Security Forum, the China-Africa Peace and Security Forum and the China-Africa Security and Law Enforcement Forum (Shinn & Eisenman 2023, p. 42). In this vein, it is not surprising that China aspires to transplant its successes in Africa in this regard to the PICs, where China's interest has grown rapidly over the last two decades in the new century. When addressing his counterparts in the PICs, Wang Yi, Chinese Foreign Minister, stated that China supports not just the PICs, but the other developing countries in Asia, Africa and Latin America in terms of keeping economic growth, domestic stability and regional peace. Wang's statement makes it clear that China's sweeping proposal of a comprehensive cooperation with the developing states, including the PICs, displays China's intention to institutionalize arrangements of security-related cooperation with its counterparts across the Global South.

It is in this context that some Chinese scholars (e.g., Zhao Shaofeng and Yu Lei 2023) view China's security cooperation with the Solomon Islands as an example of a mutually beneficial partnership, whose aim is to guarantee a safe business and investment environment. In their viewpoints, to provide a safe and stable environment that is conducive to economic cooperation and trade, one imperative is to ensure that the local police force and other security services would suffice to withstand possible future social unrests, riots and other disruptions. The Chinese foreign policy elites have learnt much from the last riots in the South Pacific and are guarding against riots that may occur in the future. Chen Hong and Guo Chunmei note the roles played by some traditional players in the riots. When interviewed by the authors, Chen Hong accuses Australia and pro-Taiwan secessionist elements of instigating the riots in the Solomon Islands. In his view, the motivation behind their instigation was to create obstacles and even a dangerous environment for the Chinese businesses and investors in the Solomon Islands.

Zhao Shaofeng at the Liaocheng University did fieldwork in the Solomon Islands and he had conversations with some Chinese nationals there, who told him that the riots were far more severe than those of 2006: the rioters burned schools, banks and even police stations, and the Chinatown bore the brunt of the most severe damage. The Chinese nationals suffered incalculable losses in the riots and some Chinese merchants have reported an estimated loss of more than US$6 million. Many Chinese nationals suffered from "homelessness and loss of income" with the China Town in Honiara was burned and looted (Fan & Shan 2021). Many Chinese nationals in the Solomon Islands highly suspect the United States and Taiwan's influence behind the riots when they concluded: what the riots reflect is the scope of influence that the United States has over the country in particular and the region in general. The suspicion was further deepened by the remarks made by Manasseh Sogavare, former Prime Minister of the Solomon Islands, on the crisis. Sogavare accused some foreign powers of "encouraging" and "influencing" the riots because they did not like to see an intensified relationship of cooperation between China and the Solomon Islands (Rising & McGuirk 2021, Pryke 2021).

Some Chinese analysts (e.g., Chen Hong, Yang Honglian and Guo Chunmei) hold fast to the belief that the riots in the Solomon Islands are literally a fierce "geopolitical competition among major powers." (Fan & Shan 2021). The Chinese watchers and analysts believe that the United States views the Pacific islands as "a geopolitical battleground" and supports an anti-China movement in the Solomon Islands, as part of a wider resistance to growing Chinese presence and influence in the Pacific region. They note that the United States switched its proffer of financial aid to the island of Malaita, the major opposition of the country's central government, immediately after China and the Solomon Islands exchanged diplomatic recognition in late 2019. Statistics provided by the Lowy Institute showed that the US pledged to Malaita was 500 times more than the aid that the province received from all countries in 2018 (Wasuka & Bahmani 2020). The Australian Broadcasting Company disclosed in a 2020 report that the United States pledged $25 million in aid for Malaita directly, sparking concerns of misappropriation of aid funding as a weapon in a "geopolitical tussle, which triggered speculation on the role played by the United States in the riots. There have been concerns that the United States is seeking support for its own geostrategic struggle with China in the Pacific.

Some Chinese observers and analysts (e.g., Chen Hong and Zhao Shaofeng) note that Australia had been closely cooperating with the United States in the last turmoil. Australian Prime Minister Scott Morrison said after the riots occurred that it was not Australia's role to "interfere in their democracy" as he sent troops to help maintain peace in Honiara. Chen Hong therefore believed that the overall attitude of Australia and the United States was in fact to "condone and even encourage the riots" (Fan & Shan 2021). Shortly after the riots in the Solomon Islands, China has tried to have security cooperation with the PICs to keep peace and stability in the region and protect the Chinese nationals as well as their interest in the region. In 2023, a China-proposed sweeping security deal with the PICs was rejected at the second China-Pacific Islands Foreign Minister's meeting in Fiji. Zhao Shaofeng and Ni Peng note that the deal goes well beyond an interpretation of the Chinese interests as solely concerned with establishing a basing facility and demonstrates China's willingness to become a long-term actor in the region.

Despite the refusal of the sweeping deal, China has indeed concluded security agreements with Tonga and the Solomon Islands by providing them with defence, police, and military training. When interviewed by the authors, Chen Hong argues that "If necessary, China and the Solomon Islands, as well as other countries in the regions that face similar challenges and potential risks, shall further their cooperation". But he insists that "Such cooperation shall adhere to the principle of mutual respect and equality, to the effect of joint success" (Yang & Liu 2022). When interviewed, Niu Li at Beijing Foreign Studies University views the conclusion of the security pact between the Solomon Islands and China as a clear-cut reflection of the former's determination to maintain domestic stability and defend its national sovereignty by resisting the pressure from the United States and its allies like Australia[33].

Situated outside the second island chain, the Pacific islands have geopolitical significance, which is a crucial part of the US strategy to contain China as some American military scholars (e.g., James Holmes at the US Naval War College) claim. In this context, the location of the Pacific Islands between Australia, Japan and the United States is of military and strategic interest to both the traditional and new players in the region. When interviewed by the authors, Chen Hong at East China Normal University said that Washington and Canberra attempt to form a regional alliance to contain China by incorporating the South Pacific into its "Indo-Pacific Strategy", which, in his view, aims to deter China's rise. Guo Chunmei argues that the United States is trying to contain China with its "Indo-Pacific Strategy" and encircle China with the so-called first and second island chains. But China's footprints are ubiquitous in the region outside the second island chain, which shows that the US containment strategy can hardly work.

---

33 Niu Li, executive director of the Pacific Research Center at Beijing Foreign Studies University.

The US-China competition sheds light on the geostrategic drivers to the Chinese interests in the region that has been the traditional "sphere of influence" of the former colonial powers headed by the United States. China has increasingly realized the military significance of the PICs and increased its presence in the South Pacific by dispatching there much more vessels and warships than ever before for information collection, reciprocal visits and military trainings (Harding & Pohle 2022). Most recently, the modern Typ. 680 training ship *Qi Jiguang* of the People's Liberation Army Navy (PLAN) has been active in the South Pacific. It visited Indonesia, Papua New Guinea and Fiji in turn. The 163m-long *Qi Jiguang* conducted bilateral training in each country that it visited. It is designed to improve the operational adaptability and capability of Chinese naval officer cadets, strengthen maritime practical cooperation and mutual trust with the countries visited, and contribute to serving and building a maritime community with a shared future.

The PLA views such activities as to intensify the friendly military ties with their counterparts of the PICs. These activities provide the Chinese navy opportunities to improve its capability of deploying forces overseas far away from China and gain experience of modern warfare that the it lacks. It is one of China's military goals to develop a navy that has the capability of traveling beyond its coastal waters into the world's oceans (Poulin 2016). China has impressively boosted its naval power by increasing its projection of power in the Pacific to counterattack the US encirclement and containment. In the eyes of the United States, China is seeking to expand its overseas logistics and basing infrastructure to allow the PLA to project and sustain military power at greater distances. If realized, a global PLA military logistics network could disrupt US military operations as China's global military objectives evolve (Arthur 2023).

Apart from the aim to hone its navy's skills, China takes advantage of its naval presence in the South Pacific to display its rapid transformation from a regional military power to an international one with the capability of a military revenge on any intervention into its territorial disputes and containment of its rise. It is reported that China has recently approached Vanuatu and Tonga about setting up a military presence in the South Pacific in a significant move that could see the Chinese Navy sail warships in the "backyard" of the United States and its military "anchor", Australia, in response to their "freedom of navigation operations" in the South China Sea (Wroe 2018). The Chinese authorities consider the "free navigation operation" in the South China Sea and particularly in the Taiwan Strait as "provocative" and detrimental to China's security. The increased presence of Chinese warships and the planned naval bases in the South

Pacific reveals China's ambition to overcome the US military encirclement by breaking through the so-called "three island chains"[34].

Some international scholars, such as James Holmes (Holmes & Yoshihara 2007, p. 132) at the U.S. Naval War College, observe that the Chinese government has devoted substantial attention to its energy security dilemma posed by the United States. Apparently, China worries that 'American naval prowess will hold China's sea-dependent economy hostage in times of crisis' (e.g., Taiwan and the South China Sea). Some American military analysts (e.g., Holmes 2020) portray the island chains from Japan southward to Australia as a 'Great Wall in reverse' to militarily encircle China. This statement revives the Chinese collective memory of having been encircled by the US-led military alliances since 1949 when the People's Republic of China (PRC) was founded (Brown 2021, p. 32). In this context, the PICs are of increasingly military and strategic significance for China alongside its rise at the systemic (global) level and more so, in its competition with the United States, the solely remaining superpower, for regional dominance in the Pacific.

IR scholars inside and outside China are concerned with the likelihood of a sharp clash of interests between China and the United States as a consequence of their escalating competition in the Pacific. A growing number of Chinese foreign policy-makers and IR scholars (e.g., Zhang 2018, p. 159, Su et al 2005, p. 268) take the view that relations between China and the United States can never be good, but that they may become quite bad. As noted in *The Economist* (2010): 'Many Chinese scholars suggest that the [Chinese] government should give up the illusion of American partnership and face squarely the profound and inevitable strategic competition.' The ongoing trade war launched by former President Trump against China and his "Indo-Pacific Strategy", a perceived master plan to contain China's rise, seemingly justify the Chinese argument. It is in this context

34 The three island chains theory provides a lens through which to analyse PICs' relevance to China's military strategy. Countries in the northern Pacific – including Guam and the Northern Mariana Islands – sit along the second island chain. This 1950s United States-created theory has been an important driver of PLA Navy development. Successive PLA Navy leaders have developed different strategies to break through these island chains, including 'coastal defence' (1950-85), 'offshore waters defence' (1985-2008) and a 'combination of offshore waters defence and open-seas protection' (since 2008). The island chains have also appeared in PLA reports, a testimony to their military relevance. https://www.policyforum.net/chinas-military-engagement-with-pacific-island-countries/.

that the Chinese political leadership and military authorities have come to realize the magnitude of China-PICs strategic partnership as a counterweight against US attempts to contain China's rise.

The interests of China's involvement for the PICs

It is no denial that the primary motivations behind the Chinese vigorous involvement in the PICs are to gain economic as well as geopolitical and strategic interests as shown by the previous section of this chapter. The cooperation between China and the PICs has been focused on economic cooperation and trade, rather than on the US-imagined military expansion to pursue a military hegemony in the South Pacific (Brown et al 2019). Some Chinese academics (e.g., Lyu Guixia, Niu Li, and Cheng Hong) note that China's involvement in the region and its rapid growth of economic and infrastructural cooperation and trade with the PICs reveal a fact that China's increasing involvement in the region does not lack appreciation and support by the authorities and public in the PICs alike. There are many reasons for the political and commercial elites in the region to welcome China's increasing involvement in the region. The PICs like countries elsewhere are acutely aware of the significance of China's investment in local infrastructure and business, which means better commercial facilities and environment, more ensured economic growth, and more job opportunities. When interviewed by the press, Sogavare, former Prime Minister of the Solomon Islands, said frankly:

> We need to use the Belt and Road Initiative to share development experience, so as to transform the country's potential into prosperity"; we need to transcend the idea of using ideology and geopolitics to divide the world, stay united and keep exploring creative cooperation roads to narrow the gap between rich and poor (Yang et al 2023).

As a catch-up economy, China has been focused on economic growth over the last four decades since the late 1970s, which witnesses China's nominal GDP skyrocket to US$18 trillion in 2023 from less than US$300 billion in 1980, and its GDP per capita rapidly rose to US$12,800 in 2021 from less than US$200 in 1980 (Department of Foreign Affairs and Trade, Australia 2023). Some scholars (e.g., Ivanov et al 2023) are impressed by China's economic growth over the last decades and describe it as a "textbook example" of rapid development. It is no denial that China has gained rich experience in advancing economic growth, which helps the Chinese investors and enterprises find investment and commercial opportunities in the other parts of the developing world, such as Africa, Latin America, and Southeast Asia. China's vigorous involvement in the developing world is also driven by Deng Xiaoping's strategy of "South-South Cooperation". Deng, the late Chinese political leader, initiated the "South-South" strategy in the late 1980s when the Western countries withdrew their investment and business from Africa.

The large-scale withdrawal was primarily a result of the pessimistic conception of the African continent that was described by the *Economist Journal* (2000) as a "hopeless" continent. The Western withdrawal compelled the African countries to turn to China for investment and economic assistance, which has proven an invaluable opportunity for the Chinese involvement in Africa. The Chinese investors and enterprises have thereafter rushed into the African countries to seek business opportunities, and the two-way trade has now skyrocketed to US$282 billion in 2022, more than Africa's trade volume with the EU and the United States combined (Ministry of Commerce of China 2023). China's vast engagement with African countries since the late 1990s has contradicted 'the idea of international marginalization of Africa' and brought significant economic and political consequences for China, Africa and the rest of the world (Staden 2017, Tull 2008, p. 213). More importantly, Africa's economic prosperity and African elites' revenue are increasingly connected to China's economic involvement in Africa and China's ever-increasing engagement with and assistance to Africa. China's unprecedented presence and influence on the African continent, to some extent, reflects the appreciative attitudes of local elites towards China.

Similar to the African countries, the PICs, be it Tonga or PNG, need to take economic growth, employment and climate change as priorities on their national agenda whereas geopolitics and power competition are literally meaningless for them. As the policy analysts in the Lowy Institute note that the political leaders of the PICs refuse to choose between major powers, which they consider as detrimental to their countries' interest and regional peace. Instead, they would like to maintain cooperative relations with both the traditional and new players in the region by announcing their countries to be "friends to all and enemies to none". The strategy allows the PICs to leverage the big power competition for their political and national advantage, and maximize their interest arising from their interactions with the traditional and new players (Keen & Tidwell 2024). China is widely assumed a major aid donor to the PICs, but the scale of its economic and infrastructural involvement in the region obviously overshadows the amount of its aids to the PICs.

Xu Xiujun at China Academy of Social Sciences notes that the Chinese authorities have long emphasized a "win-win" cooperation as a two-way street benefiting both partners rather than a one-way street. It is in this context that China has redoubled its efforts in intensifying economic and infrastructural involvement in the PICs since the 21st century. Within less than two decades, China has rapidly risen as the largest trading, economic and infrastructural partner of some PICs, and become indispensable part of local economy (Zhao & Yu 2023, p. 162). A journalist from the Solomon Islands, wrote in *The New York Times* in June 2022 that "little remaining legacy of the US help can be seen in the South Pacific countries", adding that "meanwhile, Chinese-run businesses — construction, hardware, fishing, transport and other sectors — have quickly become part of the local economy" (Dorothy 2022). The United States has apparently felt the pressure by the Chinese economic involvement in the region and had recently hosted two summits in Washington with some PICs. The topics of the PICs-US summit included assistance in meeting the challenge arising from the climate change, facilitating a sustainable growth of local economy, opening embassies, promising new investment in infrastructure, improving connectivity through undersea cables, bettering Pacific Islands medical service, and cracking down the illegal fishery in the region (U.S. Department of State 2022).

The audience could easily find by the topics of the summits that the concerns of the PICs, such as the climate change, precede those of the United States (e.g., the hegemonic competition between the United States and China in the region). The topics on the summit agenda and the order itself are commendable as they primarily reflect the concerns of the Pacific Islands rather than those of the United States. Obviously, Washington heard the voice of the Pacific Islands and accepted the advice by her friends in Canberra and Wellington to be focused on climate change and economic growth, rather than the so-called hegemonic competition between the United States and China. The PICs though small in size and population have good command of diplomatic finesse at "achieving the best from both worlds" by balancing the traditional and rising powers, and playing them against each other, rather than rushing to side with either of them. Wallis (2017, p. 5) note that the smaller countries can play competing big powers against each other for their own benefit. As some policy analysts in the Lowy Institute note that on the one hand, the governments of the PICs generally adopt the strategy of "being friends to as many as possible when it comes to trade, and looking for opportunities to expand markets". To the PICs, all aid and assistance either from the traditional players or from the new ones are helpful for their countries. On the other hand, the PICs do not want to over-depend on either the traditional players or the new players. Rather, they would like to diversify and hedge relationships for maximum gain (Keen & Tidewell 2024).

According to the data released by the Lowy Institute based in Sydney, the traditional players, rather than China, have been the major donors to the PICs over the last decades since their independence, of which the United States and Australia have been the largest donors (Guardian 2013, McKenzie 2013). Notably, Australia had provided more than US$7 billion from 2006 to 2016, which accounted for half of Australia's international aids and one third of the aids received by the PICs. The Australian authorities have markedly reduced their international aids to the other parts of the developing world, such as Africa; but increased its aids to the PICs partially due to their efforts to counter China's increasing presence and influence in the South Pacific. It is reported that the Australian government has responded to accusations that Australia was neglecting its Pacific neighbors by increasing aid to the region by 50 percent. Australia provided $1.721 billion of development assistance to Pacific nations in 2020/21, a 56 percent nominal increase on 2012/13 aid spending in the region (Summers 2022). Out of the same motivation, other traditional players and especially the United States have also scaled up their attention to the South Pacific and increased their aid to the PICs. The attention and aid from either the new players or the traditional players to the PICs are obviously in the interest of the PICs.

The Biden administration announced in September 2023 that it planned to invest $1 billion a year in the 14 PICs, which is widely described as the South Pacific version of the "Marshall Plan" (The White House 2022). The reliance of the PICs on external aid provided by both the traditional and new powers is inescapable given their economic hardship and vulnerability to natural disasters. The aid flows and particularly the investment by both the traditional and new powers, to a certain degree, benefit the PICs as they open the access to new technology, markets, commerce, and opportunities. Equally importantly, the diversification of aid flows from the rising powers has provided a degree of political and strategic autonomy to the PICs, which has markedly enhanced the status of the PICs vis-à-vis the traditional players. The PICs are awaiting the US promised economic assistance worth $810 million and $130 million, which is earmarked for the programs to stymie the impacts of climate change, both of which are most unlikely to be materialized in view of the tightened control by the US Congress on international aid.

As well, the PICs are awaiting the US' promised infrastructural assistance, for instance, better internet service. The PICs' geographic isolation and distance from major markets lead to high costs of doing business and delivering public services. Huawei, a world-class Chinese telecommunication company, has been undertaking upgrade of the telecommunication network in some PICs, which led to jointed efforts made by the United States and Australia in blocking Huawei with their alternatives (Clark 2021). It is a typical case of the PICs to benefit from the big power competition, particularly between China and the United States and its military allies in the South Pacific as a number of IR scholars and local watcher note. The same is true of climate change. China's vigorous involvement in the PICs and its promised commitment to help combat the challenges from climate change partially show China's understanding of the PICs' concern with climate change.

No matter what the motivations behind China's promised commitment to climate change are, China has shown its concerns with the impacts of climate change, and promised to provide the PICs with aid and assistance. As some scientists note, the impact of climate change extends to alterations in ocean climate, sea level, acidity, water circulation, and ice distribution, directly affecting coastal ecosystems and the species essential for coastal economic benefits (Mimura 1999, p. 139). Alongside rising temperatures, climate change is also causing an increase in extreme and adverse weather events such as sea-level rise, floods, heatwaves, and droughts. The climate change has severely impacted the PICs' tourism, fisheries, seafood production, and maritime transport. The anticipated increase in the frequency and intensity of hydrological, meteorological, and climatological disasters, including floods, tropical cyclones, and drought, further exacerbates the vulnerability of the blue economy that the PICs have determined to pursue (Mcleod et al 2019).

China has indeed intensified cooperation with the PICs to help them address climate change since the early 2010s, such as to provide the PICs with meteorological services, disaster relief and clean energy (UN Development Program 2023). In addition to the provision of material assistance, China has provided training programs to the officials and scholars of the PICs on addressing the climate change as shown in the previous chapter. It is safe to say that China's commitment to climate change provides additional impetus to the United States in assisting the PICs to address the climate change, which is in the interest of the PICs in particular and the world in general. Some social elites in the PICs comment 'it has not gone unnoticed here that China has taken meaningful measures to reduce carbon emissions, while American and Australian politicians have dithered or, in the case of Australia, even made light of climate concerns in the Pacific' (Wickham 2022). President Donald Trump has for years "dishonestly" dismissed the existence and impact of climate change by claiming that "the oceans may rise, over the next 300 years, 1/100th of an inch" (Dale 2023). In reality, rising sea levels are expected to have devastating consequences not only for many seafront properties but for areas further inland – rendering some communities uninhabitable and others more dangerous, increasing the frequency and reach of flooding, making storms more destructive, and damaging infrastructure and ecosystems.

To counter China's cooperation with the PICs in the sphere of climate change, President Biden and the Pacific islands leaders gathered in September 2023 in Washington D.C. for a summit, many of whom have been critical of rich countries for being responsible for climate change and refusing to do enough to control climate change (Shea et al 2020, p. 91). The political leaders of the PICs claim that their countries have to bear the brunt of the impact of climate change and become the victims of climate change. No matter whether China's commitment to climate change is relevant or not, President Joe Biden told the political leaders from the PICs at their summit that he heard their warnings about the impact of climate change on their region, and that his administration is committed to helping them meet the challenge (Madhani 2023). Biden announced that his administration is requesting Congress to approve US$200 million in assistance for the region, including financing to help the Pacific islands prepare for climate and natural hazards, and improve infrastructure in the region. The stance of President Biden constitutes a contrast with that of former President Donald Trump who kept using inaccurate figures to minimize the threat of climate change and blamed the Paris Agreement as being "a terrible deal for" and "unfair to" the United States. In this sense, China's involvement in the PICs seemingly contributes to attracting the US attention to the climate change in the South Pacific region, and concerted efforts made by the international community in combating the challenges arising from climate change.

The climate change once again explains why the political leaders in the South Pacific refuse to take sides in the big power competition and adopt a stance of being "friends to all and enemy to none", which is apparently in the PICs' interest in maximizing their interest. Some politicians in the PICs (e.g., Sogavare, former prime minister of Solomon Islands, and Bainimarama, former prime minister of Fiji) publicly express their willingness to see China's expanding presence and influence in the region, and are willing to create a strategic partnership with China. These politicians are smart and know how to take advantage of big power competition to best serve their countries' interest. They obviously use China's expanding presence and influence in the region as a counterbalance to those of the US-headed traditional players in their countries and in the South Pacific, enabling them to 'shrug off sanctions' imposed on them by the traditional players like that on Fiji in the wake of a military coup in 2006 (Special Broadcasting Service 2019).

In a 'thinly veiled swipe at Australia and New Zealand', Frank Bainimarama, former Prime Minister of Fiji, embraces China as "a true friend" as the latter gives the PICs 'greater leverage over the traditional powers' in the region (Wallis et al 2023, p. 459). It is safe to say that the politicians of the PICs are playing the "China card" and employing the Chinese alternative to resist western pressure on their governments and re-shape their relations with the traditional players. It is no denial that China's increasing involvement and influence in the South Pacific helps the PICs politically and diplomatically re-gain attention of the traditional players to the much-neglected region after the end of the Cold War. The *New York Times* notes:

> At the very least, the United States and Australia have been forced to notice us again. They are pledging to be more involved, there are plans to reopen the U.S. embassy in Honiara, and Peace Corps volunteers are returning (Wickham 2022).

In the view of some Chinese policy analysts and scholars (e.g., Zhao Shaofeng, Chen Hong, Guo Chunmei and Lyu Guixia), the US neglect of the PICs in the early period of the post-Cold War era, to a large extent, reveals a fact that the US involvement in the region particularly after the Second World War is more relevant to its hegemonic competition with the former Soviet Union, rather than to the benefits of the PICs. Chen and Lyu argues that it is safe to conclude that the US "returning to the South Pacific" in the late 2010s has little to do with the benefits of the PICs, but much with its hegemonic competition with China. The United States and some other traditional players in the region have since scaled up their attention to the PICs by intensifying their presence in and assistance to the PICs thanks to China's fast-growing presence and influence in the region. It is good, anyway, for the PICs to re-gain attention of the United States and other traditional players as the region is absolutely in need of much attention and assistance of the rest of the world, particularly in terms of economic growth, environmental protection and climate change.

Joe Biden, the US President, announced to make a historic visit to PNG in early 2023, which was widely appreciated by the political leaders and general public alike in PNG and other PICs. President Biden would be the first sitting US president to visit the country in at least a century if he made it, and draw close US relations with the PICs. Unfortunately, Biden had to cut short his Asia trip and cancel the scheduled visit to PNG when he was confronting the US debt-ceiling crisis (Kuku 2023). The good news is that the Biden administration decided to re-open its embassy in the Solomon Islands after a 30-year absence. Moreover, a lengthening list of the US plans on opening embassies, such as in Tonga, Vanuatu and Kiribati was frequently reported. The last time for the United States to open a lot of embassies in the PICs was in the Cold War era when it confronted growing Soviet influence in the region. However, the United States soon closed a number of embassies in the South Pacific after the demise of the former Soviet Union, the US Cold War rival. For instance, the United States officially opened an embassy in the Solomon Islands in 1988 to reinforce its hegemony in the region, but closed the embassy in 1993 shortly after the disintegration of the former Soviet Union.

The PICs have thereafter been cast a cold eye in the US geopolitical spectrum in the following decades and failed to re-gain the US attention until China rapidly expands its presence and influence in the region, and rises as a leading economic and political partner for the PICs. It is not surprising in the context of China's rise that the US officials and media outlets are being quite explicit, noting it is all about China. This argument is plausible if a glance is cast upon the Solomon Islands that has long been neglected by the United States and other traditional players in the region since the end of the Cold War. Most recently, the country has suddenly become one of the "focuses" of the US foreign policy immediately after it signed a security pact with China, which is viewed by the United States as a "threat" to its long-term hegemony and its vested interest arising from the hegemony. The *New York Times* ran a lengthy article, hyping that "a Chinese security deal in the Pacific ripples through the world" as China will "have a foothold in an island chain that played a decisive role in World War Two" (Cave 2022).

A number of Chinese academics, such as Chen Hong and Lyu Guixia, comment: "Apparently, China's expanded security footprint in the region literally poses a "threat" to the US hegemony in the region, rather than to the security and interest of the PICs. As the former colonial powers, the United States and the traditional players can not represent the PICs. They owe much to the PICs." Chen Hong notes that high-ranking officials from the United States, Australia and Japan have thereafter rushed to the Solomon Islands, trying to force the government of Solomon Islands to annul the pact through both military threats and the suspension of economic aid. At noted, Daniel Kritenbrink, assistant secretary of state for East Asian and Pacific Affairs, threatens to take military action if China "establishes a base in Solomon Islands".

President Joe Biden nominated Laura Stone[35], a senior career diplomat with a background in China affairs to be US ambassador to the Marshall Islands, a move widely deemed by media and policy analysts as part of US efforts to contain China's expanded presence in the country (Reuters 2023a). The Marshall Islands is one of three PICs covered by the so-called Compacts of Free Association (COFA) with the United States (the other two are Palau and the Federated States of Micronesia), under which the United States gains exclusive access to huge strategic swathes of the Pacific (Yu 2023, p. 3). To create its military supremacy and hegemony, the United States detonated 67 nuclear bombs on, in and above the Marshall Islands Between 1946 and 1958 — vaporizing whole islands and exiling hundreds of people from their homes (Rust 2019). The United States has renewed agreements in 2024 with the Marshall Islands, Palau and the Federated States of Micronesia under which it remains exclusive access to huge swaths of the Pacific.

Take one more example of the new embassy in Tonga. Daniel J. Kritenbrink, US Assistant Secretary for East Asian and Pacific Affairs, explicitly acknowledged that 'this is part of efforts to step up US diplomatic presence in the Pacific region to counter China' (Reuters 2023b). To this end, the United States is continuing to engage with Vanuatu, Kiribati and others about opening proposed new embassies in those countries. When having a face-to-face conversation with the authors in late 2023, Latu at the National University of Samoa said that a number of high-level Western officials visited the South Pacific, a region that they had long neglected, after China's increasing involvement in the PICs and particularly after China concluded the security pact with the Solomon Islands. In his opinion, the best way to attract the attention of the western countries is not to beg them, but to create close ties with China.

Apart from much political and diplomatic attention, the PICs have re-gained much more military attention of the United States as a result of China's expanding footprints in the region. It is reported that the United States intends to draw the PICs into the Quad (a quadrilateral security mechanism composed by Australia, India, Japan, and the United States) (Grossman 2022b). The military mechanism dominated by the United States is widely conceived by regional watchers as an

35 Laura Stone was deputy coordinator at the State Department's Office of COVID Response and previously served as deputy assistant secretary for India, Nepal, Sri Lanka, Bangladesh, Bhutan and Maldives. A Chinese speaker, Stone also worked previously as coordinator of efforts to counter Chinese "malign economic influence".

instrument to implement the "Indo-Pacific" Strategy, and bring together the United States, Australia, India, Japan and others to contain the rise of China (Jaishankar 2021, Khurana, Gurpreet 2020, p. 2012). Zhao Shaofeng and Ni Peng note that the United States rushes to dispatch its para-military Coast Guard ship to patrol the South Pacific in the name of cracking down illegal fishery. It is no need to tell the Pacific Islanders why the United States is efficient with the dispatch of the Coast Guards to the region whereas not with the other issues, such as to address the challenges arising from climate change. The Pacific islanders are, in their own words, "smart elephants", not the "white elephants". To strengthen their military build-up in the region, the United States and Australia have sped up the construction of naval and air bases in the South Pacific to enhance their capabilities of power projection in the region. It is reported that the United States and Australia committed $175 million in 2021 to upgrade the Lombrum naval base on Manus Island, PNG, "in response to China's growing presence in the region" (Faa 2021). When works are finished, the base will be able to double the number of military personnel.

As mentioned previously, the Marshall Islands, Palau and the Federated States of Micronesia (FSM) are covered by the Compacts of Free Association (COFA) with the United States. By the compact, the United States takes responsibility for the defense of the three countries while gaining exclusive access to huge strategic swaths of the Pacific. Think the military and strategic significance of the three countries: the three countries sit across the shipping lanes connecting Asia to the North and South Americas. To control the three countries have long been a strategic priority of imperialist powers as the militarist Japan did in World War One and World War Two (Firth 2019, p. 32). The United States grabbed them from Japan in the waning period of WWII and the U.S. military forces have thereafter been stationed there, controlling the shipping routes connecting Asia to North and South Americas.

In the view of some Chinese academics, the U.S. presence in the three countries and beyond is military- and geopolitical-driven, and the United States enjoys military privilege to construct military facilities and operate military bases in the three countries and control the North Pacific (Yu 2023, p. 51). Of the military bases in the three countries, the Ronald Reagan Ballistic Missile Defense Test Site is of strategic significance. It is a world-class range and test facility for technologies involved in long-range missile testing, missile defense, and space domain awareness, is located in the Marshall Islands. It is well noted that the United States has around 300 military bases in the West Pacific, including those in PNG, Guam, Hawaii and Australia. In the eyes of Chen Hong and Zhao

Shaofeng, it is ironic that the United States has been keeping hyping up the "China threat" thesis and blames China to militarize the Pacific though it has a lot of military bases in the region whereas China has none.

The United States regards the renewal of the pacts as a key part of its efforts to push back against China's involvement and influence in the Pacific. A final deal with the Marshall Islands had been held up by disagreement over how to address the legacy of historical mass of the U.S. nuclear testing. The Marshall Islanders are still plagued by health and environmental effects from 67 U.S. nuclear bomb tests from 1946 to 1958, which included "Castle Bravo" at Bikini Atoll - the largest U.S. bomb ever detonated (Miller 2010, p. 134). The nuclear tests yielded as much radiation as 1.6 Hiroshima bombings every day for more than a decade. The United States not only detonated the bulk of its weapons tests but also conducted a dozen biological weapons tests, and dumped 130 tons of soil from an irradiated Nevada testing site (Rust 2019). It then deposited the most lethal debris and soil into a concrete dome that has recently been at risk of collapsing from rising seas and other effects of climate change. Pohle blames the United States for 'subjecting the Marshallese people to scientific study without their consent; destroyed their health and their environment; lied to them about their radiation exposure; evacuated them too late, or not at all; knowingly resettled them on contaminated land; and displaced them – often indefinitely – from their homes' (Pohle 2024).

The Marshall Islanders have to date continued to suffer from their legacy, including high cancer rates, environmental degradation, and cultural dislocation, which the U.S. government has done little to redress. The government of Marshall Islands has long requested the U.S. government for help, but the latter declines, saying the dome is on Marshallese land and therefore the responsibility of the Marshallese government. Many arms-control, environmental and other activist groups urged the Biden administration to formally apologize to the Marshall Islands and provide help and fair compensation (Brunnstrom & Martina 2023). Some regional watchers argue that as Washington seeks to reengage in the Pacific during a new Cold War, nuclear justice has become even more essential for positive relations with the Marshall Islands and improving U.S. standing in the region (Pohle 2024).

Probably, the growing competition between the United States and China will force Washington to alter its stance on the issue and help the Marshall Islanders to get U.S. apology and fair compensation. Ironically, China's expanding presence and influence in the Pacific islands has, to a large extent, helped the PICs regain attention from the United States and other traditional players, bringing them respect for sovereignty and self-determination, as well as investment, economic and infrastructural development, and aids for social development and climate change. Not surprisingly, China's expanding presence in the South Pacific region is meant to seek interest economically, politically and militarily as other players do. It has no intention to bring back the attention of the traditional players to the region, which will most likely undermine its interest and tighten regional competition. However, it is well noted that China's involvement in the region and the "back to the region" by the United States and other traditional players, to some extent, benefit the PICs as intimated above.

Some political leaders of the PICs may appreciate China's involvement in the region and assistance to their countries, which is usually attached no political strings, such as human rights and good governance. This explains why some international watchers assert that the Chinese economic involvement in and aids to the PICs more often than not empower some authoritative governments and corrupt politicians (Dayant et al 2023). This also explains why some social activists worry about the inter-governmental deals between China and the PICs, and demand more transparency. Probably this partially explains why Moisés Naím (2009) describes China's aid as a 'rogue aid' and Joseph Nye (2013) who coins the term of "soft power" denies China's "soft power" in the developing world. Over the last decades since China's vigorous involvement in the developing world, China has been preoccupied with undertaking economic cooperation and trade with the developing countries, including the PICs, and particularly with regional political and commercial elites regardless of human rights, social morality, or justice — China's strategy of "non-interference in their internal affairs".

But from China's own experiences over the past decades since Deng Xiaoping launched the market reform in the late 1970s, it is safe to conclude that good governance, respect for human rights and environmental protection are vital to the long-term economic growth and social progress (Yu 2018, p. 491). The aims of China's involvement in the PICs since the beginning of the 21st century have been not merely to reap economic benefits, but also strategic benefits deriving from China's "soft" power with a view to elevating China's status at the systemic (global) and sub-systemic (regional) levels. Some international IR scholars argue that China's "non-interference" strategy may become 'an obstacle' when it concerns the question of Chinese soft power that presumably constitutes alongside China's increasing "hard" power the basis for China's rise at global level (Jafrani 2012).

Concluding remarks

The chapter examines the economic and geopolitical interests for China and for the PICs arising from the BRI, and China's extended presence in and intensified cooperation with the PICs. The main argument of the chapter is that China's expanding involvement in the South Pacific and its efforts in creating a strategic partnership with the PICs demonstrate the country's desire to intensify its economic cooperation and political relations with the PICs. A closer look into China's interests sheds light on the potential shape of future sub-regional order, and illustrates the prospective value of a much-neglected region (the South Pacific) by the United States. China's BRI and its economic involvement in the PICs have reaped economic and political benefits by creating close relations of collaboration particularly with political and commercial elites in the PICs. Strategically, China's increasing involvement in the South Pacific, the traditional "backyard" of the United States and Australia, the sheriff and deputy sheriff in the Pacific, has served its interest of breaking through the U.S. containment and encirclement by virtue of the Second islands chain.

China has kept in mind two interconnected objectives whilst pursuing its strategic partnership with the PICs: one is the commitment to China's economic growth, which was identified by Deng Xiaoping as the country's paramount task in the next 100 years; the other, the long-cherished dream of restoring China's past glory of *fuqiang* (wealth and power) by enhancing its 'hard' and 'soft' power, and boosting its rise at the systemic (global) level. Two noteworthy points in the discussion above emerge. One is China's adoption of economic diplomacy as a means of advancing its partnerships with the PICs. China's adoption of economic diplomacy is first due to China's strategy of economic priority and second to an assumption prevailing in the Chinese IR narratives. The narratives predict that the states that have neither territorial disputes nor strategic competition with China will, in view of the enormous economic benefits derived from their economic cooperation and trade with China, accept the basic premise of its economic strategy: China's rise is not a threat, but an opportunity to gain wealth and prosperity. This is likely to help China gain more 'soft' power in and leverage over its economic partners, and thereby help it rise in the global power hierarchy.

The other noteworthy point is that the PICs though small in size and population have long been good at playing big games both in the Cold War and post-Cold War eras, and maximizing their interest by achieving "the best from both worlds" through the strategy of balancing the big powers instead of siding with either of them. Some politicians and political elites in the Pacific islands are aware of the fact that the attention of the traditional players to the PICs as well as their assistance will surely diminish if the China's presence and influence in the region disappear. However, as they enjoy increasing attention from the traditional and new powers, the PICs need to avoid the risk that the influx of investment and aid may bring the converse effects of excessive of external influence. They may result in over-exploitation of resources, excessive debt dependence and a destruction of the fragile ecology in the region. The PICs also need to ensure that the region does not become the site of great power contestation, which is obviously detrimental to their interest, and the peace and stability in the region and beyond.

References

Arthur, Gordon 2023, 'Chinese Navy Continues To Fly The Red Flag In The South Pacific', *Naval News*, 31 December, https://www.navalnews.com/naval-news/2023/12/chinese-navy-continues-to-fly-the-red-flag-in-the-south-pacific/

Backman, M. 2008, *Asia Future Shock: Business Crisis and Opportunity in the Coming Years*, Palgrave Macmillan: New York.

Birnbaum, Michael and Pannett, Rachel 2023, 'U.S. and China battle for influence in Pacific Island nations', *The Washington Post*, 26 July, https://www.washingtonpost.com/national-security/2023/07/25/blinken-tonga-biden-china-pacific-islands/.

Brunnstrom, David and Martina, Michael 2023, 'Activists urge U.S. apology, fair compensation, for U.S. Pacific nuclear testing', Reuters, 11 January, https://www.reuters.com/world/activists-urge-us-apology-fair-compensation-us-pacific-nuclear-testing-2023-01-10/.

Blasko, Dennis 2016, *China's Contribution to Peacekeeping Operation: Understanding the Numbers*, Jamestown Foundation, 5 December, https://www.refworld.org/docid/584ab9434.html.

Brown, Gordon 2021, Seven Ways to Change the World: How To Fix The Most Pressing Problems We Face, Simon & Schuster: London.

Brown, Robert, Lackey, Blake and Forester, Brian 2019, 'Competing with China for a Free and Open Indo-Pacific', *Military Review*, September/October, https://www.armyupress.army.mil/Journals/Military-Review/English-Edition-Archives/September-October-2019/Brown-Indo-Pacific/.

Canuto, Otaviano 2019, 'How Chinese Investment in Latin America Is Changing', *Americas Quarterly*, 12 March, https://www.americasquarterly.org/article/how-chinese-investment-in-latin-america-is-changing/.

Carbone, Maurizio 2012, 'European Union and China's rise in Africa', Taylor, Ian; Kopinski, Dominik and Polus, Andrzej (eds), *China's Rise in Africa: Perspectives on a Developing Connection*, Routledge: New York, p. 287.

Cave, Damien 2022, 'Why a Chinese Security Deal in the Pacific Could Ripple Through the World', *New York Times*, 20 April, https://www.nytimes.com/2022/04/20/world/australia/china-solomon-islands-security-pact.html.

China National Bureau of Statistics 2020, the monthly income of over 610 million people less than 1000RMB, China Central TV Station, 15 June, https://news.cctv.com/2020/06/15/ARTIl2cVjRx3y8y0dEnNxJh5200615.shtml.

China State Administration of Foreign Exchange 2019, Spokesman of the Administration interviewed by Media on China's foreign reserves, 6 October, http://www.safe.gov.cn/safe/2019/1006/14286.html.

Chun, Z. 2018, 'China-Africa Cooperative Partnership for Peace and Security', Alden, C., Alao, A., Chun, Z., Barber, L. (eds), *China and Africa*, Palgrave Macmillan, Cham.

Clark, Emily 2021, 'Undersea cables bring Pacific nations online, but there are concerns China is trying to tap in', Australian Broadcasting Company, 24 July, https://www.abc.net.au/news/2021-07-24/china-huawei-build-png-cable-that-connects-to-sydney/100249922.

Coleman, Katharina and Job, Brian L 2021, 'How Africa and China may shape UN peacekeeping beyond the liberal international order', *International Affairs*, Vol. 97, Issue 5, pp. 1451-1468.

Dale, Daniel 2023, 'Fact check: Trump's latest false climate figure is off by more than 1,000 times', CNN news, 24 April, https://edition.cnn.com/2023/04/24/politics/fact-check-trump-sea-levels-ocean-climate-change/index.html.

Dayant, Alexandre, Keen, Meg and Rajah, Roland 2023, Chinese aid to the Pacific: decreasing, but not disappearing, Lowy Institute, 25 January, https://www.lowyinstitute.org/the-interpreter/chinese-aid-pacific-decreasing-not-disappearing.

Deng, Xiaoping 1993, *Selected Deng Xiaoping works* (Volume 3), People's Publishing, Beijing, p. 380.

Department of Foreign Affairs and Trade, Australia 2023, *The China Fact Sheet*, November, https://www.dfat.gov.au/sites/default/files/chin-cef.pdf.

Economist 2000, 'Africa: the hopeless continent', 13 May, p. 17.

Economist 2010, 'Less biding and hiding', 2 December, <http://www.economist.com/node/17601475?story_id=17601475&CFID=163907680&CFTOKEN=58532039>.

Economist (2015) Made in China. 14 March, http://www.economist.com/news/leaders/21646204-asias-dominance-manufacturing-will-endure-will-make-development-harder-others-made.

Embassy of the PRC in the Solomon Islands 2022, China and the Solomon Islands concluded agreement on bilateral security cooperation, 31 March, http://sb.china-embassy.gov.cn/chn/sgxw/202203/t20220331_10658139.htm.

Faa, Marian 2021, 'Australian Defence Force to fund $175 million major upgrade for Papua New Guinea's naval base on Manus Island', Australian Broadcasting Company, 15 June, https://www.abc.net.au/news/2021-06-15/major-naval-base-on-png-manus-island-lombrum-adf/100216040.

Fan Lingzhi and Shan, Jie 2021, 'GT investigates: Funding opposition, cultivating influence through cult - US, Taiwan island lurk in shadows of Solomon Islands riots', *The Global Times*, 28 November, https://www.globaltimes.cn/page/202111/1240115.shtml

Ferguson, Niall 2010, 'In China's orbit', *Wall Street Journal*, 18 November, http://online.wsj.com/article/SB10001424052748704104104575622531909154228.html?KEYWORDS=in+china%27s+orbit, accessed 6 Aug. 2015.

Firth, S. 2019, 'The Military and Security in the Pacific Islands Past and Present', In: Ratuva, S., Compel, R., Aguilar, S. (eds), *Guns & Roses: Comparative Civil-Military Relations in the Changing Security Environment*, Palgrave Macmillan, Singapore.

Friedrichs, Jörg 2019, 'Explaining China's popularity in the Middle East and Africa', *Journal of Third World Quarterly*, Vol. 40, Issue 9, pp. 1634-1654.

Fukuyama, F. 1992, *The end of history and the last man*, Hamilton, London, p. 10.

Fujita, Kimio 1993, 'China and its Asian neighbors: a Japanese perspective', Kau, Michael Ying-Mao and Marsh, Susan (eds), *China in the era of Deng Xiaoping: a decade of reform*, M.E. Sharp: New York, p. 464.

Global Times, 'Hegemonic and colonist mentality behind Australia's threats to invade Solomon Islands', 28 March, https://www.globaltimes.cn/page/202203/1256947.shtml.

Grossman, Derek 2022a, China's gambit in the Pacific: implications for the United States and its allies and partners, the Rand, August, https://www.rand.org/pubs/testimonies/CTA2198-1.html.

Grossman, Derek 2022b, *America's Pacific Island Summit: The Good, the Bad, and the Ugly*, Rand, 7 November, https://www.rand.org/pubs/commentary/2022/11/americas-pacific-island-summit-the-good-the-bad-and.html.

Guardian, 'Australia's foreign aid spending: how much and where? – get the data' 2013, 22 August, https://www.theguardian.com/global-development/datablog/2013/aug/22/australia-foreign-aid-spending-data.

Hammond, Joseph, 2023, 'China's Security Agreement with the Solomon Islands: Wider Implications for Geopolitics in the South Pacific', *Journal of Pacific Affairs*, 15 November, https://www.airuniversity.af.edu/JIPA/Display/Article/3588465/chinas-security-agreement-with-the-solomon-islands-wider-implications-for-geopo/.

Harding, Brian and Pohle, Camilla 2022, 'China's Search for a Permanent Military Presence in the Pacific Islands', 21 July, United States Institute of Peace, https://www.usip.org/publications/2022/07/chinas-search-permanent-military-presence-pacific-islands.

Holmes, James 2020, 'Great Wall In Reverse: To Take Down China, Look To The Pacific's Many Islands', *National Interest*, 11 August, https://nationalinterest.org/blog/reboot/great-wall-reverse-take-down-china-look-pacifics-many-islands-166628.

Holmes, James R. and Yoshihara, Toshi 2007, Chinese Naval Strategy in the 21st Century: The Turn to Mahan, Routledge: New York.

Information Office of the State Council of the PRC 2013, *the White Paper on China-Africa Economic and Trade Cooperation*, IOSC, August, Beijing.

Iroga, Robert 2022, 'Gold Ridge Mine to open tomorrow (Tuesday)', *Solomon Business Magazine*, 28 November, https://sbm.sb/gold-ridge-mine-to-open-tomorrow-tuesday/.

Ivanov, P., Duan, K., & Werner, R. 2023, 'Deciphering the Chinese Economic Miracle: The Resolution of an Age-Old Economists' Debate — and its Central Role in Rapid Economic Development', *Review of Political Economy*, https://doi.org/10.1080/09538259.2023.2180200.

Jafrani, N. 2012, *China's growing role in Africa*, Carnegie endowment for international peace, Washington D.C., 9 February, <http://carnegieendowment.org/ieb/2012/02/09/china-s-growing-role-in-africa-myths-and-facts/9j5q>.

Jaishankar, Dhruva and Madan, Tanvi 2021, 'How the Quad Can Match the Hype: It's the Best Hope for Balancing China in the Indo-Pacific', *Foreign Affairs*, 15 April, https://www.foreignaffairs.com/articles/united-states/2021-04-15/how-quad-can-match-hype.

Jones, Bruce 2023, TEMPERATURES RISING: THE STRUGGLE FOR BASES AND ACCESS IN THE PACIFIC ISLANDS, Foreign Policy, Brookings, February, https://www.brookings.edu/wp-content/uploads/2023/02/FP_20230207_pacific_basing_jones.pdf.

Keen, Meg and Tidwell, Alan 2024, *Geopolitics in the Pacific Islands: Playing for advantage*, Lowy Institute, 31 January, https://www.lowyinstitute.org/publications/geopolitics-pacific-islands-playing-advantage

Khurana, Gurpreet 2020, 'South China Sea: geopolitical connectedness to the Indian Ocean', Buszynski, Leszek and Hai, Thanh (eds), The South China Sea: From a Regional Maritime Dispute to Geo-Strategic Competition, Routledge: London, p. 2012.

Kirkwood, Jamieson and Chaisse, Julien 2020, 'Chinese Puzzle: Anatomy of the (Invisible) Belt and Road Investment Treaty', *Journal of International Economic Law*, No. 23, pp. 245-269.

Kuku, Rebecca 2023, 'Disappointment in Papua New Guinea after Biden cancels first visit by a U.S. leader', *The Guardian*, 17 May, https://www.theguardian.com/world/2023/may/17/disappointment-in-papua-new-guinea-after-biden-cancels-first-visit-by-a-us-leader.

Li, Qiang 2023, *Following the Vision of a Community with a Shared Future for Mankind and Bringing More Certainty to World Peace and Development*, Premier Li Qiang's speech at the Boao Forum for Asia Annual Conference 2023, Information Office of the PRC, 30 March, http://english.scio.gov.cn/topnews/2023-04/01/content_85206125.htm.

Liu, Huaqiu 1997, 'Zhong guo shi zhong bu yu de feng xing du li zi zhu de he ping wai jiao zheng ce (China adheres to the independent foreign policy of peace)', *Journal of Qiushi*, No. 23, pp. 2-9.

Mabera, F. 2021, 'China's Evolving Approach to the African Peace and Security Agenda: Rationale, Trends and Implications', Mthembu, P. and Mabera, F. (eds), *Africa-China Cooperation*, International Political Economy Series. Palgrave Macmillan, Cham.

Madhani, Aamer 2023, Biden tells Pacific islands leaders he hears their warnings about climate change and is committed to act, 25 September, https://www.pbs.org/newshour/world/biden-tells-pacific-islands-leaders-he-hears-their-warnings-about-climate-change-and-is-committed-to-act.

McGuirk, Rod 2021, 'Solomon Islands PM blames 'foreign powers' for unrest after Australia sends troops', *The Sydney Morning Herald*, 26 November, https://www.smh.com.au/world/oceania/solomon-islands-pm-blames-foreign-powers-as-unrest-grows-20211126-p59ce9.html

McKenzie, Joe 2013, 'Australia should fund foreign aid', ABC news, 12 September, http://www.abc.net.au/news/2013-09-12/mckenzie-australia27s-aid-budget/4951302.

Mcleod, Elizabeth; Bruton-Adams, Mae and Förster, Johannes et al 2019, 'Lessons From the Pacific Islands – Adapting to Climate Change by Supporting Social and Ecological Resilience', *Marine Science*, Vol. 18, No. 1, https://www.frontiersin.org/journals/marine-science/articles/10.3389/fmars.2019.00289/full.

McVeigh, Karen 2023, 'James Cameron supports deep-sea mining. Scientists say it's a huge risk. Who's right?', *Guardian*, 27 July, https://www.theguardian.com/environment/2023/jul/27/james-cameron-supports-deep-sea-mining-activists-say-its-a-disaster-whos-right.

Miller, Michael 2022, 'China's growing reach is transforming a Pacific island chain', *The Washington Post*, 11 August, https://www.washingtonpost.com/world/2022/08/11/solomon-islands-china-australia-pacific/.

Miller, Frederic P. Vandome, Agnes F., McBrewster, John 2010, *Castle Bravo*, VDM Publishing: *Saarbrücken*.

Mimura, Nobuo 1999, 'Vulnerability of island countries in the South Pacific to sea level rise and climate change', *Climate Research*, Vol. 12, No. 2/3, pp. 137-143.

Ministry of Commerce of China 2023, the statistics of China-Africa economic cooperation and trade, 25 July, http://xyf.mofcom.gov.cn/article/tj/zh/202307/20230703423421.shtml

Ministry of Foreign Affairs of the PRC 2022, The Second Foreign Ministers' meeting between China and the PICs, 30 May, http://new.fmprc.gov.cn/wjbzhd/202205/t20220530_10694549.shtml.

Ministry of Foreign Affairs of the PRC 2023a, China's relations with Palau, October, https://www.mfa.gov.cn/web/gjhdq_676201/gj_676203/dyz_681240/1206_681666/sbgx_681670/.

Ministry of Foreign Affairs of the PRC 2023b, China's relations with Pacific Island Countries, October, https://www.mfa.gov.cn/web/gjhdq_676201/gj_676203/dyz_681240/1206_681666/sbgx_681670/.

Morgan, Wesley 2021, 'Ripple Effect: the cost of our Pacific neglect', *Australian Foreign Affairs*, July, https://www.australianforeignaffairs.com/articles/extract/2021/08/ripple-effect.

Myers, Lucas, 2022, 'Don't Overreact to China's Solomon Islands Plans', Foreign Policy, 13 June, https://foreignpolicy.com/2022/06/13/china-solomon-islands-asia-pacific-security/.

Naím, M. 2007, 'Rogue Aid', *Foreign Policy*, 14 February, <http://www.foreignpolicy.com/articles/2007/02/14/rogue_aid>.

Nye, J. 2013, 'What China and Russia Don't Get About Soft Power', *Foreign Policy*, 29 April, <http://www.foreignpolicy.com/articles/2013/04/29/what_china_and_russia_don_t_get_about_soft_power>.

Observatory of Economic Complexity (OEC) 2023a, Palau and the United States, December, https://oec.world/en/profile/bilateral-country/plw/partner/usa.

Observatory of Economic Complexity (OEC) 2023b, The United States and the Marshall Islands, October, https://oec.world/en/profile/bilateral-country/usa/partner/mhl.

Pan, X., Wang, L., Dai, J., Zhang, Q., Peng, T. and Chen, W. 2020, 'Analysis of China's oil and gas consumption under different scenarios toward 2050: An integrated modeling', *Energy*, Vol. 195, No. 15, pp. 1-10.

Panda, Ankit 2018, 'One More Down, 19 to Go: Beijing's Diplomatic Isolation of', Diplomat, 19 May, viewed 7 May 2019, https://thediplomat.com/2018/05/one-more-down-19-to-go-beijings-diplomatic-isolation-of-taipei-continues/.

Peterson, Michael and Tawake, Akuila 2017, Deep sea minerals in the Pacific, *State, Society and Governance in Melanesia*, September, http://dpa.bellschool.anu.edu.au/sites/default/files/publications/attachments/2017-05/ib_2017_9_pettersontawake_0.pdf.

Pohle, Camilla 2024, 'Ashes of Death': The Marshall Islands Is Still Seeking Justice for U.S. Nuclear Tests', *Diplomat*, 1 March, https://thediplomat.com/2024/03/ashes-of-death-the-marshall-islands-is-still-seeking-justice-for-us-nuclear-tests/.

Poulin, Andrew 2016, 'Going Blue: The Transformation of China's Navy', *Diplomat*, 15 April, <http://thediplomat.com/2016/04/going-blue-the-transformation-of-chinas-navy/>.

Pryke, Jonathan 2021, 'Solomon Islands unrest not helped by foreign powers behaving badly', *Australian Financial Review*, 26 November, https://www.afr.com/world/pacific/solomon-islands-unrest-not-helped-by-foreign-powers-behaving-badly-20211126-p59ckv.

Reuters 2023a, Biden nominates China specialist to be ambassador to strategic Marshall Islands, 12 July, https://www.reuters.com/world/biden-nominates-china-specialist-be-ambassador-strategic-marshall-islands-2023-07-11/.

Reuters 2023b, the United States opens embassy in Tonga in new pushback against China in Pacific, 10 May, https://www.reuters.com/world/us-opens-embassy-tonga-new-pushback-against-china-pacific-2023-05-09/.

Rich, T. S., & Banerjee, V. 2015, 'Running Out of Time? The Evolution of Taiwan's Relations in Africa', *Journal of Current Chinese Affairs*, Vol. 44, No. 1, pp. 141-161.

Rising, David and McGuirk, Rod 2021, 'Solomon Islands leader blames foreign powers for unrest', *Los Angeles Times*, 25 November, https://www.latimes.com/world-nation/story/2021-11-25/solomon-islands-leader-blames-foreign-powers-for-unrest.

Rotberg, R. 2008, 'China's quest for resources, opportunities and influence in Africa', Rotberg, R. eds, China Into Africa: Trade, Aid, and Influence, Brookings Institution Press: Baltimore.

Rust, Susanne 2019, 'How the U.S. betrayed the Marshall Islands, kindling the next nuclear disaster', *Los Angeles Times*, 10 November, https://www.latimes.com/projects/marshall-islands-nuclear-testing-sea-level-rise/.

Seneviratne, Kalinga 2024, 'Guest Opinion: For South Pacific, China is opportunity, not threat', *Malaysia Sun*, 9 August, https://www.malaysiasun.com/news/274487645/guest-opinion-for-south-pacific-china-is-opportunity-not-threat.

Shea, M.M., Painter, J. & Osaka, S. 2020, 'Representations of Pacific Islands and climate change in the United States, UK, and Australian newspaper reporting', *Climatic Change*, Vol. 161, No. 2, pp. 89-108.

Sheldon-Duplaix, Alexandre 2016, 'Beyond the China Seas: Will China become a global "Sea Power"?', China Perspectives, No. 3, pp. 43-52.

Shinn, David and Eisenman, Joshua 2023, *China's Relations with Africa: A New Era of Strategic Engagement*, Columbia University Press: New York.

Silver, Laura; Devlin, Kat and Huang, Christine 2019, *People around the globe are divided in their opinions of China*, Pew Research Center, 5 December, https://www.pewresearch.org/fact-tank/2019/12/05/people-around-the-globe-are-divided-in-their-opinions-of-china/.

Song, Xiuju and Ye, Shengxuan 2016, 'The BRI and China-PICs cooperation', *Contemporary World*, No. 8, pp. 69-72.

Special Broadcasting Service 2019, 'Solomon Islands switch diplomatic ties from Taiwan to China', SBS news, 16 September, https://www.sbs.com.au/news/solomon-islands-switch-diplomatic-ties-from-taiwan-to-china.

Staden, Cobus Van 2017, 'Here's How China Is Changing Africa's Future: moving away from Western influence, Africa is already getting a glimpse of a different future', *Huffington Post*, 30 August, https://www.huffingtonpost.com/entry/china-africa-bor_us_59a4372ce4b05710aa5dcd02.

Information Office of the State Council of the PRC 2021, China urges the United States to stop supporting 'Taiwan independence' separatist forces, 5 October, http://english.scio.gov.cn/pressroom/2021-10/05/content_77791111.htm.

Su, Ge; Jin, Canrong; Fu, Chengli; Zhang, Tuosheng and Yan, Xuetong 2005, 'how does the Bush Administration deal with China?', Liu, Jiangyong and Song, Nianshen (ed), *World and China*, Tsinghua Uversity Press: Beijing, p. 267.

Sui, Sophia and Yu, Lei 2023a, 'China-Russia Strategic Partnership: the strategic fulcrum of China's rise?', *International Journal* (SSCI), 2023, Vol. 79, No. 1, pp. 217-239.

Sui, Sophia and Yu, Lei 2023b, 'China-Russia Strategic Partnership and the Oil and Gas Collaboration', *Innovation: The European Journal of Social Science Research*, https://doi.org/10.1080/13511610.2023.2289827.

Sui, Sophia and Yu, Lei 2024, 'Ontological Security in China–Pacific Islands Countries (PICs) Geopolitics', *Journal of Island and Marine*, Vol. 1, No. 1, pp. 1-23. http://islandandmarinestudies.press/10-59711-jims-11-110010/#:~:text=The%20article%20concludes%20that%20China%E2% 80%99s%20ontological%20security%20has.

Summers, William 2022, 'Did the Morrison government increase Pacific aid 50 per cent?', Australian Associated Press, 1 April, https://www.aap.com.au/factcheck/did-the-morrison-government-increase-pacific-aid-50-per-cent/

Szadziewski, Henryk 2021, 'A Search for Coherence: The Belt and Road Initiative in the Pacific Islands', *The China Alternative: Changing Regional Order in the Pacific Islands*, Australia National University Press.

The White House 2022, *FACT SHEET: Roadmap for a 21st-Century U.S.-Pacific Island Partnership.* 29 September, https://www.whitehouse.gov/briefing-room/statements-releases/2022/09/29/fact-sheet-roadmap-for-a-21st-century-u-s-pacific-island-partnership/.

Tull, D. 2008, 'the political consequence of China's return to Africa', Alden, C., Large, D. and Oliveira, R.S., ed, *China Returns to Africa: a rising power and a continent embrace*, Columbia University Press: New York.

UN Development Program 2023, *China's policy and practice: the report on international cooperation on climate change*, July, https://www.undp.org/sites/g/files/zskgke326/files/2023-08/0821_zhongguoqihouguojifazhanhezuoyanjiucn1_0.pdf

U.S. Department of State 2022, U.S.-Pacific Island Country Summit, 28 September, https://www.state.gov/u-s-pacific-islands-country-summit/

U.S. Department of Defense 2023, Military and security deployments involving the PRC, annual report to Congress, March, https://media.defense.gov/2023/Oct/19/2003323409/-1/-1/1/2023-MILITARY-AND-SECURITY-DEVELOPMENTS-INVOLVING-THE-PEOPLES-REPUBLIC-OF-CHINA.PDF.

Wallis, Joanne 2017, Crowded and Complex: the Changing Geopolitics of the South Pacific, Barton: Australian Strategic Policy Institute.

Wallis, Joanne, Xie, Geyi, Waqavakatoga, William, Habru, Priestley, Koro, Maima 2023, Ordering the Islands? Pacific Responses to China's Strategic Narratives, *The Chinese Journal of International Politics*, Volume 16, Issue 4, pp. 457-481.

Wang, J. 2015, 10 industrial sectors of the China Manufacturing 2025 strategy, *China Daily*, 30 March, http://www.chinadaily.com.cn/business/2015-03/30/content_19946139_1.htm.

Wang, Xinhua 2007, 'The American-Soviet cold war and the collapse of Soviet economy', *Journal of Ningxia University*, Vol. 29, No. 6, pp. 112-115.

Ward, Bob 2018, President Trump's fake news about climate change, London School of Economics and Political Science, 30 January, https://www.lse.ac.uk/granthaminstitute/news/president-trump-fake-news-climate-change/

Wasuka, Evan and Bahmani, Nazli 2020, 'The United States denies geopolitical motives are behind a massive aid increase to the Solomon Islands' Malaita province', Australian Broadcasting Company, 16 October, https://www.abc.net.au/news/2020-10-16/us-aid-increase-solomon-islands-china-independence-malaita/12765310.

Wickham, Dorothy 2022, 'Can You Blame Poor Countries Like Mine for Turning to China?' *The New York Times*, 27 June, https://www.nytimes.com/2022/06/27/opinion/international-world/china-us-solomon.html.

Wickham, Dorothy 2022b, 'Australia rejects claim its security forces in Solomon Islands were told not to protect Chinese-built buildings', *The Guardians*, 21 April, https://www.theguardian.com/world/2022/apr/21/australia-rejects-claim-its-security-forces-in-solomon-islands-were-told-not-to-protect-chinese-built-buildings.

Wroe, David 2018, 'China eyes Vanuatu military base in plan with global ramifications', *The Sydney Morning Herald*, 9 April, https://www.smh.com.au/politics/federal/china-eyes-vanuatu-military-base-in-plan-with-global-ramifications-20180409-p4z8j9.html.

Xu, Quan 2022, 'Rethinking Investment Treaties for Sustainable Development: From the 'New Delhi Declaration, Principles to Modern Investment, Law & Policy', *Asian Journal of WTO & International Health Law and Policy*, Vol. 17, No. 2, pp. 405-448.

Yang, Sheng and Liu, Caiyu 2022, 'China launches diplomatic activities to boost ties with South Pacific islands; 'U.S., Australian containment strategy doomed to fail', The Global Times, 24 May, https://www.globaltimes.cn/page/202205/1266449.shtml.

Yang, Sheng, Zhao, Yusha and Zhang, Changyue 2023, 'China, Solomon Islands ink comprehensive strategic partnership', *The Global Times*, 10 July, https://www.globaltimes.cn/page/202307/1294095.shtml.

Yu, Le 2018, 'China's expanding security involvement in Africa: a pillar for 'China-Africa community of common destiny', *Global Policy*, Vol. 9, Issue 4, pp. 489-500.

Yu, Lei 2020a, 'Contending Chinese Perspectives on China-Russia Military Partnership', *Communist and Post-Communist Studies*, Vol. 53, No. 4, pp. 239-258.

Yu, Lei 2020b, 'China-Pacific Island Countries Strategic Partnership: China's strategy to reshape regional order', *East Asia: An International Quarterly*, 2021, Vol. 39, Issue 1, pp. 81-96.

Yu, Le 2021, 'China-Pacific Island Countries Strategic Partnership: China's strategy to reshape regional order', *East Asia: An International Quarterly*, Vol. 39, Issue 1, pp. 81-96.

Yu, Lei 2023, *From the U.S. trusted territory to the freely associated states: relations between the United States and Federated States of Micronesia, the Marshall Islands and Palau*, China Social Sciences Press: Beijing.

Yu, 2024, 'Ontological Security in China–Pacific Islands Countries (PICs) Geopolitics', *Journal of Island and Marine*, Vol. 1, No. 1, pp. 1-23.

Zhang, Chun 2018, 'China-Africa cooperative partnership for peace and security', Alden, Chris, Alao, Abiodun, Zhang, Chun, Barber, Laura (eds), *China and Africa: Building Peace and Security Cooperation on the Continent*, p. 125, Palgrave MacMillan: Cham.

Zhang, Weiyu 2018, 'the aggravation of China-America relations in 2018 and the likelihood of a new Cold War', *Quarterly Journal of International Politics*, Vol. 9, No. 1, pp. 158-160.

Zhao, Shaofeng and Yu, Le 2023, Relations between China and the Pacific Island Countries, China Social Sciences Press: Beijing.

Zhong, Hongming 2018, 'the strategic conception of China's relations with world major countries in Africa', *West Asia and Africa*, Vol. 262, No. 5, pp. 21-41.

Zhou, Tianyong 2011, *The Chinese Dream and the Chinese Road to Development*, Social Sciences Literature Press: Beijing. The Information Office of the State Council of the PRC 2019, *China and the world in the new era*, September, http://www.scio.gov.cn/ztk/dtz.

5

Perceptions of BRI and China's Involvement: the Chinese and Pacific Perspectives

Introduction

The BRI is one of China's most ambitious economic policies, which is aimed to intensify China's economic cooperation with its partners across the world by enhancing connectivity and communication with the rest of the world through a vast program of infrastructure building. From the Chinese perspectives, the key drivers behind the BRI are primarily motivated by China's pursuit of sustained economic growth through intensified economic cooperation, investment and trade. China hopes that its enhanced cooperation and trade with the rest of the world will spur its economic growth, which underlies the legitimacy of the communist rule of China and the "hard" and "soft" power that China needs to rise at the systemic (global) level. China also employs the BRI as a platform to address the country's overcapacity in manufacturing and industry. In this context, the BRI has a heavy domestic and economic focus.

The South Pacific was not incorporated into the BRI when it was first proposed in 2013 by Xi Jinping, Chinese President (2013-), until four years later when the relations between China and the United States worsened as a result of the U.S. "pivot to Asia". Xi Jinping referred to the South Pacific as a 'natural' extension of the BRI, implying the increasing significance of the PICs in the context of the great picture of America-China competition for supremacy, and China's rise at the systemic (global) level (Yu & Zhao 2019, p. 27). A development strategy notwithstanding, many policy analysts particularly in the United States and its military allies view the BRI largely through geopolitical lens, perceiving it as China's attempt to compete with the United States for regional and global hegemony (Westad 2019 & Colton 2018). This partially explains why the United States and its military allies have recently fastened their "return to the South Pacific" that has long been neglected economically and politically since the end of the Cold War.

China's involvement in the South Pacific, including the BRI, is widely conceived by the Chinese foreign policy elites (e.g., Zhao Shaofeng, Chen Hong and Lyu Guixia) as a strategy to intensify China-PICs economic cooperation and trade, and by extension, their political, diplomatic and security relations (Zhao & Yu 2023, p. 143). With the aggravation of China-America relations, the Chinese foreign policy elites (e.g., Gao & Zhang 2017; Sui & Yu 2020) conceive the U.S. strategies, such as the "pivot to Asia", "the freedom of navigation operations" in the South China Sea and the ongoing trade war, as designed by the United States to contain China's rise (Gao & Zhang 2017, p. 48, Sui & Yu 2020, p. 326) despite Washington's denial (Löfflmann 2016, p. 93). In this context, they increasingly view the BRI and the intensification of China-PICs strategic partnership as a strategy to counterattack the U.S. containment by opening up a "new battlefield" in the traditional "sphere of influence" of the United States and its military allies.

China's BRI and its expanding presence and influence in the South Pacific have aroused diverse responses by the PICs. Economically, the political and commercial elites, and local governments perceive the BRI and China's presence in the region as being beneficial for local economic growth and infrastructural development (Park et al 2020, p. 74). Politically, they view China's BRI and its vigorous involvement in the region as a way to achieve "the best from both worlds" by balancing the traditional players and regaining their attention (Zhao & Yu 2023, p. 132, Yu 2021, p. 82). It is noted that some activists and NGOs in the PICs, however, hold a critical attitude towards the BRI and China-PICs cooperation, and call for transparency on the BRI and other projects from project planning to budgeting and procurement, as well as public reporting of debt levels, and environmental standards.

The main argument of the chapter is that China's BRI in the South Pacific helps enhance China's capability of reaping economic and political benefits from the Chinese perspectives. The BRI in the PICs is not merely an economic initiative, but one with a combination of economic, political and strategic objectives and consequences. The BRI in the region is aimed to advance China-PICs infrastructural and economic cooperation, and by extension, to intensify China's political and strategic partnership with the PICs. China has long defined the vast developing states in Africa, Latin America and elsewhere as the "basis" of her international relations, underlying China's global power and influence (Yu 2018, p. 491). China wants to show its partners in the PICs that its peaceful rise shall not be misconstrued as a threat, but an opportunity for economic prosperity both for the PICs and China as well as China's economic partners across the world (Guo 2017, p. 7). The chapter finds that the political elites in the PICs more often than not welcome the BRI and particularly China's increasing involvement in the region as they may "achieve the best from both worlds" by playing the traditional and new players against each other to maximize their economic and political interest. In this context, the chapter concludes that China is increasingly able to reap economic and geopolitical interest in the South Pacific by intensifying "connectivity" and "exchanges of people" between China and the PICs through the BRI and other cooperation.

An Appraisal from the Chinese perspectives

The Chinese foreign policy elites and academics are generally of the view that the BRI and China's economic cooperation and trade with the PICs are in their common interest. Some Chinese economists and IR scholars (e.g., Shi 2019, p. 37, Ding & Cui 2017, p. 42) are acclaiming for China's expanding economic presence in and trade with the PICs, which, in their viewpoints, constitutes solid groundwork underpinning China-PICs strategic partnership and China's ambitious BRI. When interviewed by the authors, Niu Li at the Beijing Foreign Studies University, Zhao Shaofeng at Liaocheng University, Chen Hong at East China Normal University, and Yu Changsen at Sun Yatsen University are unexceptionally supportive of China's economic cooperation and trade with the

PICs[36]. In their view, China's involvement in the PICs is primarily economy- and development-centric, a view completely different from the presence of the United States, which is primarily hegemony- and military-centric. In this context, these Chinese scholars insist that the increasing economic cooperation and trade between China and the PICs are beneficial to the well-beings of the peoples of both China and the PICs.

Intensified economic and infrastructural cooperation notwithstanding, the volumes of two-way trade and Chinese investment in the PICs remain less than $10 billion in 2022 due to the limited markets and investment opportunities based on the data released by the Chinese Ministry of Commerce (Ministry of Foreign Affairs of the PRC 2023). Obviously, China's economic involvement in the PICs has not yet and probably unlikely reaped as many economic dividends as it does in the other parts of the developing world, such as in Africa and Latin America, as a result of the limited markets and commercial opportunities in the PICs (Zhao & Yu 2023, p. 145). Both the PICs and China have displayed much interest in furthering their economic cooperation by exploiting the deep-sea resources in the vast economic exclusive zones (EEZ) of the PICs. It is speculated that the PICs are abundant in deep-sea resources. For instance, the area that borders the territorial waters of the Cook Islands, Kiribati, Nauru, and Tonga, is a deep-sea trench approximately the size of Europe.

It is estimated that this area holds a calculated 21 billion tons of polymetallic nodules that contain mostly manganese, but also iron, nickel, copper, titanium,

36 The interviews conducted are aimed to help explore the dynamics that contributes to the rapid intensification of China-PICs economic cooperation and their strategic partnership, and the constraints that hamper China-PICs cooperation particularly in the spheres of security and military cooperation. Some IR academics in China were interviewed. The criteria of choice are as follows: (1) interviewees are academically specialized in the China-PICs relations; (2) interviewees have been committed to the studies on China-PICs relations for more than a decade; (3) interviewees had field work or academic exchanges in the counterpart countries in the last decade. The authors concluded from the interviews that the growing economic cooperation and trade between China and the PICs have helped intensify their relations whereas aroused concerns and worries among the traditional players.

Niu Li is director of Pacific Center, Beijing Foreign Studies University. Zhao Shaofeng is director of the Research Center for PICs, Liaocheng University. Chen Hong is director of the Center for Australian Studies, East China Normal University. Yu Changsen is director of the Center for Oceanian Studies, Sun Yatsen University.

and cobalt. The polymetallic nodules here contain more cobalt and nickel, the key ingredients in electric batteries, than all known land deposits. Such metals are in increasing demand amid a push to develop batteries for electric vehicles and renewable energy (Mcdonald, Joshua 2019). However, the deep-sea resources are hardly accessible to and the exploitation of them are money-consuming in view of the complicated technology required, let alone the fragile environment and biodiversity in the South Pacific. The deep-sea mining would likely destroy the marine habitats and particularly the ocean floor where there are many rare and sensitive organisms. The noise pollution created by the mining would drive marine mammals, such as dolphins, away from their natural areas. Much worse, much of the biodiversity and habitat loss by mining will be permanent. The scientific consensus is that deep-sea mining would cause significant permanent damage to ocean ecosystems (McVeigh 2023).

In the viewpoints of the Chinese academics (e.g., Zhao Shaofeng and Chen Hong), the rapid involvement of China in the South Pacific is primarily attributable to China's strategies of "non-interference", "economic priority" and China's resonance with the concerns of the PICs, such as climate change and better livelihood of the local residents. When interviewed by the authors, Zhao Shaofeng explains that China's policy of "non-interference" signals to the PICs China's willingness to treat them as equal partners by respecting their sovereignty and self-determination (Zhao & Yu 2019, p. 31). The PICs have long valued their countries' sovereignty and self-determination since they gained their independence after centuries of colonialization by the colonial powers (the traditional players). Niu Li at the Beijing Foreign Studies University explains that China's strategy of economic priority signals to the PICs China's aspiration of conducting economic cooperation and trade with the PICs in the spirit of mutual benefits and regardless of their differences in ideological values and political systems (Lyu 2022, p. 72). In the viewpoints of Niu, China would like to conduct win-win cooperation with countries across the world, including the PICs, and refuses to politicalize and ideologize the relations of cooperation with the rest of the world.

Some Chinese scholars (e.g., Xu Xiujun at the China Academy of Social Sciences and Lei Yu at the Shandong University) are of the view that China's adoption of the "non-interference" strategy in the South Pacific and elsewhere (e.g., Africa and Latin America) is not aimed to counter the "ideological diplomacy" pursued by the United States and other traditional players. In their opinions, China's adoption of the strategy in the South Pacific and elsewhere can be expressed in the following ways. First, China had long been bullied and invaded by the colonial and imperial powers in the "Chinese century of humiliation"

(Hsu 2000, p. 477, Liu 2004, p. 129, Mao 1995, p. 583), that started from the first Chinese-British Trade War (the first Opium War, 1839-1841), and resulted in Qing China's rapid decline (Bregolat 2015, p. 64), to the founding of the People's Republic of China (PRC) in 1949. As a victim of foreign invasion and bullying by the big powers, the founders of PRC (e.g., Mao Zedong and Deng Xiaoping) have insisted that China should refrain from interfering in the internal affairs of other developing states (or the countries in the Third World).

Second, the PRC had been confronted with a critical challenge of military encirclement and political isolation imposed by the United States and its military allies over the decades from the birth of the PRC in late 1949 to Nixon's trip to Beijing in 1972. Apart from the states in the Soviet Blocs, the majority of the developing states in Asia, Africa and Latin America had balked at exchanging diplomatic recognition with Beijing over the 1950s and 1960s for fear of communism and China's export of revolution (Xia 2005, p. 75). To overcome the diplomatic predicament, China proposed with India and Burma the "Five Principles of Peaceful Coexistence (commonly known as "non-interference" overseas) to govern their relations with the rest of the world, and particularly with the developing states. China has thereafter pursued the strategy to win the diplomatic recognition and political endorsement of the developing states[37]. It is noteworthy that the Chinese authorities had indeed abandoned the strategy of "non-interference" in the so-called "Cultural Revolution" (1966-1976), during which time, Beijing claimed itself as the "champion of the world revolution" and exported revolution to the Third World states. China restored the "non-interference" strategy in the late 1970s after the death of Mao Zedong and particularly after the reinstatement of Deng Xiaoping as China's top political leader.

It is safe to say that the memory of the "Chinese century of humiliation" and the concern of the developing states with the communist ideology make the Chinese foreign policy makers reluctant to interfere in the internal affairs of

37 The Chinese foreign policy makers and IR scholars have long viewed the "five principles" as the utmost important principles governing its external relations with the rest of the world. The Five Principles are: mutual respect for territorial integrity and sovereignty; mutual non-aggression; mutual non-interference in internal affairs; equality and mutual benefit; and peaceful co-existence. For more details, see Zheng, Ruixiang 2004, 'heping gongchu wuxiang yuanze chansheng de lishi beijing he shidai yiyi (the historical background of the creation of the five principles of peaceful co-existence and its significance for the current time), Contemporary Asia-Pacific Studies, *No. 6, pp. 3-8.*

the developing states. This explains why Hu Yaobang, General Secretary of the Communist Party of China (1980-1987), reassured the political leaders of the PICs in his visit to Samoa, Fiji and PNG in 1985 that China respects the sovereignty and self-determination of the PICs. Hu further assured the governments of the PICs that China refrains from interfering in the internal affairs of the PICs and imposing on them the communist ideology (Xiao 2010, p. 243). Hu was the first top Chinese political leader to visit the South Pacific and promise non-interference with the internal affairs of the PICs. Hu's promise has thereafter been repeated by the Chinese political leaders, including Xi Jinping who visited the PICs in 2009 in the capacity of vice president and in 2014 and 2018 in the capacity of president. Xi Jinping stressed that relations between China and the PICs are based upon the 'five principles of peaceful co-existence', which prohibits the interference by one sovereign state in the internal affairs of the others (Tsai 2012, p. 56, Yu 2021, p. 87). China's 'non-interference' strategy has been appreciated by some of the political leaders and commercial elites in the PICs, which is partially evidenced by their willingness to create with China a strategic partnership and by China's rapidly expanded presence and influence in the region.

As well, China's strategy of economic priority towards the PICs and elsewhere is not aimed to counter the traditional players in the region and elsewhere, but reflects the philosophy of the Chinese governance. Deng Xiaoping, the late Chinese political leader, prioritized economic growth by launching a market reform after his return to the top Chinese leadership in the late 1970s (Laursen 2009, p. 224). Deng (1993, p. 370) held fast to the belief that China's economic growth and the better livelihoods of the Chinese people granted the legitimacy of the communist rule of China, and constitutes the basis underlying China's "hard" and "soft" power, and its re-emergence at the systemic (global) level. The disintegration of the former Soviet Union in 1991 enhanced Deng's doctrine of economic priority. Deng and the Chinese academics rejected Fukuyama (1992, p. 11)'s perception that the Soviet demise marked the superiority of the U.S. political system over the communist system. Rather, they theorized that the Soviet demise was the tragic aftermaths of the country's failure in economically backing the Soviet pursuit of a military hegemon and its hegemonic competition with the United States, which lasted for half a century and exhausted the resources of the former Soviet Union.

Deng further argued that the strategy adopted by the Soviet authorities that military hegemony preceded better livelihoods of the general public undermined the interest of the general public and resulted in the loss of their political loyalty to and support of the Soviet regime (Wang 2007, p. 113, Yu 2020, p. 240). Deng (1993, p. 371)'s argument provides insights into his doctrine that China's priority should be given to the country's economic growth and the improvement of the Chinese people's livelihood, rather than to the pursuit of military hegemony. In Deng's views, China should be focused on economic growth and modernization in the 100 hundred years ahead starting from the late 1970s and cultivate relations of cooperation in economic development and trade with all countries across the world albeit their differences in ideological values and political systems. Deng's theory explains why China's involvement in the PICs and elsewhere (e.g., Africa and Latin America) has been primarily focused on trade and economic and infrastructural cooperation.

In the viewpoints of some Chinese academics and governmental officials (e.g., Lyu 2022, p. 70 and Yu 2023, p. 175), China's has been focusing on economic and infrastructural involvement in the PICs whereas the United States on military hegemony, ideological value and political system. Some Chinese foreign policy elites (e.g., Chen Hong, Niu Li and Yu Changsen) share the perception. When interviewed by the authors, Chen, Niu and Yu contrasted the strategies adopted by China and the United States towards the PICs: China prioritizes economic relations with the PICs and other countries across the world whereas the United States prioritizes military and security ties with the PICs and others to keep its global hegemony. This contrast is reminiscent of the speeches respectively addressed by President George Walker Bush and President Hu Jintao to the Australian Parliament one day apart in 2003 when they visited Australia. Members of the Australian Parliament were profoundly impressed by the contrast of their speeches as President Bush was extremely focused on "war" with Iraq and Afghanistan whereas President Hu on "trade, economic growth and cooperation" with Australia and others (Sui & Yu 2023, p. 63). In hindsight, such a dichotomy of war and peace in their respective foreign policies reflected by their speeches posited the different trajectories of the United States and China in the later couple of decades.

However, this perception hardly means an agreement has been reached by the Chinese academics on the roles of the United States and other traditional players in the South Pacific. Rather, the viewpoints of the Chinese academics differ dramatically on the engagement of the traditional players with the PICs. Some scholars (e.g., Zhou 2023, p. 119 and Wu 2020, p. 124) accuse the United States and other traditional players of trying to maintain their hegemony in the region, and disrespecting the sovereignty and self-determination of the PICs by imposing their ideological value, political system and mode of development on the PICs (Zhou 2023, p. 121, Wu 2020, p. 125). In the eyes of these scholars, China has long displayed respects for the sovereignty and self-determination of the PICs by treating them as equal partners and by refraining from interfering in their internal affairs. When interviewed by the authors, Guo Chunmei, Lyu Guixia and Li Jianjun quote Xi Jinping when Xi reassured Manasseh Sogavare, former Prime Minister of the Solomon Islands, in the latter's visit to China in 2023, that China respects the sovereignty, independence and cultural traditions of the Solomon Islands and other PICs[38]. The joint announcement made by Xi and Sogavare on the strategic partnership, and the commitment to strengthening their mutual help and assistance under the framework of South-South cooperation show China's willingness to treat the PICs as equal partners despite the huge differences in the land surface size, population and "hard" power (Ministry of Foreign Affairs of the PRC 2023a). In the viewpoints of these Chinese scholars, this partially explains why the PICs and other developing states in the other parts of the world appreciate China's "non-interference" policy and are enthusiastic with working with China economically and politically for a new order that they deem as "fairer" and "more rational".

Other Chinese scholars (e.g., Zhao & Yu 2023, Zhang 2019, p. 94) argue that for such least developing countries as the PICs, to ensure the improvement of the livelihoods of the PICs by providing them aid in boosting their economic growth and addressing climate change shall precede the American-style democracy. In their view, this partially explains why the governments and businesses of the PICs welcome China's economic and infrastructural involvement in the region. The Solomon Islands, PNG and Fiji have been at the forefront of China's BRI and economic cooperation with the PICs. When meeting Prime Minister Manasseh Sogavare, Xi Jinping promised that China will share the development opportunities brought about by China's economic growth with the Solomon Islands, expand imports of advantageous products from the Solomon Islands and help it achieve economic growth, stability and long-term prosperity.

Still some others (e.g., Yu 2021, p. 87) hold fast to the belief that the economic growth in the region shall go hand in hand with democracy and good governance. They argue that China's own experiences over the past decades since

38 Guo Chunmei is deputy director and associate research professor in the Institute of Southeast Asian and Oceanian Studies, China Institutes of Contemporary International Relations. Lyu Guixia is a professorial research fellow at the Center for the Pacific and Pacific Countries History, China Academy of Social Sciences. Li Jianjun is director of the Center for Australian Studies at Beijing Foreign Studies University.

Deng Xiaoping launched the market reform in the late 1970s show that good governance, respect for human rights and environmental protection are vital to the long-term economic growth and social progress. The same is true of PICs' economic growth and people's well-being as well as the sustained cooperation and trade between China and PICs. Good governance and transparency in the region are in the interest of the PICs and help both the PICs and China to reap the long-term interests arising from their economic cooperation and political partnership. The goals of the Chinese engagement with the PICs are aimed to reap the economic and trading interest, which is, however, "meagre" in contrast to the country's interest in the other parts of the developing world, such as Africa and Latin America. More importantly, China is aimed to reap strategic benefits, deriving from the combination of China's "hard," and "soft" power in the South Pacific to reshape the regional system and order. It is a little out of expectation that though difference in their viewpoints, the Chinese scholars when interviewed have reached consensus that the traditional and new players in the region should conduct cooperation rather than military confrontation to help address the challenges confronted by the PICs.

As the partnership and BRI in the South Pacific evolves, the interests of both China and the PICs are dramatically expanding and diversifying with further resources, investment, trade, security and other priorities added. In this context, some policy analysts and watchers inside and outside China (e.g., Graeme Smith, Terence Wesley-Smith 2021, Zhao Shaofeng and Lei Yu 2023) predict that the partnership with and BRI in the Pacific islands may serve as a two-pronged instrument to re-shape the economic and geopolitical landscape in the South Pacific, and eventually re-shape the regional power hierarchy and order. China's strategy evolves and interests diversifies in conjunction with its increasing economic involvement in the South Pacific though China's cooperation with the PICs has long been focused on economic cooperation and trade. For example, Zhao Shaofeng and Ni Peng and others note that China's cooperation with the PICs has gradually expanded to bilateral cooperation on climate change, cultural exchanges, education and other spheres. Lyu Guixia notes that Xi Jinping made a promise to Manasseh Sogavare in his visit to China in 2023, that China supports the PICs in implementing the 2050 Strategy for the Blue Pacific Continent, and cooperates with them to contribute to a peaceful, inclusive and prosperous Blue Pacific (Ministry of Foreign Affairs of the PRC 2023c).

The Chinese foreign policy elites are acutely aware that their country's rapidly increasing interest in the South Pacific needs to be protected by both conducting security cooperation with the local authorities and by winning the hearts and minds of the local people. In the view of Zhao Shaofeng and Ni Peng, this partially explains why the Chinese authorities incorporate the China-PICs cooperation in the domains of security, climate change, education, culture, medical service and people-to-people exchanges into the framework of BRI. The authors note that a growing number of Chinese academics are attaching significant importance to China's "soft" power in the PICs by reading the Chinese literature, attending a dozen of academic conferences on the China-PICs cooperation over the last five years, and lecturing the trainees from the South Pacific who participated in training programs held by the Chinese institutions and universities. The Chinese foreign policy elites and scholars advise the Chinese authorities to intensify cooperation with the PICs in the spheres of climate change, education and people-to-people exchange in tandem with China's growing presence and influence in the PICs.

Zhao Shaofeng notes that situated at the frontline of climate change, the PICs are more vulnerable to climate change than most countries in the other parts of the world as a result of their limited land size, geographic location prone to tropical cyclones, and incapacity to adapt to climate change (Morgan et al 2024). The PICs span 25,000 islands and encompass approximately 15 percent of the Earth's surface albeit being labeled as "small" island countries. While the PICs' contribution to global greenhouse gas emissions is minimal (only responsible for 0.03 percent), the PICs have long been disproportionally facing many of the compounding threats of climate change (Parsons 2022). As small island countries, the PICs are among the most vulnerable to climate change, whose primary impacts include increased risk of inundation and coastal flooding, exacerbation of erosion, saltwater intrusion, cyclones and tsunami (Mimura 1999, p. 137). The disasters caused by climate change are becoming more frequent and widespread, posing a lethal threat to local ecosystem, communities, the livelihoods and economic growth (Almulhim 2024, p. 1). Most importantly, the sea-level rise is devastating for the low-lying PICs that sit at or just above sea level, and many coastal communities in the PICs are being forced from their homes by rising sea levels and erosion, and relocating to higher ground. It is reported that 94 percent of households in Kiribati have been affected by natural hazards in the past decades (Oakes et al 2016).

Ni Peng who just finished fieldwork in the PICs in August 2024 notes that the marine environments of the PICs are characterized by a variety of ecosystems, such as mangroves, coral reefs and seagrass beds, which are crucial for biodiversity and livelihoods. These ecosystems are now threatened by climate change that results in rising sea temperatures, rising sea level and ocean acidification, which affect regional ecosystems, natural food chain, and the PICs' food supply, economy and tourism. Climate change not only harms marine environment and life, but also disrupts fishing activities and the PICs' well-being (Carlson et al 2021). Climate change is affecting marine organisms at multiple trophic levels, displacing wild fisheries, driving the reorganization of marine food systems, impacting fisheries, and disrupting food production with implications for food production and human communities (Teshome 2023). As a result, areas in the tropics are predicted to see declines of up to 40 percent in potential seafood catch by 2050 (Marine Stewardship Council 2024).

The PICs are witnessing ocean acidification as a result of human-driven increased levels of carbon dioxide in the atmosphere, which are increasingly dissolving into the ocean, and resulting in a decrease in the pH and an increase in acidity (Wu et al 2018). According to the Secretariat of the Pacific Regional Environment Programme (SPREP), the pH of the tropical Pacific Ocean has decreased by 30 percent (0.11 pH units) since the early 19th century, now decreasing by ~0.02 units per decade. A further decline of 0.3 units (150 percent drop) is expected by the end of the 21st century. It is well noted that rising ocean temperatures and especially the ocean acidification are increasingly impacting the coastal ecosystems in the South Pacific. For instance, nearly half of coral reefs in the South Pacific are currently threatened, with about 20 percent rated as "highly threatened" according to the Intergovernmental Panel on Climate Change.

Ni Peng expressed his concerns with the raised sea temperatures that are causing widespread coral bleaching in a huge swathe of the Pacific, which leads to the loss of coral cover and biodiversity. The disappearance of corals in the South Pacific would increase coastal damage tenfold as they provide sand for beaches, ensure the limitation of coastal erosion, and absorb up to 97 percent of wave energy (Tesan 2022). It is reported that bleaching of unprecedented severity hits most of the atolls and islands of the Marshall Islands and more than 50 percent of coral reefs around Tahiti and Moorea of French Polynesia have been bleached. Climate change-driven ocean acidification is rapidly changing Pacific ecosystems and poses a significant threat to marine life. The main issues resulting from ocean acidification include the loss of biodiversity and significant losses in fisheries and mariculture production (farming marine life for food).

Zhu Xuan (an associate professor at the Liaocheng University) who just came back from her fieldwork in the PICs concerns with the decreasing seawater concentration of carbonate ions, which makes it hard for the marine life (e.g., calcifying plankton and algae, shellfish) to build their skeletons and shells with. This will lead to a reduction in the growth for many of these species and ecosystems, jeopardizing the ocean's role as a nutrition provider, and decreasing the ability of reefs to reduce erosion and storm wave impacts (Agostini et al 2018). The PICs have reef-dependent communities and are highly dependent on fisheries resources, vulnerable to declines in reef conditions, demersal and invertebrate fisheries, and aquaculture. Fish are a cornerstone of food security for the PICs, which provide 50-90 percent of animal protein in the diet of coastal communities across a broad spectrum of the Pacific islands (Tesan 2022). Ocean acidification has therefore done harm to coral reef health, undermined fisheries and tourism in the South Pacific, and consequently, impacted the livelihoods of the local people in the PICs. In this context, climate change and ocean acidification have threatened PICs' economies and food security as evidenced by the loss of fisheries productivity.

As well, Climate change and climate variability pose significant challenges to groundwater systems and to freshwater supply in the Pacific islands (Bouchet et al 2019, p. 579). Groundwater is a critical source of freshwater for island ecosystems in the Pacific islands that heavily depend on ground water from shallow coastal aquifers and rainwater to meet their freshwater needs. These important coastal aquifers in the South Pacific are vulnerable to various threats of climate change, such as saltwater intrusion, over-extraction, and coastal erosion (Pacific Community Centre for Ocean Science 2024). Moreover, the degradation of mangroves that protect coastal communities from coastal hazards (coastal erosion, tidal bores and cyclones) further exacerbates the PICs' vulnerability to erosion and storm surges (UNEP-WCMC 2006). These multifaceted impacts of climate change accentuate the urgent need for the application of AI solutions to monitor, mitigate and manage the effects of climate change on the PICs' blue economy. Recognizing the vulnerability to climate change, the PICs are committed to enhancing the sustainability of coastal and marine systems through strengthening the management of coastal and marine resources, thus preventing environmental degradation and preparing for the challenges posed by climate change impacts. The PICs have adopted a proactive stance in addressing climate change through a multifaceted approach and particularly through policy formulation, regional policy coordination and international collaboration. As early as in 2005, the PICs coordinated their stances on climate change and adopted an action plan to carry out the Pacific Islands Framework for Action on Climate Change, 2006 to 2015, in which national activities of the PICs were complemented by regional programming (Secretariat of the Pacific Regional Environment Programme 2011).

In addition to climate change aid to the PICs, the Chinese government provides funding annually to the China-PICs Climate Change Cooperation Center (The Research Center for PICs Studies) based at the Liaocheng University, Shandong Province. The funds are earmarked for studies on the climate change and climate change cooperation with the PICs. As part of China-PICs climate change cooperation, the Center in collaboration with other Chinese universities and research institutions provides the PICs training opportunities on climate change (Du 2023). When interviewed, Chen Dezheng, vice director of the Center, told the authors that the Center has to date provided hundreds of training opportunities on the climate change to the scholars and officials from the PICs. At the invitation by the Center, the authors have lectured the trainees on the China-PICs green energy cooperation since 2018. The training programs make it possible for the authors to carry face-to-face conversations with the scholars and officials from the PICs.

The last training program on climate change was held in November 2023 and the authors had the opportunity to hold detailed conversations with around 30 trainees from the PICs, most of whom were governmental officials, scholars and employees of NGOs. The trainees told the authors that they were markedly impressed by the Chinese efforts in reducing carbon emissions when they saw millions of electricity-powered cars, buses and motorcycles on the streets in cities and countryside in China. Some of them were surprised to see electricity-powered tractors on the farms and pickup trucks in the countryside. Their comments remind the authors of an article in the *New York Times*:

> It has not gone unnoticed here that China has taken meaningful measures to reduce carbon emission, while American and Australian politicians have dithered or, in the case of Australia, even made light of climate concerns in the Pacific (Dorothy 2022).

Confronted with the aftermath of climate change, both China and the PICs have come to the realization that to combat the challenges arising from climate change necessitates the utilization of cutting-edge technology. Of the breakthrough innovations, AI emerges as a pivotal force to revolutionize the existential approach to climate change, and reshape the paradigm of environment, ecosystem and biodiversity protection. AI has been widely used for extraction of meaningful patterns and analysis on datasets and correlations from them, which can revolutionize predictions and markedly enhance decision-making. The truism applies here that AI can extremely increase the efficiency and efficacy to combating climate threats and better managing ecosystem in the South Pacific. However, these technologies are mostly of dual use, in that they can be used as much to serve malicious purposes as they can be harnessed to enhance social and economic development. Moreover, these technologies are viewed by established and rising powers as central to national security. In this context, growing strategic and hegemonic competition between the world's leading powers, especially in high-tech sectors, will not be conducive for international efforts in addressing climate change and may lead to a delay to the much-needed application of AI in climate change.

On the advice of the Chinese scholars, China has recently provided scholarship opportunities in marine, environmental, and climate-related areas to the PICs through initiatives, such as the "The Marine Scholarship of China", which aligns with China's commitment to offer 2,500 government scholarship opportunities to PICs from 2020 to 2025 (Ministry of Foreign Affairs of the PRC 2022). Apart from the Confucius institutes in the PICs, hundreds of volunteering teachers from the Chinese high schools and universities are working in the middle and high schools, and universities in the PICs, teaching Chinese, mathematics, science, agricultural skills and etc. During their fieldwork in the PICs, the authors had detailed conversations with the Chinese volunteering teachers. Kang Jian and Qu Sheng had been in the PICs for three years as volunteering teachers. When interviewed by the authors, they both emphasized the magnitude of educational and cultural exchanges between China and the PICs, and appealed for more volunteering teachers to go to work in the South Pacific. Zhao Shaofeng, director of the Research Center for the Pacific Island Countries at the Liaocheng University told the authors that his university is going to set up the Liaocheng-Tonga College according to a memorandum signed by the two governments in 2018. The college is aimed to help Tonga cultivate high-level talents in applied science, and conduct joint research in marine studies (Li 2022). Zhao highlights that the cooperation between China and the PICs on climate change and education has contributed much to drawing close their relations, and enhancing China's "soft" power in the South Pacific.

As above mentioned, some Chinese academics (e.g., Chen Hong and Zhao Minhao) are of the view that the United States and some other traditional players in the South Pacific have been focused on ideological and political values, and military hegemony in the region. From their perspectives, the primary objectives of the United States and its military allies in the region are aimed at keeping control of the PICs and their own supremacy in the region in the name of promoting "democracy", "good governance" and "human rights protection".

They quote Francis Fukuyama (2011) that 'the Iraq war and the close association it created between military invasion and democracy promotion tarnished the latter'. Zhao Minhao at Fudan University blames the traditional players and particularly the United States and Australia for their intention to maintain their traditional status of "paternalism", rather than to keep an equal relationship with the PICs. In the view of Zhao, the United States has always employed this region as a testing ground for U.S. nuclear weapons and a geopolitical pawn for its Pacific hegemony (Chen 2023).

When interviewed (personal communication, May 12, 2022), Chen Hong at the East China Normal University argues that most of the aid provided by the United States and its military allies are carried out in political and ideological fields, including programs training the civil servants, police and those working in the judiciary system with Western values. After much fieldwork in the PICs, Zhao Shaofeng argues that these training programs are aimed to brainwash the local people and impose the western ideological values on the PICs. These programs provide no concrete benefits to the local people, nor do they advance local economic growth and employment. In the opinions of Chen and Zhao, this partially explains why the United States fails to counter China's growing presence and influence in the PICs though they have provided much more aid than China has, leaving open an opportunity for China and other new players to expand their involvement in the region. In this sense, the Chinese scholars conceive China's intensified economic and infrastructural cooperation with the PICs as an effective way to counter the containment campaign launched by the United States and its military allies in the South Pacific.

Chen Hong added that the PICs are disappointed with the policies adopted by the traditional players in the region, which have hardly helped the PICs improve their economic and infrastructural situation. In this context, an increasing number of PICs have adopted a strategy of 'looking north', which is aimed to cultivate close relations of economic cooperation and trade with Asia, and leverage the latter's capital, technology and modernization experience to advance the PICs' economic growth and infrastructural development. Chen notes that over 140 countries across the world have signed on to the BRI, in which China lends them large sums of money for roads, dams, railways, ports and sports facilities. In view of the enormous benefits arising from the BRI, countries around the globe, including the PICs, would like to shape closer relations of cooperation with China to advance infrastructure connectivity under the BRI. Chen Hong believes that the BRI helps the PICs to be connected both "internally" and "externally", and integrate the economies of the PICs into the global economic system. Niu Li at the Beijing Foreign Studies University added that as the second largest economy in the world, China is home to a complete industrial chain that complements the economic structure of the PICs (Cave 2022). In her opinion, the economic complementarity helps advance the China-PICs relations of partnership.

In the eyes of some Chinese academics, every step of the U.S. promotion in ties with the PICs is saying "America is back". Chen Hong argues that what is really back is U.S. military hegemony, as well as the weaponization of the South Pacific region. In his view, the United States is struggling with a strong sense of "strategic and tactic anxiety" when Washington witnesses that China's cooperation with the PICs has gained a strong momentum. Chen argues that it is in this context that the United States is ramping up efforts to engage with the PICs, including holding the U.S.-PICs summit for two consecutive years. Zhao Shaofeng shares Chen, arguing that the "return of the United States to the region" is primarily out of growing anxiety, resulting from its perception of China as a major challenge to its hegemony in the South Pacific. Zhao hence insists that the South Pacific is merely a tool employed by the United States to keep its regional hegemony.

Chen notes that Washington is eager to regain its influence in the region with a series of high-profile, hustle and bustle diplomatic offensive, including establishing new embassies or carrying out blitz tours there. When interviewed (personal communication, September 10, 2022), the six Chinese scholars who have been devoted to studies on the PICs, namely, Chen Hong, Zhao Shaofeng, Niu Li, Yu Changsen, Guo Chunmei and Li Jianjun, predict that the trend of the U.S. "offensive" in the South Pacific will continue. They conclude that this is not because the United States wants to help the PICs advance their economic growth, employment and the well-beings of the local people, but because it needs the region to contain China in its Indo-Pacific Strategy. The views of these scholars conform to the mainstream Chinese literature of international relations on the U.S. relations with the PICs.

Can China draw geopolitical dividends from its expanded presence and influence in the South Pacific as some of Chinese scholars and strategists expect? A number of Chinese IR scholars (e.g., Chen & Chang 2022, p. 21, Zhao &Yu 2019, p. 27) acknowledge that the United States has to date remained the most important player in the South Pacific and particularly in the Micronesia and northern part of Polynesia. It is no denial that the United States has profound economic, political and cultural influence in the PICs, and incomparable capabilities of military projection in the region and beyond (Chen & Chang 2022). As well, Australia, New Zealand and Japan, the traditional players and allies of the United States in the Pacific, remain impressive presence and influence in the region. In the opinions of Zhao Shaofeng, Lyu Guixia and Li Jianjun, the combined prowess and influence of the United States and its regional allies outweigh qualitatively those of China, which may constrain China's ability to reap geopolitical dividends in the PICs and in the South Pacific. These scholars conclude that in this context, the PICs are most likely to proceed cautiously in their relations with both the traditional players and the new comers though they may perceive with favor a reduction in the presence and influence of the traditional players, particularly the United States, Australia and New Zealand, and their dependence on the traditional players.

It is noteworthy that even if Beijing does not have the capability of subverting or marginalizing the United States and its allies in the region, China may see its increased presence and influence in the South Pacific as a way to 'squelching' Taiwan, and to resisting the U.S.-led "Indo-Pacific" strategy. The Chinese foreign policy elites are generally of the view that the "Indo-Pacific" strategy means bringing Western allies together to contain China's rise (Jennings 2019). Jain (2006) at the Adelaide University argues that 'it is not politically sensible for a select group of nations to gang up and exclude others — a Cold War-type response' and 'a cooperative and inclusive framework rather than exclusion and containment would be a better way forward'. This sheds light on the strategic thinking of the Chinese foreign policy makers in the post-Cold War era to create a strategic partnership with the PICs in the hopes of dissuading them, among others, from being involved in any U.S.-led military encirclement or containment of China.

When interviewed (personal communication, June 18, 2022 and September 7 2022), Guo Chunmei and Yu Changsen take the view that China has no interest in undertaking a geopolitical or military competing with the United States in the South Pacific, but only looks forward to having mutually beneficial cooperation with the PICs for their interest. However, the United States and Australia, as well as some Western media and think tanks, are describing China's cooperation with the PICs as a "security risk", or even accuse China of "militarizing" the South Pacific. Zhao Shaofeng argues that the United States and Australia have a number of military bases in the South Pacific whereas China has none, which is self-evident who is militarizing this region.

The Chinese scholars note that China's rapidly increasing engagement with the PICs has aroused concerns in the United States, Australia and New Zealand, the "Sheriff" and "Deputy Sheriffs" of the South Pacific. An article published in the *Wall Street Journal* claimed that China is becoming 'a political rival' of the United States in its own backyards, such as in the South Pacific and Latin America (O'Grady 2004, p. 7, Jiang 2008, p. 4). Another article published in the *Foreign Affairs* claimed that 'there is a U.S.-Chinese cold war, and American policy makers need an updated version of Kennan's containment' (Westad 2019). Apparently, the United States and its major allies in the Pacific are unlikely to sit on their hands and do nothing about their declining influence and China's increasing presence and influence in their 'backyard'. Regional watchers and analysts surmise the U.S. "Indo-Pacific" Strategy and Australia's South Pacific "Set Up" as a joined response to China's rapidly expanding presence and influence in the PICs and the Pacific region (Colton 2018, p. 9, Zhao & Yu 2019, p. 73).

Some Chinese scholars (e.g., Song & Ye 2016, p. 51, Chen & Change 2022, p. 23) note that against the backdrop of intensified relations between China and the PICs, the United States hastily "returns to the South Pacific". Instead of addressing the concerns of the PICs, the United States and other traditional players give priority to maintaining their hegemony by intensifying their military and security relations with the PICs as the military and strategic importance of the PICs has become increasingly prominent in competition with China for hegemony (Song & Ye 2016, p. 52, Chen & Chang 2022, p. 21). Zhao Minghao at the Fudan University argues that the United States has put the PICs into its Indo-Pacific strategic deployment, accelerating the security cooperation with other U.S.-dominated multilateral or trilateral pacts, such as Quad, AUKUS and the U.S.-Japan-Philippines security ties (Chen 2023). Zhao notes that the United States has extended its military alliance under the framework of "Indo-Pacific" strategy to the South Pacific, and urged Vietnam, South Korea and New Zealand to join the alliance. In the opinions of these Chinese scholars, the ultimate goal of the United States is to instrumentalize and militarize the South Pacific region to serve its hegemonic interests, making it an important pivot in the southern hemisphere to weaken the China-PICs relations of cooperation.

Concurrent with the U.S. "returning to the South Pacific", Zhao Shaofeng, Lyu Guixia and Chen Hong note that the United States and other traditional players are demonizing the China-PICs cooperation by spreading the theses of the "China threat", "the debt trap" and "the neo-colonialism". When interviewed (personal communication, May 10, 2022), Chen Hong attributed the demonization of the China-PICs cooperation and China's presence and influence in the South Pacific to the intensified partnership between China and the PICs, which is sounding alerts to the United States. Washington fears China's expanding involvement in the region and the intensified cooperation between China and the PICs to diminish its hegemony in the South Pacific and beyond.

Chen Hong argues that it is in this context that the United States and Australia have hence sought to intimidate the PICs with the so-called "China threat thesis".

Vis-à-vis the "China threat thesis", the Chinese academics raise the question: who is on earth the biggest source of instability for the South Pacific and for the world? Who brings benefits to the region and other parts of the developing world? In the eyes of Chen Hong and Zhao Shaofeng, it is ironic that the United States that has launched most wars on other countries in the post-Cold War era blames China that has not launched no war on countries over the decades since the late 1970s "a security threat". They argue that after the PICs refuse to buy into the "China threat", the United States and its military allies, began hyping the so-called "debt trap" to deter the PICs from intensifying their cooperation of mutual benefits with China. In the viewpoints of Chen Hong, the unrelenting slander against the China-PICs cooperation exposes that the pursuit of hegemony is deeply rooted in the philosophy of the United States and its military allies. When the authors talked to the trainees who attended the climate training program in China in November 2023, at least half of the 30 trainees from the PICs told the authors that they value their personal experiences in China. What they see in China is completely different from what they read in the Western media and they will tell their friends and colleagues a "true" China after they are back to their countries.

Zhao Shaofeng shares Chen, arguing that the pursuit of hegemony drives the United States and its "Deputy Sheriff", namely, Australia to "ideologize" and "politicize" China's cooperation with the countries in the South Pacific that they have long perceived as their "backyard". In Zhao's opinions, the hype of the thesis of the "China threat" and the thesis of the "debt trap" by the United States and other traditional players in the South Pacific are aimed to prevent the PICs from intensifying their cooperation with China. Zhao has had a lot of fieldwork in the South Pacific over the decade since the founding of the Research Center for the Pacific Island Countries, Liaocheng University. He told the authors that, Australia, the "deputy sheriff", has long tried to block and undermine the BRI projects in the South Pacific apart from the "demonization" of China-PICs cooperation. He finds from his conversations with the officials and businessmen in the PICs that the Australian politicians have kept badmouthing the BRI projects in the region, and that the consultants sent by Australian government to the governments of PICs have tried to distance the local governments from China and the BRI.

In his fieldwork, Zhao finds that it is extremely difficult for the Chinese nationals to secure an Australia transit visa, when the fastest and most convenient way for them to fly to the PICs and back home is to transit through

Australia. Zhao Shaofeng argues that the so-called China "debt trap" by some critics, and particularly by the former colonial powers are without foundation (the authors provide more detailed analysis on "the debt trap" from an academic perspective in the later part of this chapter). He questions the objectivity of such narratives against China and the PICs. In Zhao's views, the so-called "debt trap" is merely a "narrative trap" created by the United States and its military allies with ulterior motives to disrupt and undermine the China-PICs cooperation. Zhao claims that debt is a problem in the PICs, and one that appears to be increasing in importance. But for most PICs, it is debt to China is not a concern.

Zhao highlighted that China has exercised caution over the potential debt sustainability implications of the BRI and has taken steps to address the issue. He said that China has helped improve the debt management capacity of its BRI partners across the world in cooperation with an IMF training center. The Chinese Ministry of Finance has also established a new cooperation platform with some financing institutions. Zhao quotes a report released by the Lowy Institute based in Sydney, Australia:

> China committed itself to the G20 Operational Guidelines for Sustainable Financing in 2017, and to the G20 Principles for Quality Infrastructure Investment in 2019, both of which contain debt-related provisions including complying with World Bank and International Monetary Fund policies for countries where debt sustainability is already a concern (Rajah et al. 2019, p. 7).

These Chinese scholars note that many of the PICs have remained the least developed countries since they had been colonialized by the colonial powers for a couple of centuries, and since they have gained their independence for decades. It is in this context that they argue that what the PICs could anticipate from the U.S. "returning to the South Pacific" is further militarization of the region without economic growth and prosperity. Chen Hong argues that the cooperation conducted by the United States with the PICs is never about economic growth and development, but about U.S. exploitation of the PICs, making them unsinkable aircraft carriers to counter its hegemonic rivals, such as militarist Japan, the formal Soviet Union and now rising China. The United States is now trying to entice the PICs into the Quad that is widely considered by policy analysts inside and outside China as a main framework of Washington's Indo-Pacific Strategy of containment of China (Zhang & Wang 2022, p. 61, Menon 2021, Grossman 2020).

When interviewed (personal communication, June 18, 2022) by the authors, Guo Chunmei and Li Jianjun argue that the geopolitical competition between big powers is meaningless for the PICs, and merely serves the interests of the United States and the traditional players. The two scholars are of the view that the South Pacific region is the home to PICs, not the backyard of external powers, and that the region is a stage for cooperation, rather than an arena for geopolitical competition. Guo said that the PICs are all sovereign and independent states, with the right to make their own choices, rather than being vassals of others. However, the scholars welcome the growing involvement of the United States and others in the PICs as long as they are committed to addressing issues, such as local economic growth, peace and stability, climate change.

China has long been preoccupied with economic cooperation and trade with the developing states, including the PICs, and pursued the strategy of non-interference in other states' internal affairs. The "non-interference" strategy as opposed to the one adopted by the United States and Australia has been appreciated by some governments and politicians in the PICs and helped advance the China-PICs relations of cooperation. This strategy has, however, aroused concerns in both the PICs and the West over the local corruption and class disparities that have long plagued this region. Such concerns with the negative impact of the Chinese involvement in the PICs first came to the fore in the early 2000s when the Chinese companies began to rush into the PICs and invest in resources. Most recently, the Solomon government has concluded a package of pacts with some Chinese companies to exploit local resources and develop real estate, about which some businessmen inside and outside the PICs articulate complaints of lack of transparency (Barret 2019).

Empirical analysis on the Chinese economic development over the last four decades since Deng Xiaoping adopted the "open door" policy towards the rest of the world in the late 1970s reveals that transparency, good governance and a concern for environmental protection are of much significance for sustained prosperity and social progress (Long & Wang 2009, p. 67). The same is true of the PIC's economic growth and people's well-beings as well as the cooperation and trade between China and the PICs. The non-interference strategy and China's mercantilist approach to economic development may reap dividends in the short run, but they are detrimental to the long-term interests of both the PICs and China, arising from their economic cooperation and political partnership in the region. A World Bank report finds that China's BRI could speed up economic development and reduce poverty for dozens of developing countries—but it must be accompanied by deep policy reforms that increase transparency, improve debt sustainability, and mitigate environmental, social, and corruption risks (Ruta et al. 2019, p. 12).

Caroline Freund, the World Bank's Director for Macroeconomics, Trade, and Investment, concludes that "BRI's success depends on the implementation of policy measures in three broad categories: transparency, country-specific gaps, and multilateral cooperation". In her view, greater transparency is necessary at all levels, from project planning to budgeting and procurement and public reporting of debt levels, and environmental standards need to be strengthened. In this context, China needs to adopt the precautionary approach to avoid harm to natural resources and ecosystems starting from the decision-making stage and based on the independent scientific judgment through a transparent process (Xu 2022, p. 407). The extent to which China's BRI investments will be regulated by law needs to be made clear after China becomes a major source of capital flows to the South Pacific region over the past decades (Kirkwood & Chaisse 2020, p. 247). The contention around environmental impacts and corruption shows the need for China's investment finance to reckon with risks and the fallout from environment and governance issues (Canuto, 2019). Official guidelines on environment and social policies for Chinese companies investing abroad have been issued, signaling the matter has caught the attention of the Chinese authorities.

Much worse, the "non-interference" strategy may work against the goals of the Chinese engagement with the PICs, which is primarily aimed to reap the economic and trading interest though it is "infinitesimal" in contrast to the country's interest in the other parts of the developing world, such as Africa and Latin America. Moreover, it may work against China's efforts in reaping strategic benefits that derive from the combination of China's "hard", and more importantly, "soft" power in the South Pacific to reshape the regional system and order more to its liking (or in the official Chinese terms, a more rational and fairer order) (Yu 2018, p. 491). In this sense, China's non-interference strategy and mercantilist approach might turn out to be a barrier precluding its efforts in pursuit of the 'soft' power that, along with the growing 'hard' power at its disposal, boosts China's rise at the systemic (global) level.

An Appraisal from the PICs' Perspectives

China's vigorous involvement in the PICs has aroused diverse responses by the local governments and the general public in the region. From the local perspectives, there is no agreement among the local governments and general public in the PICs on China's expanding presence and influence in the region. Some political leaders, such as Sitiveni Rabuka, Prime Minister of Fiji, distance their governments from China. For instance, Rabuka delayed his visit to China, which coincided with a period of heightened rivalry between the United States and China in the South Pacific (Dziedzic 2023). Fiji's relations with China have burgeoned over the past couple of decades since the beginning of the 21st century, but have been less cordial since Rabuka was elected prime minister in late 2022.

Fiji's relations with China had blossomed under the rule of Frank Bainimarama since the traditional players in the region sought to punish Fiji for Bainimarama's 2006 coup. Immediately after taking power, Rabuka has put under review the police cooperation agreement with China, which was signed in 2011 by the Bainimarama's government as Rabuka views the agreement as being inconsistent with Fiji's democracy (Pacific News Service 2023). Moreover, Rabuka tried to elevate the status of Taiwan's representation in Fiji, but reversed that move after China filed strong protests. In his visit to Australia in October 2023, Rabuka told the press: "We're more comfortable dealing with traditional friends, that we have similar systems of government, that our democracies are the same brand of democracy, coming out of the Westminster system" (Associated Press 2023).

Fiame Naomi Mataafa, Samoa's new prime minister, cancelled a $100 million port development project backed by China in 2021 because it was excessive for the country's needs, and would increase the country's debts (Barrett 2021). Apparently, Prime Minister Mataafa had done the assessment on the governmental debts and a risk benefit analysis on whether the project would add to the total figure. The project had been backed by former prime minister Sa'ilele Malielegaoi, who claimed that it would benefit local economy and families. The project divided opinions in the country and became an issue in the elections in early April 2021 and Malielegaoi lost his majority in the Parliament. Once completed, the port would have the capacity of accommodating 12 vessels at once, which triggered speculations and fears among the traditional players, and particularly in the United States and Australia about the military significance. Prime Minister Mataafa cancelled the port project, but she is obviously unwilling to be dragged into big power competition and she dispersed the "China threat thesis" by saying "they are not our narratives" (Yu 2021, p. 83). Mataafa said that she hoped to maintain good relations with China, but that Samoa had more pressing needs than a wharf in Vaiusu Bay. Mataafa provided a detailed explanation for the cancellation of the project:

> Samoa is a small country. Our seaports and our airports cater for our needs. It's very difficult to imagine that we would need the scale that's being proposed under this particular project when there are more pressing projects that the government needs to give priority to (Global Construction Review 2021).

However, as some local media (e.g., *Samoa Observer*) note that China's BRI has got the political leaders of some PICs excited since it was first proposed by China under President Xi Jinping in 2013 (Rheeney 2018). Of them, Manasseh Sogavare, Prime Minister of Solomon Islands, James Marape, Prime Minister of PNG, Sa'ilele Malielegaoi, former Prime Minister of Samoa, and Frank Bainimarama, former Prime Minister of Fiji, are particularly appreciative of China's BRI and economic involvement in the region. Politically, they view their cooperation with China as a counterweight to the interference by the "traditional players" in their internal affairs, and a significant step towards terminating the hegemony of the "sheriff" and "deputy sheriff" in the region (Special Broadcasting Service 2019). To a lesser degree, China's increasing involvement in the region has elevated the PICs status in the global geopolitics and forced the United States and other traditional players to notice them again.

Politically, the United States has to scale up attention to the PICs and pledge to be more involved in the region, including reopening embassies in and re-sending Peace Corps volunteers to some PICs (Perry 2023). Economically, they view their cooperation with China as an opportunity for economic growth and better livelihoods for the local people. Many PICs are facing an existential threat from rising sea levels and suffering from high levels of deprivation and low levels of basic infrastructure, particularly in sanitation. China has become a substantial source of trade, infrastructure and aid for the PICs over the last decades. Manasseh Sogavare, former Prime Minister of the Solomon Islands, made positive remarks on the China-proposed initiatives, including the Belt and Road Initiative, Global Development Initiative, and Global Civilization Initiative in his speech to the General Debate of the UN General Assembly (United Nations 2023). Peter O'Neill, former Prime Minister of PNG, referred to poverty as one of the most critical challenges that his country is confronting. He showed his appreciation in a speech in July 2023 of China's ability to bring a large population to a middle-class income and a better standard of living by saying 'that is something that PNG has been aspiring to lead that kind of example and follow':

> You are able to move over 300 or 400 million people from low based income level to a middle-income situation, which is really lifted the standard of living for your people. That is the experience that countries like PNG need (O'Neill 2023).

Peter O'Neill witnesses that China has become a huge investor in PNG over the last 20 years by providing access to finance and to the experience of many of their contractors who were able to build infrastructure in PNG: "we lack foreign direct investment and China is now starting to become the largest investor in our country". In the viewpoints of Peter O'Neill, the BRI is a great initiative for developing countries like PNG because of the access to capital and infrastructure-building capacities. It is able to open up markets and improve the standard of living for our people (Australian Broadcasting Company 2018). The initiative is something that is good for PNG and good for the region. It will promote trade and investment for all countries globally. China's BRI and investment provide PNG an opportunity to 'build many schools, many hospitals, many roads, many airports, and infrastructure that is changing the lives of individual families and individuals'. Peter O'Neill (2023) argues:

> PNG's challenges are that we must continue to stay away from the issues that are running around with the geopolitics of our region. Countries in the Pacific, especially the smaller countries, they have no ability to advance the course of geopolitics that is going on. But unfortunately, we get dragged into it. My views have been very public and very upfront that particularly Pacific Island countries to stay clear of those discussions, we should focus on economic and trade and people to people relationships. That's where it matters most.

Tuilaepa Sailele Malielegaoi, former Prime Minister of Samoa, has been a strong supporter of the BRI, and has described criticism of China's lending as patronizing. He said that the BRI is opening a vast market and bringing lots of opportunities for the world, particular for "the small countries like Samoa in the South Pacific region in this difficult time and challenges posed by climate change". He dismissed the "debt trap" thesis by saying: "We are fortunate to have grants from China. I think all the allegation (of the China debt trap) is based completely on misunderstanding of the issues involved." (Rheeney 2018). As for the China threat thesis, Malielegaoi responded that he would not allow geopolitical fears to stifle the development of much-needed infrastructure, and that Samoa would "follow our own line of thought", not that of the United States and its allies.

Similar to Tuilaepa Sailele Malielegaoi, Charlot Salwai, Prime Minister of Vanuatu, shows his appreciation of the BRI by saying that his country will seek additional finance from China as a result of the need for projects in hard infrastructure, like roads, ports, telecommunications, utilities, health and education. Salwai argues that to funnel money into productive projects would help the country pay back its existing debt, provide employment and develop the economy. Vanuatu owes nearly $130 million to China, which accounts for roughly half its external debt and represents over 13 percent of its annual GDP. When interviewed, he said:

> We are an independent country, and we can't wait for grants to come. Whether through grants or through loans we have to have money to build our infrastructure, we want to invest this money into economic sectors (Greenfield 2019).

As well, China's BRI has got some officials of the local governments excited and the recent memorandum of understanding on a fishery park signed in late 2020 by a Chinese company and the authorities of the Solomon Islands is a case in point. The memorandum was signed by Fujian Zhonghong Fishery Company, Lino Tom, Fisheries Minister of PNG, and Taboi Yoto, Governor of Western province, to build a multifunctional fishery industrial park on Daru Island (Ministry of Commerce of the PRC 2020). The project is part of the BRI, worth around US$150 million, which signals a major boost to PNG's ambition to establish itself as a significant exporter of seafood to the Chinese market and to other parts of the world. The Fujian Zhonghong Fishery has long been involved in PNG, mainly in fishing and seafood processing and exports of seafood to China. The fishery park is located in an impoverished region of the PNG, which is rich in fish resource and has no capacity to commercially fish its share of the quotas under the Torres Strait Treaty concluded by Australia and PNG (Smith 2020). The PICs as a whole are heavily dependent on marine resources, especially tuna, for their export earnings. The local government hopes the fishery park to bring more jobs and improve the livelihoods of the local people. The multifunctional park is therefore commissioned with a task by the local authorities to boost local economic growth and employment.

The fishery park attracted criticism particularly from Australia about the potential security risks to Australia, and the possibility of depletion of fishery resources after the fishery park begins to process fish taken from the Torres Strait that divides PNG and Australia (Smith 2020b). Some analysts, such as Leon Perera, CEO of international research and consulting firm Spire, dismiss the fears by saying that the claims have no basis. Leon Perera explains that the region is known to be abundant in marine resources, including fish, prawns and lobsters, and that the fishery park could create the foundation for PNG's seafood export industry (Wilson 2021). As is the case with many least developed countries, PNG can hardly work towards realizing its goal of economic development without financial help from other countries. Some Chinese companies have increased their investment in the PNG in cooperation with the local authorities to boost PNG's exports to the Chinese market.

The Chinese government has concluded an agreement with PNG, allowing the PNG's seafood to directly export into China and granting it "zero-tariff". In so doing, China wishes to help PNG fulfill its aspiration of growing as a major seafood exporter in the South Pacific (Vari 2020). More PNG fishery companies are expected to be registered by China's General Administration of Customs as key exporters of seafood after the health certificates for live seafood are submitted and the administrative requirements are satisfied. The rapidly growing Chinese market is in need of more seafood that the Chinese producers can hardly meet while the PICs, including PNG, are rich in fish resources, but have no capacity to commercially fish. The local governments in the South Pacific, such as the one of the Western Province in PNG, is eager to have fishery cooperation with China in the hopes of boosting their economic growth and reducing poverty.

A delegation from Australia's Foreign Affairs Department and the Australian High Commission in PNG traveled to Daru soon after the fishery cooperation memorandum was signed, according to a report from the Australian Broadcasting Corporation (Whiting 2021). The delegation met the local authorities of PNG, asking the latter to abandon the fishery project in Daru, which was rejected by the local authorities. Yoto reassured the local people after the meeting that he would not abandon the project even under foreign pressure: "I will not sway". Yoto explained why: "I do not want my people to remain living in poverty". One day later, Yoto criticized Australia on a Facebook post: "as usually, the Australian government proposes nothing to counter the Chinese proposal. They came with no alternative plans to counter and deter any foreign direct investment, especially to alleviate our poverty and improve social services".

After she failed to dissuade the PNG authorities, Marise Payne, Australian Foreign Affairs Minister, threatened the PNG with force by announcing that "commercial-scale fisheries would not be permitted" and the Australian Border Force would be patrolling the Torres Strait (Smith 2020b). Minister Lino Tom responded that "PNG is within its sovereign rights" to be considering the fishery project and that "it can boost economic growth and reduce poverty in the area". He criticized the Australian government for its neglect of the economic benefits that the fishery project would bring to PNG, including jobs for local people (Whiting 2021b). Yoto added:

> Australians are working behind my back to have my people not to support any foreign direct investment. It's regrettable that all they want is for us to be subsistence farmers and fishermen, and maintain our current status quo. This is about improving the lives of the individual population that each country has.

In addition to the Chinese investment in fishery, some officials in the PICs express their appreciation of the BRI and China's investment in the PICs' infrastructural development. Jerry Agus, chief executive officer of PNG Tourism Promotion Authority, expresses that infrastructure is very important for the PICs: "without infrastructure, you cannot do anything." (Xinhua 2018). A report released by the Asian Development Bank justifies Jerry Agus' argument, which claims that "the Pacific has enormous investment needs in the range of US$2.8 billion a year up to 2030", and that investment in critical infrastructure, such as airports, highways, bridges and ports can hardly meet on its own (Asia Development Bank 2019).

Emma Veve, director of social sectors and public sector management in the Pacific Department of Asia Development Bank, highlights that the economies of the PICs are too small and too isolated. In this sense, continued grant and concessional assistance from development partners will remain absolutely critical in supporting sustainable, inclusive, and resilient development in the PICs. Joseph Cajetan is acting administrator for the Southern Highlands Provincial Government in PNG and he shares Jerry Agus that PICs need more foreign investment in infrastructural development. In this context, Joseph Cajetan expresses his idea that he is ready to sign more cooperation contracts with organizations or businessmen from China. In his eyes, he has many reasons for his decision:

> Our (geological) environment is very unforgiving. We need roads, airports, bridges. PNG has been undertaking infrastructure projects to meet the demand of its growing economy. In our province, we are building a university, expanding an airport, and planning to build a new port. Also we wanted to upgrade our hydro-power generation station, for the power generation capacity could not meet demand of the province. The BRI can really benefit PNG, especially with electric power supply, as PNG is developing fast and there is great demand for energy and we are running out of capacity.

Yogesh Karan, Permanent Secretary for the Prime Minister Office of Fiji, points out that the Chinese expertise and know-how in the field of renewable energy can be of tremendous help to the PICs. In Karan's view, the PICs are rich in renewable energy resources, such as hydropower, solar power and wind power (Xinhua 2018). When interviewed, Keshmeer Makun, a lecturer at the University of the South Pacific based in Suva, Fiji, says that the BRI is a process of inclusive and common development, which is in the interests of both PICs and the international development partners if they can work together and take concrete actions. In his eyes, the BRI has become a platform for cooperation between China and the participating countries across the world, including the PICs:

> The world has already witnessed China's expanding trade and investment ties with countries along the Belt and Road over the years. The Chinese-run projects and businesses have become part of the local economy in the Pacific islands, generating jobs and incomes for the people (Xinhua 2022).

The controversial Pacific Game project in the Solomon Islands that is contributed by China, Australia and others probably provides a typical case of varied responses from the local people. China has contributed half of the games' approximate 1.85 billion Solomon Island dollars (about US$220 million) cost and the Solomon Islands government nearly one third. Australia, Japan and Indonesia also have made significant contributions (Maka'a 2023). Manasseh Sogavare, then Prime Minister, argued that the country's economy would have collapsed "without the financial and economic boost brought in by the 2023 Pacific Games projects". He further argued that the investment brought in by the Games injected a boost into local economy and facilitated progress on other infrastructure projects, such as the new airport terminal and Japan's repairing of a highway between the airport and capital.

However, Matthew Wale, the Solomon Islands' opposition leader, criticized spending on the games wasteful, particularly when the country struggles to provide basic healthcare (Radio New Zealand 2023). Other critics complained that the Games would reinforce lopsided development in the country as they mainly benefit the capital, and questioned if the country can afford to maintain the facilities. Gina Maka'a, a journalist from Benar News, saw David Tutukiri, a high school principal, among the crowd at the Stadium handover ceremony, who said that young people will benefit from having proper sports facilities. Tutukiri added that "these facilities are greatly appreciated by ordinary citizens. We are fortunate to have them". Unity Galekausua, a student at King George VI High School in Honiara, said it was a thrill to attend the ceremony: "this stadium signifies hope for the future. With better sports facilities, young people aiming to excel in sports can receive proper training."

In the eyes of some elites in the PICs, the involvement of China and the United States in the South Pacific constitutes a stark contrast as the former expects a relationship of economic cooperation and trade with the PICs, whereas the latter a "reliable backyard" for its global hegemony. Dorothy Wickham, a journalist in the Solomon Islands, notes that the United States has little concrete legacy in the PICs, and its trade with some of the PICs, such as with the Solomon Islands, is negligible. In contrast, China is the biggest trading partner of a number of PICs, and its aided and constructed highways, bridges, factories can be seen everywhere in the region, and become part of the local economy (Wickham 2022). The political and commercial elites (e.g., Rabuka, O'neil and Mataafa) usually show little interest in the geopolitical competition between the traditional and new players, and try to downplay the game by arguing that geopolitical competition is not in the interest of the PICs that want to be friends to all and enemies to none. When interviewed by the authors (personal communication, June 18, 2022), Guo Chunmei at China Institutes of Contemporary International Relations attributes the attitudes held by the political and commercial elites in the PICs to the West's neglect of the region and China's increasing cooperation with the PICs[39]. "After years of neglect by the West", the political and commercial elites as well as the general public have come to realize the significant roles played by China in terms of economic, political and environmental spheres, and "they are not buying into vicious rhetoric against China".

Prime Minister Mataafa who stopped a China-funded port project in Samoa after she took into power refuses to be involved in the America-China competition by clarifying that "the 'China threat thesis' is their (the traditional players) narratives, not ours" (Yu 2021, p. 85). PNG Prime Minister James Marape issued a statement contradicting Major General Toropo's comments about China's presence in his country: 'I do not perceive China as a security threat, but rather as an important development, investment and trade partner with shared values conducted under mutual friendship and understanding' (Australian Broadcasting Company 2021). Prime Minister Sitiveni Rabuka, who put Fiji-China police cooperation under review, calls for the PICs to declare their ocean territories a "zone of peace" when he sees that the United States and China are jostling for geopolitical influence in the region (Wright 2023). Rabuka claimed that "it is our manifest duty to carry banners for peace and speak out for harmony in our time and forever" when he addressed the policy analysts in the Lowy Institute based in Sydney, Australia. Like Prime Minister Mataafa, Rabuka said that his government continued to value its relationship with China, the world's No. 2 economy, 'even as its rivalry with the U.S. appeared to be intensifying'. Peter

39 Guo Chunmei is deputy director and associate research professor in the Institute of Southeast Asian and Oceanian Studies, China Institutes of Contemporary International Relations.

O'Neill (2023), former Prime Minister of PNG, provides a detailed explanation why the PICs have no interest in the geopolitical competition:

> We are not really interested in issues of security arrangements. We are not in any conflict with anyone. I think the Pacific is big enough for everyone. There are greater challenges before us like climate change and population growth that many of the other countries within the region, especially the Asia-Pacific region, are facing. That needs our immediate attention. I think those are focuses that we should be focusing on.

As the Chinese investment flows into the South Pacific, some critics in the PICs and in the West articulate their concerns with the growing debt of the PICs to China and blame China for its "debt-trap diplomacy", especially when it comes to the PICs (Varrall 2021, Foster 2021). Some justify the blame by arguing that the PICs obviously do not have the capacity to pay back the Chinese loans, and that the rapidly growing debts on the part of the PICs have posed a threat to the sustained economic growth and sovereignty of the PICs. In this context, it is prudent for Prime Minister Fiame Mataafa to cancel the country's port project funded by China given Samoa's mounting debt as discussed above. However, a number of scholars and policy analysts beg to differ in the assertion of China's "debt-trap" diplomacy. Roland Rajah, Alexandre Dayant and Jonathan Pryke in the Lowy Institute, an independent policy think tank in Sydney, conclude in their recently published report, titled "Oceans of debt? Belt and Road and debt diplomacy in the Pacific": "our analysis of debt in the Pacific strongly suggests that China has not been engaged in such problematic debt practices in the Pacific as to justify accusations of debt trap diplomacy, at least not so far" (Rajah et al. 2019).

The three researchers in the Lowy Institute argue in their report that "for most countries it is not debt to China that is of concern. Keep that in mind next time you hear that the Pacific is drowning in Chinese debt". The researchers attribute the accusation of debt-trap diplomacy first to the increasing geopolitical competition and the rush from larger players to win influence in the region, and second to the lack of objective economic analysis. James Laurenceson at the University Technology Sydney, is of the view:

> The very concept of Chinese debt-trap diplomacy is an odd one. If a Chinese loan goes bad, it is the Chinese lender at risk of losing its capital. The port or road can't be taken away from the host country. And the evidence that loan default to China or any other country provides coercive leverage is shallow.

Bob Jurriaan Van Grieken and Jaroslaw Kantorowicz note that there is a growing concern among the established powers about China's sway over the aid-dependent PICs concurrent with China's expansion of its aid program in the region (Grieken et al 2021, p. 862). Drawing on project-level data from AidData for the period 2000-2014, they disaggregate China's official financing into its constituent parts and systematically explores the determinants of China's Official Development Assistance (ODA) and its commercially-oriented finance flows to the Pacific. The two scholars find through panel data analysis that, contrary to the popular belief, China does not reward voting compliance in the United Nations nor is its allocation of financing to the Pacific influenced by the countries' level of indebtedness. As for Sri Lanka and Malaysia, the two most widely cited 'victims' of China's 'debt-trap diplomacy', they find that the most controversial BRI projects were initiated by the recipient governments that pursued their own domestic agendas. The two scholars conclude that their debt problems arose mainly from the misconduct of local elites and the Western-dominated financial markets. China has faced negative reactions and pushback in both countries, though to a lesser extent than is commonly believed, given the high-level interests at stake in the recipient countries.

After having analyzed six countries–Sri Lanka, Maldives, Malaysia, Laos, Kenya, and Djibouti that have confronted debt problem, Michal Himmer and Zdeněk Rod fail to detect the Chinese intention to burden borrowing countries with debt in order to gain strategic assets in any case (Himmer & Rod 2022, p. 252). Their statement is supported by various Chinese actions that go straight against a potential strategic gain:

> For example, China postponed the payments of Kenyan debts by six months due to the COVID-19 pandemic, slightly reduced Maldivian debt due to the same reason, or reduced Malaysian debt by a third. In any of those cases, China could have requested the payment of its debt with the relinquishment of a strategic asset (port, airport, mining rights, etc.) but the opposite happened. Additionally, we did not uncover any non-material assets (e. g., rising Chinese influence within internal matters of the borrowing states) either. China simply used the existing relations with other states' politicians to its advantage as would probably any other country. Therefore, we tend to believe that China did not engage in a relationship with the borrowing country with malicious intentions.

Yang Honglian, a Fiji-based senior research fellow at the Research Center for Pacific Islands Countries, Liaocheng University, notes that some observers and political commentators worry that China's large-scale infrastructure projects may lead to debt problems and put some countries in a disadvantaged position of being dependent on China. However, the debt problem of the PICs has long existed, long before China proposed cooperation under the BRI in the region. The key to the debt issue lies in how the PICs evaluate their economic development and how they make feasible plans. On the premise of ensuring that loan and contract conditions are transparent and fair, Yang concludes that the PICs can meet the needs of local people's livelihood development through reasonable loans and allow their people to benefit from such investment. Yang notes that with the escalation of geopolitical competition in the region, the PICs' debt has been purposely used by the United States and its military allies to attack the PICs and the new players in the region. Rohan Fox and Matthew Dornan in the Development Policy Centre of the Australian National University in Canberra find that China is the largest bilateral lender, but the Chinese lending comprises less than half of lending in any single country apart from Tonga (Fox & Dornan 2018). Based on their research, China held around 12 percent of the total debt by the Pacific nations, or US$1.3 billion out of US$11.2 billion.

A report published by the Asian Development Bank in 2019 highlighted that funding from international partners will be vital for investments in infrastructural projects. This is because countries in the Pacific have a small amount of fiscal space to provide tax incentives and exemptions to boost these projects thanks to their stable fiscal footing and public debt profile (Asia Development Bank 2019). In late 2019, the Asian Development Bank approved a proposed US$62.3 million grant to rehabilitate and upgrade Apia Port, Samoa's gateway to the rest of the world. When completed, the project will open up trade channels particularly to Asia and North America with the potential to boost the local economy and employment. The Asian Development Bank insists that the investment is necessary for Samoa. The report reasons that with a population of about 200,000 and a gross domestic product of just over US$800 million, the country is small and geographically isolated, with limited access to global value chains and financial markets, and exposed to disaster risk. Despite strong efforts to improve revenue collection and cap spending to limit budget deficits, the International Monetary Fund (IMF) still rates Samoa as at high risk of distress. This does not reflect poor financial management, rather it shows the Catch-22 faced by the Pacific: the small slow-growing economies are unable to access the very investment funds needed to raise economic performance and drive development. Despite doing much to rein in expenditures and boost revenues, the small and isolated nature of the Pacific Islands provides them with limited options to mitigate exposure to shocks from international price fluctuations, as well as natural hazards and climate change.

The report concludes that Samoa's situation is indicative of the broader Pacific Islands region that has enormous investment needs for infrastructure, economic growth and others. Among numerous other development projects, ADB is supporting the climate-proofing and rehabilitation of the sole seaport in Nauru, a country that relies almost totally on maritime transport. ADB also funds the construction of a seawater desalination plant and rehabilitation of the water distribution network in Kiribati, which is aimed to increase the local supply of fresh water and access to the same in a major urban area. As these economies of Nauru and Kiribati are even smaller, each less than a quarter the size of Samoa's, the costs of these projects alone reach the equivalent of about two-thirds of annual GDP in Nauru, and one-fifth of GDP in Kiribati.

The report notes that the average debt-to-GDP ratio in 2018 for ADB's Developing Member Countries (DMCs) in the Pacific stood at 35 percent, well below the emerging and developing Asia average of almost 52 percent. Only one country in the Pacific had a debt-to-GDP ratio higher than that regional average. Debt-to-GDP ratios of eight of ADB's 15 Pacific DMCs are also currently below the subregional average and none are actually in debt distress, according to IMF ratings. The report notes that the broader trend line is encouraging as the Pacific's average debt-to-GDP ratio stood at over 53 percent in 2009 but fell to just over 36 percent in 2014. The trend line is on the rise again, forecast to exceed 44 percent of GDP by 2024, precisely due to the necessary investments to bridge remaining gaps in access to basic services, such as health care and education; expand land, sea, and air transport networks; and climate-proof, maintain, or repair disaster damage to public assets. Veve summarized that "This trendline shows that the broader debt situation in the Pacific countries has improved impressively over much of this decade. But the projected rise in average debt-to-GDP is the result of spending that is absolutely critical to the long-term economic stability of these countries."

Conclusion

The main argument of this chapter is that the Chinese foreign policy elites have generally viewed China's BRI and its increasing involvement in the South Pacific as mutually beneficial for China and its partners in the South Pacific. They also believe that the BRI and China's involvement in the region help China reap economic and political benefits as they expect. From the Chinese perspectives, the BRI in the PICs is not merely an economic initiative, but one with a combination of economic, political and strategic objectives and consequences. The BRI is aimed to advance China-PICs cooperation in the spheres of infrastructural and economic development, and by extension, political and strategic partnership.

The responses from the PICs to the BRI and China's increasing involvement in the region are diverse, with some being supportive and others opposed. However, the rapidly expanding presence and influence of China in the region reveal a fact that the PICs and particularly their political and commercial elites would more often than not like to embrace the BRI and China's vigorous involvement in the region. Otherwise, it is hard to explain why China, as a new comer, can expand its presence and influence in the traditional "sphere of influence" of the United States and other former colonial powers at such a rapid rate. From the PICs' perspectives, the BRI and China's vigorous involvement in the region provide the small states in the region an opportunity to play big games and "achieve the best from both worlds" by playing the traditional and new players against each other.

References

Agostini, S., Harvey, B.P., Wada, S., Milazzo, M., Inaba, K., Hall-Spencer, J.M., 2018, 'Ocean acidification drives community shifts towards simplified non-calcified habitats in a subtropical–temperate transition zone', *Scientific Report*, 8, 11354.

Almulhim, A.I., Alverio, G.N., Sharifi, A. *et al 2024*, 'Climate-induced migration in the Global South: an in-depth analysis', *npj Climate Action*, Vol. 3, No. 47, pp. 1-12.

Asia Development Bank 2019, *The Pacific: Urgent Development Needs Remain Despite Stable Debt and Higher Revenues*, 18 September, https://www.adb.org/news/features/pacific-urgent-development-needs-remain-despite-stable-debt-and-higher-revenues.

Associated Press 2023, 'Fijian prime minister 'more comfortable dealing with traditional friends' like Australia than China', *Financial Post*, 17 October, https://financialpost.com/pmn/business-pmn/fijian-prime-minister-more-comfortable-dealing-with-traditional-friends-like-australia-than-china.

Australian Broadcasting Company 2018, PNG becomes first Pacific nation to sign onto China's One Belt, One Road, 25 June, https://www.abc.net.au/pacific/programs/pacificbeat/png-china-trip/9905346.

Australian Broadcasting Company 2021, 'Major naval base on PNG manus island lonbrum', 15 June, https://www.abc.net.au/news/2021-06-15/major-naval-base-on-png-manus-island-lombrum-adf/100216040.

Barrett, Jonathan 2019, 'Solomon Islands government says Chinese lease of island unlawful', *Sydney Morning Herald*, 26 October, https://www.smh.com.au/world/oceania/solomon-islands-government-says-chinese-lease-of-island-unlawful-20191026-p534gv.html.

Barrett, Jonathan 2021, 'Samoa's new leader scraps Belt and Road port deal', *Sydney Morning Herald*, 30 July, https://www.smh.com.au/world/oceania/samoa-s-new-leader-scraps-belt-and-road-port-deal-20210730-p58egu.html.

Bouchet, Louis; Thoms, Martin C. and Parsons, Melissa 2019, 'Groundwater as a social-ecological system: A framework for managing groundwater in Pacific Small Island Developing States', Groundwater for Sustainable Development, Vol. 8, No. 2, pp. 579-589.

Bregolat, Eugenio 2015, *the Second Chinese Revolution*, Palgrave Macmillan: New York, p. 64

Canuto, Otaviano 2019, 'How Chinese Investment in Latin America Is Changing', *Americas Quarterly*, 12 March. https://www.americasquarterly.org/article/how-chinese-investment-in-latin-america-is-changing/.

Carlson, Rachel R., Evans, Luke J., Foo, Shawna, A. et al 2021, 'Synergistic benefits of conserving land-sea ecosystems', *Global Ecology and Conservation*, Vol. 28, No. 2, https://www.sciencedirect.com/science/article/pii/S2351989421002341.

Cave, Damien 2022, 'Why a Chinese Security Deal in the Pacific Could Ripple Through the World', *New York Times*, 20 April, https://www.nytimes.com/2022/04/20/world/australia/china-solomon-islands-security-pact.html.

Chen, Qingqing 2023, 'U.S. arrogance, strategic intentions to counter China laid bare amid 2nd U.S.-Pacific Islands summit', *The Global Times*, 25 September, https://www.globaltimes.cn/page/202309/1298888.shtml.

Chen, Xiaochen and Chang, Yudi 2022, 'The impact of the Indo-Pacific strategy on the regional order in the South Pacific', *Social Sciences*, Vol. 21, No. 3, pp. 20-33.

Colton, Greg 2018, Stronger together: Safeguarding Australia's security interests through closer Pacific ties, Lowy Institute: Sydney.

Das, Shaheli 2016, 'How Important Is Latin America on China's Foreign Policy Agenda?', *Diplomat*, 16 November, https://thediplomat.com/2016/11/how-important-is-latin-america-on-chinas-foreign-policy-agenda/.

Deng, Xiaoping 1993, *Selected Deng Xiaoping works* (Volume 3), People's Publishing, Beijing, p. 370.

Ding, Peng and Cui, Yuzhong 2017, 'a review of China-PICs cooperation', *Journal of Shandong Science and Technology University*, No. 6, pp. 40-43.

Du, Wenhui 2023, The China-PICs climate change training programs, the Research Center for PICs/China-PICs Climate Cooperation Action Center, 19 December, https://rcpic.lcu.edu.cn/f/information/news/detail/bd13855194d14455b078400cbb963366.

Dziedzic, Stephen 2023, 'Fiji's Prime Minister Sitiveni Rabuka delays China visit after injuring his head while looking at his phone', Australian Broadcasting Company, 26 July, https://www.abc.net.au/news/2023-07-26/fiji-prime-minister-delays-china-visit/102647554

Foster, Kendrick 2021, 'Modern Island Hopping: The Geopolitical Battle for the Pacific', Harvard International Review, 1 April, https://hir.harvard.edu/modern-island-hopping/.

Fox, Rohan and Dornan, Matthew 2018, 'China in the Pacific: is China engaged in "debt-trap diplomacy"?', *Devpolicyblog*, Australian National University, 8 November, file:///C:/Users/mark7/Downloads/is-china-engaged-in-debt-trap-diplomacy-20181108.pdf.pdf.

Fukuyama, F. 1992, *The end of history and the last man*, Hamilton, London, p. 10.

Fukuyama, Francis 2011, 'U.S. democracy has little to teach China', Financial Times, 18 January, https://www.ft.com/content/cb6af6e8-2272-11e0-b6a2-00144feab49a

Gao, Fei and Zhang, Jian 2017, 'The strategic triangle of China-America-Russia in the post–Cold War era', Gao, Fei. & Li., Mingjiang (eds.) *China's neighborhood diplomacy: Peaceful development vs strategic hedging*. Beijing, Global Press, p. 48.

Global Construction Review 2021, Samoa set to cancel $100m Chinese-funded port project, 21 May, https://www.globalconstructionreview.com/samoa-set-cancel-100m-chinese-funded-port-project/.

Greenfield, Charlotte 2019, *Vanuatu to seek more Belt and Road assistance from Beijing: PM*, Reuters, 22 May, https://www.reuters.com/article/idUSKCN1SS0RW/.

Grieken, Van; Jurriaan, Bob and Kantorowicz, Jaroslaw 2021, 'Debunking Myths about China: The Determinants of China's Official Financing to the Pacific', *Geopolitics*, Vol. 26, No. 3, pp. 861-888.

Grossman, Dereck 2020, 'The Quad Is Poised to Become Openly Anti-China Soon', Rand, 28 July, https://www.rand.org/pubs/commentary/2020/07/the-quad-is-poised-to-become-openly-anti-china-soon.html

Guo, Chunhai 2017, 'zhonggong shibada yilai zhongguo dui lamei waijiao zhengce yu shijian (Chinese diplomatic policy towards Latin America and its implementation since the 18th Congress of the Chinese Communist Party)', *Journal of Latin American Studies*, Vol. 39, No. 2, pp. 1-16.

Himmer, Michal and Rod, Zdeněk 2022, 'Chinese debt trap diplomacy: reality or myth?', *Journal of the Indian Ocean Region*, Vol. 18, No. 3, pp. 250-272.

Hsu, Immanuel, C.Y. (Xu, Zhongyue) 2000, *the rise of modern China*, Oxford University Press: New York, p. 477.

Jain, Purnendra (2006) 'A little NATO against China', *Asian Times*, 18 March, www.atimes.com/atimes/China/HC18Ad01.html.

Jennings, Ralp. 2019, 'First Asia, Now South Pacific: China Expands Economic Footprint in Traditional Western Stronghold', VOA news, 23 September, https://www.voacambodia.com/a/first-Asia-now-south-pacific-china-expands-economic-footprint-in-traditional-western-stronghold/5094984.html.

Jiang, Shixue 2008, 'The Chinese foreign policy perspective', in Roett, Riordan and Paz, Guadalupe (eds), *China's expansion into the western hemisphere: implications for Latin America and the United States*, Washington DC: Brookings Institution Press.

Kirkwood, Jamieson and Chaisse, Julien 2020, 'Chinese Puzzle: Anatomy of the (Invisible) Belt and Road Investment Treaty', *Journal of International Economic Law*, No. 23, pp. 245-269.

Laursen, Finn 2009, *The EU in the Global Political Economy*, P.I.E. PETER LIANG: Brussels, p. 224.

Li, Xuanmin 2022, 'China, Tonga are examples of 'building a community with shared future', long-term Chinese investments dwarf the United States, Australia', *The Global Times*, 30 May, https://www.globaltimes.cn/page/202205/1266930.shtml.

Liu, Ye 2004, *Chinese Intellectuals and Chinese revolutions*, Tianjin People's Press: Tianjin, p. 129.

Löfflmann, Georg 2016, 'The Pivot between Containment, Engagement, and Restraint: President Obama's Conflicted Grand Strategy in Asia', *Asian Security*, Vol. 12, No. 2, pp. 92-110.

Long, Fu and Wang, Jinzhao 2009, 'the non-linear relationship between China's economic development and social harmony in the era of China's reform and opening to the outside world', *Jianghai Journal*, Vol. 29, No. 2, pp. 66-74.

Lu, Guixia 2022, 'China-PICs cooperation in the context of the BRI and its prospect', *Academic Frontier*, Vol. 86, No. 7, pp. 70-77.

Maka'a, Gina 2023, 'Solomon Islands leader credits China-aided Pacific Games as economic lifeline', Benar News, 21 August, https://www.benarnews.org/english/news/pacific/china-hands-stadium-to-solomon-islands-for-pacific-games-08202023235227.html

Mao, Haijian 1995, *Studies on the Opium War*, Sanlian Press: Beijing, p. 583.

Marine Stewardship Council 2024, *Climate change and fishing*, August, https://www.msc.org/what-we-are-doing/oceans-at-risk/climate-change-and-fishing.

Mcdonald, Joshua 2019, 'Pacific Island Nations Consider Deep-sea Mining, Despite Risks', *Diplomat*, 18 June, https://thediplomat.com/2021/06/pacific-island-nations-consider-deep-sea-mining-despite-risks/.

McVeigh, Karen 2023, 'James Cameron supports deep-sea mining. Scientists say it's a huge risk. Who's right?', *Guardian*, 27 July, https://www.theguardian.com/environment/2023/jul/27/james-cameron-supports-deep-sea-mining-activists-say-its-a-disaster-whos-right.

Menon, Rajan 2021, 'The Quad Is a Delusion', Foreign Policy, 28 June, https://foreignpolicy.com/2021/06/28/quad-delusion-china-power-containment/.

Mimura, Nobuo 1999, 'Vulnerability of island countries in the South Pacific to sea level rise and climate change', *Climate Research*, Vol. 12, No. 2/3, pp. 137-143.

Ministry of Commerce of the PRC 2020, Fujian Zhonghong company invests in a multifunctional fishery park in PNG, 13 November, http://pg.mofcom.gov.cn/article/sqfb/yy/202011/20201103015468.shtml

Ministry of Foreign Affairs of the PRC 2022, *The position document on China-PICs mutual respect and common development*, 30 May, https://www.mfa.gov.cn/web/ziliao_674904/tytj_674911/zcwj_674915/202205/t20220530_10694631.shtml.

Ministry of Foreign Affairs of the PRC 2023b, *Joint Statement on Establishing a Comprehensive Strategic Partnership Featuring Mutual Respect and Common Development for a New Era Between the People's Republic of China and Solomon Islands*, 10 July, https://www.mfa.gov.cn/web/zyxw/202307/t20230710_11110974.shtml

Ministry of Foreign Affairs of the PRC 2023a, China's relations with Pacific Island Countries, October, https://www.mfa.gov.cn/web/gjhdq_676201/gj_676203/dyz_681240/1206_681666/sbgx_681670/.

Ministry of Foreign Affairs of the PRC 2023c, *Joint Statement on Establishing a Comprehensive Strategic Partnership Featuring Mutual Respect and Common Development for a New Era Between the People's Republic of China and Solomon Islands*, 10 July, https://www.mfa.gov.cn/web/zyxw/202307/t20230710_11110974.shtml.

Morgan, W., Carter, S. G., and Manoa, F. 2024, 'Leading from the Frontline: A History of Pacific Climate Diplomacy', *The Journal of Pacific History*, pp. 1-22, https://doi.org/10.1080/00223344.2024.2360093

Oakes, R., Milan, A. and Campbell, J. 2016, *Kiribati: Climate Change and Migration*, United Nations University.

O'Grady, Mary anastasia 2004, 'The Middle Kingdom in Latin America', *Wall Street Journal*, 6 September 2004, p. A7.

O'Neill, Peter 2023, *Cooperation for a Sustainable 21st Century, Center for China & Globalization*, 5 July, http://en.ccg.org.cn/archives/79725

Pacific Community Centre for Ocean Science 2024, *Pacific Island atolls fixed on water security*, 4 June, https://www.spc.int/updates/news/media-release/2024/06/pacific-island-atolls-fixed-on-water-security.

Pacific News Service 2023, Prime Minister Rabuka cancels China visit, Pacific Islands News Association, 26 July, https://pina.com.fj/2023/07/26/fiji-pm-rabuka-cancels-china-visit/

Park, Jaepil; Ye, Fang; Li, Chunlin and He, Yixiong 2020, 'The relationship between China-South Pacific island countries tourism and trade in the context of the Belt and Road Initiative', *Island Studies Journal*, Vol. 15, No. 2, pp. 73-92.

Parsons, Chris 2022, 'The Pacific Islands: The front line in the battle against climate change', U.S. National Science Foundation, 23 May, https://new.nsf.gov/science-matters/pacific-islands-front-line-battle-against-climate.

Perry, Nick 2023, 'U.S. reopens embassy in the Solomon Islands to counter China', *Los Angels Times*, 2 February, https://www.latimes.com/world-nation/story/2023-02-02/us-opens-embassy-solomon-islands-counter-china.

Radio New Zealand 2023, Solomon Islands government receives Pacific Games stadium from China, 14 September, https://www.rnz.co.nz/international/pacific-news/497965/solomon-islands-government-receives-pacific-games-stadium-from-china.

Rajah, Roland, Dayant, Alexandre and Pryke, Jonathan 2019, *Ocean of debt? Belt and Road and debt diplomacy in the Pacific*, Lowy Institute: Sydney.

Rheeney, Alexander 2018, 'Taking a breather on China's Belt and Road Initiative', Samoa Observer, 16 October, https://www.samoaobserver.ws/category/editorial/19586.

Ruta, Michele, Dappe, Matias Herrera, Lall, Somik, Zhang, Chunlin, Constantinescu, Cristina, Lebrand, Mathilde, Mulabdic, Alen, and Churchill, Erick 2019, *Belt and Road Economics: opportunities and risks of transport corridors*, World Bank: Washington D.C.

Secretariat of the Pacific Regional Environment Programme 2011, *Pacific islands framework for action on climate change, 2006-2015*, https://library.sprep.org/content/pacific-islands-framework-action-climate-change-2006-2015-2nd-edition.

Shi, Chunlin 2019, 'China-PICs cooperation: past, present and propect', *Contemporary World*, No. 2, pp. 35-39.

Smith, Aaron 2020a, 'Chinese fishing plant in Torres Strait raises alarm for Australian industry and islanders', *Guardian*, 27 November, https://www.theguardian.com/world/2020/nov/27/chinese-fishing-plant-in-torres-strait-raises-alarm-for-australian-industry-and-islanders.

Smith, Aaron 2020b, 'China's fishery deal with PNG: wolf-warrior diplomacy or just business?', *Strategist*, Australian Strategic Policy Institute, 22 December, https://www.aspistrategist.org.au/chinas-fishery-deal-with-png-wolf-warrior-diplomacy-or-just-business/.

Smith, Graeme and Wesley-Smith, Terence 2021, *The China Alternative: Changing Regional Order in the Pacific Islands*, Australia National University: Canberra.

Song, Xiuju and Ye, Shengxuan 2016, 'analysis on the new development of US-PICs ties in the context of Asia rebalance', *The Pacific Journal*, Vol. 14, No. 1, pp. 50-62.

Special Broadcasting Service 2019, 'Solomon Islands switch diplomatic ties from Taiwan to China', SBS news, 16 September, https://www.sbs.com.au/news/solomon-islands-switch-diplomatic-ties-from-taiwan-to-china.

Sui, Sophia and Yu, Le 2020, 'Sino-Russian military cooperation in the context of strategic partnership', *Asia-Europe Journal*, Asia Europe Journal, Vol. 18, No. 3, pp. 325-345.

Sui, Sophia and Yu, Lei 2023, *Complex Interdependence and China-Australia relations*, Routledge: New York.

Tesan, Maëva 2022, 'Ocean acidification: a tide of challenges for Pacific Islanders', Climate Change and Environmental Sustainability, Pacific Community Centre for Ocean Science, 17 August, https://www.spc.int/updates/blog/2022/08/ocean-acidification-a-tide-of-challenges-for-pacific-islanders.

Teshome, Martha 2023, 'Charting the systemic and cascading impacts of climate change on marine food systems and human health', BMJ Global Health, Vol. 8, Supp. 3, doi: 10.1136/bmjgh-2023-014638.

Tsai, Yuchen 2012, *Australia's responses to China-U.S. power competition in the South Pacific*, Zhizhi Academic Press: Taibei, p. 56.

UNEP-WCMC 2006, *In the front line: Shoreline protection and other ecosystem services from mangroves and coral reefs*. Cambridge: UNEP-WCMC; 2006. p. 33.

United Nations, General Debate 2023, Statement Summary, Solomon Islands, Manasseh Damukana Sogavare, 22 September, https://gadebate.un.org/en/78/solomon-islands.

Vari, Matthew 2020, PNG companies register to enter China seafood market, *Post Courier*, 18 May, https://postcourier.com.pg/png-companies-register-to-enter-china-seafood-market/.

Varrall, Merriden 2021, 'Australia's Response to China in the Pacific: From Alert to Alarmed', (eds), Smith, Graeme and Wesley-Smith, Terence, *The China Alternative: Changing Regional Order in the Pacific Islands*, pp. 107-142.

Wang, Xinhua 2007, 'The American-Soviet cold war and the collapse of Soviet economy', *Journal of Ningxia University*, Vol. 29, No. 6, pp. 112-115.

Westad, Odd Arne 2019, 'Are Washington and Beijing Fighting a New Cold War?', *Foreign Affairs*, 12 August, https://www.foreignaffairs.com/articles/china/2019-08-12/sources-chinese-conduct.

Whiting, Natalie 2021a, 'Papua New Guinea politician criticises Australia's reaction to Chinese fisheries park', Australian Broadcasting Company, 26 January, https://www.abc.net.au/news/2021-01-26/papua-new-guinea-politician-criticises-australia-chinese-fishery/13089012.

Whiting, Natalie 2021b, 'Locals in Papua New Guinea speak out as China's proposed industrial fishing park sets off alarm bells in Canberra', Australian Broadcasting Company, 10 February, https://www.abc.net.au/news/2021-02-10/png-daru-fishing-park-china-australia-tensions-james-marape/13136188.

Wickham, Dorothy 2022, 'Can You Blame Poor Countries Like Mine for Turning to China?' *The New York Times*, 27 June, https://www.nytimes.com/2022/06/27/opinion/international-world/china-us-solomon.html.

Wilson, Karl 2019, 'Australian analysts say geopolitics swamps analysis in Pacific island states', China Daily, 30 October, https://www.chinadaily.com.cn/a/201910/30/WS5db8e422a310cf3e35574630.html

Wilson, Karl 2021, 'Papua New Guinea's seafood gets MOU lift', *China Daily*, 2 February, http://epaper.chinadaily.com.cn/a/202102/02/WS601886dea31099a234353b2b.html.

Wright, Stephen 2023, 'Fiji's 'Rambo' prime minister calls for Pacific to become ocean of peace', Benar News, 19 October, https://www.benarnews.org/english/news/pacific/fiji-pm-rabuka-floats-pacific-peace-zone-10182023220058.html.

Wu, H.C., Dissard, D., Douville, E. *et al* 2018, 'Surface ocean pH variations since 1689 CE and recent ocean acidification in the tropical South Pacific', *Nature Communications*, 9, 2543, https://doi.org/10.1038/s41467-018-04922-1.

Wu, Yan 2020, 'The U.S. aids to the PICs and its policy analysis', *International Forum*, Vol. 47, No. 3, pp. 124-135.

Xia, LP 2005, 'The Bandung Conference and China's Efforts to Establish Diplomatic Relations With the Asia and African Countries', *Journal of China Foreign Affairs University*, No. 81, pp. 74-80.

Xinhua 2018, 'BRI paves way for China-Pacific islands cooperation', *China Daily*, 18 November, https://www.chinadailyhk.com/articles/28/173/13/1542535066071.html.

Xinhua News Agency 2022, China-proposed BRI boosts socio-economic development of Pacific Island countries -- Fijian expert, 12 August, https://english.news.cn/20220812/fa3087f253c748cca2e3303ff780c2cc/c.html.

Xiao, Donglian 2010, *60nian guoshi jiyao (major events in China's international relations over the last six decades)*, Hunan People's Press: Changsha, p. 243.

Xu, Quan 2022, 'Rethinking Investment Treaties for Sustainable Development: From the 'New Delhi Declaration' Principles to Modern Investment Law & Policy, *Asian Journal of WTO & International Health Law and Policy*, Vol. 17, No. 2, pp. 405-448.

Yu, Le 2015, 'China-Latin America Strategic Partnership: a fulcrum in China's rise', *International Affairs*, Vol. 91, No. 5, pp. 1047-1068.

Yu, Lei 2018, 'China's expanding security involvement in Africa: a pillar for 'China-Africa community of common destiny', *Global Policy*, Vol. 9, Issue 4, pp. 489-500.

Yu, Lei 2020, 'Contending Chinese Perspectives on China-Russia Military Partnership', *Communist and Post-Communist Studies*, Vol. 53, No. 4, pp. 239-258.

Yu, Le 2021, 'China-Pacific Island Countries Strategic Partnership: China's strategy to reshape regional order', *East Asia: An International Quarterly*, 2021, Vol. 39, Issue 1, pp. 81-96.

Yu, Lei 2023, *From the U.S. trusted territory to the freely associated states: relations between the United States and Federated States of Micronesia, the Marshall Islands and Palau*, China Social Sciences Press: Beijing.

Zhang, Jiadong and Wang, Xiangyu 2022, 'The essence, history and development of the QUAD', *International Review*, Vol. 178, No. 4, pp. 59-88.

Zhang, Ying 2019, 'the path to the implementation of the BRI in the PICs', *The Pacific Journal*, Vol. 27, No. 1, pp. 93-104.

Zhao, Shaofeng and Yu, Lai 2019, 'An analysis on the geopolitical development of China-South Pacific relations', *The Contemporary World*, Vol. 357, No. 2, pp. 26-42.

Zhao, Shaofeng and Yu, Lei 2023, *China-PICs relations*, China Social Sciences Press: Beijing.

Zhou, Shixin 2023, 'the U.S. blue Pacific partnership: motivations, characteristics and impacts', *Global Review*, Vol. 86, No. 6, pp. 119-134.

Index

The Belt and Road Initiative

Interdisciplinary Perspectives

Series Editor: Wenshan Jia

The Belt and Road Initiative (BRI) unveiled in 2013 by China has been gaining global traction and exerting global impact. Owing to the significance and impact of the BRI, there is a growing need for an academic book series that covers various essential topics related to BRI, such as five kinds of connectivity, BRI health initiatives, BRI digitization, and more.

This book series provides a scholarly and systematic understanding of BRI from global, multicultural, and interdisciplinary standpoints. It serves as a valuable resource for academics, think-tanks, policy makers, business leaders, and the public with objective, original, and cutting-edge knowledge on BRI above and beyond the existing fragmented information available through media coverages and think-tank reports.

For additional information about this series or for the submission of manuscripts, please contact:

editorial@peterlang.com

To order other books in this series, please contact our Customer Service Department at:

peterlang@presswarehouse.com (within the U.S.)
orders@peterlang.com (outside the U.S.)

Or browse online by series at: www.peterlang.com

www.ingramcontent.com/pod-product-compliance
Ingram Content Group UK Ltd.
Pitfield, Milton Keynes, MK11 3LW, UK
UKHW021838100926
8556IPUK00004B/414

9 783034 354295